Little Detours

Studies in German Literature, Linguistics, and Culture

Edited by James Hardin
(*South Carolina*)

Luise Adelgunde Victorie Gottsched.
Engraving by J. M. Bernigeroth, 1757,
after a painting by E. G. Haussmann.
Courtesy of the Bibliotheca Albertina, Leipzig.

SUSANNE KORD

LITTLE DETOURS

THE LETTERS AND PLAYS
OF LUISE GOTTSCHED
(1713–1762)

CAMDEN HOUSE

First published 2000
by Camden House

Camden House is an imprint of Boydell & Brewer Inc.
PO Box 41026, Rochester, NY 14604–4126 USA
and of Boydell & Brewer Limited
PO Box 9, Woodbridge, Suffolk IP12 3DF, UK

ISBN: 1–57113–148–5

Library of Congress Cataloging-in-Publication Data

Kord, Susanne.
    Little detours: the letters and plays of Luise Gottsched (1713–1762)/
Susanne T. Kord.
    p.   cm. – (Studies in German literature, linguistics, and culture)
Includes bibliographical references and index.
ISBN 1–57113–148–5 (alk. paper)
1. Gottsched, Louise Adelgunde Victorie, 1713–1762—Criticism and
interpretation. 2. Gottsched, Louise Adelgunde Victorie, 1713–1762—
Correspondence. 3. Authors, German—18th century—Correspondence.
I. Title. II. Studies in German literature, linguistics, and culture
(Unnumbered)
PT2253.G1 Z73 2000
832'.5—dc21

                                                            99–049774

A catalogue record for this title is available from the British Library.

This publication is printed on acid-free paper.
Printed in the United States of America

Contents

Illustrations

Preface

LUISE ADELGUNDE GOTTSCHED, who once categorically discounted the literary activity of women as "a little detour" taken from their *real* (that is, domestic) work, was herself an extremely prolific author. She was also a highly versatile one: her writing spanned the fields of literature, philosophy, translation theory, pedagogy, theology, and rhetoric. Her work, which would fill many volumes if collected, comprises nearly every genre that dominated the literary scene of her day, including comedies, one tragedy, a one-act play, letters, poetry, satires, reviews, articles in moral weeklies, translations, and even sermons. But while there are an astonishing variety of *works* by Luise Gottsched, her *work* — as a unified concept designating her authorship — does not exist: to date, there is no collection of her works, and attribution is in many cases dubious — and always has been. Many of her works were never credited to her authorship because they were published either anonymously or pseudonymously — in some cases, the identity of the author remained obscure until after her death — or because they were subsumed under her husband's work. The incredible variety of Luise Gottsched's authorial stances and interests has been obscured by the one-sidedness of her reception: the only aspect of her work that has received some scant acknowledgment in the form of re-editions have been her comedies, in German in 1908/09 and in English translation in 1994, and most recently her letters in an excerpted German edition published in 1999. Her poetry and her tragedy have never been reprinted from their original publications in the 1760s and 1770s, and there is no collection of Luise Gottsched's satires, essays, or reviews.

This book does not attempt to do justice to the versatility of Luise Gottsched's writing; it is not an introduction to her life and works, nor does it attempt to be comprehensive by including every genre or providing an interpretation of every major work. Concentrating on two genres which I view as central to the author's work, Gottsched's epistolary and dramatic writing, it does attempt to raise different questions than have traditionally been asked of these works, as well as about the conceptual and scholarly contexts in which discussions of the author's life and work usually take place. For this reason, my discussion of Gottsched's life and work tends to be more concerned with context than comprehensiveness, more interested in concepts than chronology —

chronology emerges largely in the order in which works are discussed. One major goal of the book is to provide the impetus for a true reconsideration of Gottsched's work. (Richel's book inadequately styles itself that, for two reasons: it is the *first* book introducing Gottsched to an English-reading audience, and it largely restates, rather than reconsidering, attitudes and judgments made in earlier German scholarship on the author.)

Because women authors, particularly early modern women authors whose texts are often not readily available, have a history of being severely misrepresented in paraphrases of their work, I have chosen to quote liberally from both Luise Gottsched's work and, where appropriate and necessary, scholarly sources, many of which I regard as highly and vituperatively judgmental — unusually so even for older discussions of women's writing. The purpose of these sometimes lengthy quotations is not to take up space, but to have the source material manifest in the discussion, to provide a stronger presence of the author examined, and — above all — to empower readers to argue, take issue, disagree with the points I am making. While quotations are, of necessity, always selective (so that the reader's interpretation of them can be steered by inclusion, omission or excerption alone), I hope to distinguish my work from previous scholarship on Gottsched in my attempts not to subordinate her writing to my reading, but to let important passages stand side by side with my interpretations. For reasons of accessibility and to accommodate those who are not fluent in German (or in eighteenth-century German), I quote in English translation (mine unless otherwise indicated); German originals of primary sources can be found in the notes.

The author appears throughout my text simply as "Gottsched," although I am aware that this name, in almost all other scholarly texts, is used to indicate her husband, and although even works dealing directly and exclusively with Luise Gottsched have rarely, if ever, usurped this name for their subject of inquiry. The deceptively simple issue of naming is, to me, a central concern, especially for feminist scholarship. "Gottsched," like "Goethe," "Schiller," or "Lessing," is not only a designation for a distinct male author, it is — to recall Barbara Hahn's remarks on the subject of women's authorial names — readily recognizable to feminist readers as the Single Name, a name that is permeated with (usually masculine) identity and authority. There can be no question who is designated by that name, nor about his status in the German literary canon. The Single Name stands in stark contrast to women's complicated author names with their endless string of first and last names — names which aid in identification but fatally detract from their authorial credibility ("Luise Adelgunde Victorie Gottsched, née Kulmus," "Christiane Benedikte Eugenie Naubert née Hebenstreit, erst. Holderieder," or "Caroline Dorothea Albertine Michaelis-Böhmer-Schlegel-Schelling"). Traditional ways of reading authorship view "Gottsched," "Goethe," "Neuber," the single surname, as the author's name and assign it — invariably — to the *author* (= male) of that name, the name relegated to the *woman author* of the same name is always derivative and expresses less-than-authorial status ("die Gottschedin," "die Neuberin," "die Karschin," "die Günderrode," "Bettine," "Rahel"). To my mind, circumlocutions like these imply already what most older scholarship is only too happy to confirm: the lower competence of women authors. My research on women's anonymity and pseudonyms (*Sich einen Namen machen*) has convinced me that referring to women authors by their first names ("Luise," "Adelgunde" are common appellations for Luise Gottsched even in more recent discussions) perpetuates their invisibility in the canon and in scholarly discussions. Even the polite alternative employed by Richel and Kerth/Russell ("Frau Gottsched") still implies that *Gottsched* is someone else — the real author, the man with the "Single Name"; "Frau Gottsched," while commendable over possible alternatives, is still a relegation, intentional or not, to secondary authorship status. My first move in claiming true authorship status for "Frau Gottsched" has therefore been to call her by the name that conveys this. I refer to her husband throughout the text by his full name ("Johann Christoph Gottsched") or simply "Johann Christoph," although I admit that the parallel "Herr Gottsched" was sorely tempting: it certainly would have gone some way towards illuminating the slight contempt implicit even in polite appellations like that used in the first English-language study of the author as well as the introduction to the first translation of her comedies into English.

This book owes its existence to a suggestion by James Hardin, my editor at Camden House, who read an earlier article of mine ("Eternal Love") and promptly suggested this project. I thank him for the idea, his commitment to the project over the years, and his unwavering interest in German literature and solid scholarship. Thanks are also due many others who enabled this project in less direct ways: foremost among them my best friend John Landau, who, as he does with everything I write, patiently listened to every idea as it was first formed, developed, tested, and finally adopted (and a good many that were abandoned). Magdalene Heuser (Universität Osnabrück), Gaby Pailer (Universität Karlsruhe), and Gudrun Loster-Schneider (Universität Mannheim) graciously sent me their work on Luise Gottsched; Magdalene Heuser and Mechthilde Vahsen (Universität Paderborn) also provided me with other important sources. Steffen Hoffmann and the employees at the Handschriftenabteilung of the Bibliotheca Albertina in Leipzig permitted me insight into Luise Gottsched's handwritten letters; special thanks are due Steffen Hoffmann, who generously allotted one evening of his free time to helping me decipher difficult-to-read passages from original letters by Johann Christoph Gottsched, Johann Georg Kulmus, and other correspondents with the author. For permission to reprint pictures of the author, the author's husband and some manuscripts, I owe thanks to the Handschriftenabteilung at the Bibliotheca Albertina, the Stadtgeschichtliches Museum Leipzig and the Staatsbibliothek zu Berlin/Preußischer Kulturbesitz. The Graduate School and the Faculty of Languages and Linguistics at Georgetown University each supported this project with a summer grant; my research in Leipzig and Berlin was made possible by a grant-in-aid of research travel from the Graduate School in the summer of 1997. I thank Milena Santoro from the French Department at Georgetown University for checking one of my translations from Luise Gottsched's French letters, Lynne Miles-Morillo and Jim Walker at Camden House/Boydell & Brewer for their superb editing of the manuscript, and my colleagues Peter C. Pfeiffer and Heidi Byrnes for patiently listening to my complaints about having no time to write, for their interest in and support of my research, and for helping to transform my Department into a place of ideas. While modern scholarship now seems to have developed a context almost entirely divorced from the home university of the scholar (the "profession"), writing always takes place in an institutional context as well: institutions and departments either enable or discourage feminist research. Mine enables, and for that, I am profoundly grateful.

1: Expectations: Portraits of the Author

The Birth of an Author: Failed Hopes

IN EARLY 1713, Katharina Dorothea Kulmus, née Schwenk, wife of the Danzig court physician Johann Georg Kulmus, was expecting.

She was expecting a boy.

This expectation spawns the first in a series of anecdotes about the life of her daughter, Luise Adelgunde Victorie Kulmus, later Gottsched (1713–1762), anecdotes that have set the tone for her scholarly reception and that, while clearly recognizable as unsubstantiated stories, are virtually ubiquitous in scholarship on the author. In most accounts, the story of Luise Gottsched's life begins with her mother's (disappointed) expectations. Katharina Dorothea Kulmus was expecting; she was expecting to bear a boy: she was "guter Hoffnung" (of good hope), as a rather revealing German expression has it.[1] The documentation of this failed hope is anecdotal: the hope is expressed in (unverifiable) tales of the child's liveliness in utero and in her parents' purchase of a boy-colored baptismal bonnet which then could not be used and was hastily replaced with a piece of cloth. The disappointment is masked by general expressions of astonishment at the size of the child's head, the dubbing of that head as a "poet's melon" (*Poetenkasten*) and the whimsical parental verdict that a child with a head this size was surely destined to become an author.[2]

Luise Gottsched's life story, then, begins as a tale of disappointment: contrary to her parents' hopes and expectations, it was a girl. But more interesting than this muted disappointment, which presumably remained the usual reaction to the birth of a girl for at least a century and a half after this particular birth, is the sense of premonition that the anecdote imparts on the beginning of Luise's life, a premonition chronicled in her parents' good-natured joke that she was destined for greatness, despite her sex. Upon the disappointment of the chief hope, the expectation of a son, new evidence was quickly found to support a secondary hope: the size of the baby's head was taken as indicating great intellectual and creative powers, giving rise to a new expectation — that of turning Luise into an (albeit female) author. The jocundity with which the anecdote is commonly related points to the unreasonableness of that particular expectation. Indeed, it indicates that the parents themselves may not have taken this possibility seriously, but merely sought to comfort themselves over the disappointment of their primary and reasonable hope. It is the humor that is striking, for it tells the reader that the ridiculousness of the idea lies not in the particular (the impossibility of baby Luise ever becoming an author), but in the general: women cannot be authors, no matter their cranial size. To the readers of this first of many anecdotes that now comprise Luise Gottsched's biography, and to those of us who are also aware that she did become an author and that she moreover became the most acknowledged woman author of the German Enlightenment, this tale of the Author-Despite-Her-Sex imparts two messages. One is the implication that authorship presupposes masculinity. The other is a new expectation: the Author-Despite-Her-Sex is predestined, not only for greatness, as a straightforward reading of the anecdote suggests, but also and paradoxically for failure as an author. And it is this twofold expectation that permeates both scholarly and fictional accounts of Luise Gottsched's life and of her literature.

The assumption that the author (any author) is necessarily male is another idea that has been illustrated by half-serious jokes, one of many examples being Norman Mailer's famous dictum that all a good author needs is "balls."[3] Nonetheless, this assumption is a far more subtle and universal phenomenon in literary interpretation than these jokes let on. This assumption expresses itself throughout literary history first in female anonymity and pseudonymity, but also in the default attribution of literature to male authors and in the assessment and reception of literature as a male product.[4] The Single Name[5] that alone can distinguish itself as the Author's Name is male: Goethe, Schiller, Shakespeare. A woman, burdened with a proliferation of potential author-names (the choice is usually between her birth-name, her first husband's name, her last husband's name, the name under which she became most famous, the name under which she published the most, and so on), cannot be an author; at best, she can be a "woman author," and the difference in status is considerable. Throughout the eighteenth century, "Gottsched", "Neuber," "Karsch" are designations for the man with the Single Name, the man who occupies that name, so to speak, and delegates a derivative name to the "woman author": die Gottschedin, die Neuberin, die Karschin. Barring anonymity or pseudonymity, the name serves to distinguish an "author" from a "woman author," a distinction that expresses itself in countless contemporary reviews and later scholarship.[6] It is not uncommon, for example, for biographies of "women authors" to make no reference whatsoever to their subjects' literary output,[7] an omission that would be unthinkable in works on their male colleagues. In works that do discuss women's literature, the discussion is almost invariably gendered, a fact that betrays itself most commonly in two ways:

1) *The reviewer/scholar draws conclusions about the work based on the author's gender.* Throughout the eighteenth and nineteenth centuries, reviewers of anonymously or pseudonymously published literature are very often tremendously uncertain as to whether to consider the work under review one of art or an expression of female dilettantism. Throughout both centuries, anonymously published works by women or those published under male pseudonyms fared far better in reviews than works by women whose sex was known (via a female pseudonym or orthonym). Two examples of many are the varied reviews of Amalie von Sachsen and Marie von Ebner-Eschenbach, whose plays — the same plays — received enthusiastic reviews before their authors' gender was known and highly vituperative reviews thereafter.[8]

2) *The reviewer or scholar draws conclusions about the author's gender based on her work.* The most common trait in the assessment of women's literature is the categorization of the author as a "feminine" or sometimes "masculine" type, based on facets of her works. Usually, this is achieved by an over-emphasis of content in the work that can be interpreted as "feminine" (cf. the frequent view of Marie von Ebner-Eschenbach as the kindly, compassionate mother-figure, based on her stories[9]) or by the interpreter's exclusive concentration on the portion of her work written in "typically feminine" genres (usually diaries or letters) at the expense of all other works (most obviously those written in a genre traditionally considered "masculine," such as drama).[10] Interestingly enough, the attribution of a "masculine" nature to a woman author frequently results in the critics' most extravagant compliment of all: designating the woman an "author" (*Dichter*) without the gendered qualifier. Equally revealingly, most eighteenth- and nineteenth-century women to whom this honor has been accorded were women who published anonymously or pseudonymously during their lifetimes — that is, women who could indeed, at least initially, have been mistaken for "real," which is to say male, authors (Therese Huber, Benedikte Naubert, Annette von Droste-Hülshoff, Elsa Bernstein).[11]

A Woman and An Author: Life — and Work

What this indicates is that it was highly consequential for an eighteenth-century "woman author" to be recognized as female. Indeed, this recognition — which amounts to the disappointment of the reader's expectation that the author should be male — can be seen as the single most consequential aspect of any female writer's career. And it is little wonder that the sources on which modern readers must rely for information about Luise Gottsched's life are permeated with instances of that expectation and its disappointment, that they furnish, in fact, a textbook example of gendered biographical writing. These sources tell us, for example, that Luise Gottsched received an "unusual" education for girls of her time;[12] that her parents instructed her in music, languages, geography, religion, poetry, and mathematics (of which, in fact, only mathematics can be considered "unusual" in a contemporary bourgeois girl's education); that she further distinguished herself by beginning to write occasional poetry at an early age;[13] and that she was even permitted a modicum of choice in her own education, an act of parental liberality that is viewed with nothing short of amazement. "When Luise Adelgunde Viktorie Kulmus was fifteen years old, her parents subjected her to a strange experiment. They left the child completely to herself for a while in order to discern in which activities she would engage of her own choosing. The girl chose music, poetry, reading and writing."[14] When she was fourteen, twenty-seven-year-old Johann Christoph Gottsched, an admirer of some of her early poems, requested and received her parents' permission to correspond with Luise, a permission that can be viewed as the admission of the possibility that marriage would follow once the couple had become somewhat acquainted through their exchange of letters.

Although Johann Christoph Gottsched entered that correspondence almost certainly with that objective in mind and formally proposed to her fairly early on (in 1731), the exchange of letters between the two is usually described as cool, cerebral and unromantic. Its distinguishing characteristic is the roles the couple assumed, with Johann Christoph functioning as the mentor and tutor who sent her books, instructed her to read and translate specific texts and who exhorted her to write only in German, and with Luise as his pupil who gratefully and dutifully fulfilled his instructions.[15] Johann Christoph, in his own words, "sought . . . to anchor her taste more and more in the sciences and the liberal arts: to which end he gradually supplied her with various German and French books that were suited to her abilities."[16]

The wedding had to be postponed several times due to intervening catastrophes in Luise's life (her father's death in 1731, the war and occupation of Danzig, her mother's death in 1734). Halfway into her mourning period for her mother, in April 1735, she married Johann Christoph and followed him to Leipzig. There, she became his housekeeper, secretary, editorial and research assistant — in his words, his "industrious helpmate" ("fleißige Gehülfinn," "Leben") whose task it was to support and further his career, a task she was to fulfill, with little variation, until her death in 1762.

She began this task by turning herself into a model Enlightenment erudite woman, taking music instruction from the composer Krebs (one of Johann Sebastian Bach's students), learning Latin and some Greek at her husband's request, and even listening to her husband's lectures on rhetoric and poetry, hidden behind the door to his lecture hall. Following Johann Christoph's ideas that authorship could and had to be learned according to specific rules and that creative writing was best trained through translations, she translated eleven dramas and later authored five, all at his request, most commissioned for his project *Deutsche Schaubühne* (The German Stage, 1741–5). Her first translation was the controversial drama *Die Pietisterey im Fischbein-Rocke* (Pietism in Petticoats, 1736), an adaptation/translation of Bougeant's *La Femme Docteur* (The Lady Scholar, 1730). Her translation caused a nationwide furor, was banned in several cities, and even inspired some new censorship laws in Prussia (cf. Consentius). The bulk of her subsequent work consisted of participating in her husband's projects and translating, for the most part under his direction and at his behest. When her husband planned a German edition of Addison's and Steele's moral weekly *The Spectator* (German: *Der Zuschauer*, 1739–43), she translated the bulk of the journal: "For this work, I mainly relied on my industrious and hard-working wife, who, on the one hand, possessed every inclination and capacity for this work, and on the other, could not make better use of her free hours."[17] In subsequent years, Johann Christoph Gottsched relied on his industrious wife for the translation of 330 of the 635 articles in Pierre Bayle's *Dictionnaire historique et critique* (*Herrn Peter Baylens Historisches und critisches Wörterbuch*, trans. 1741–4, a four-volume work which she then had to proofread three times, line by line) as well as for the translations of Addison's *The Guardian* (*Der engländische Guardian oder Aufseher*, trans. 1745), Leibniz's *Theodizee* (*Herrn Gottfried Wilhelms Freyherrn von Leibnitz Theodicee*, trans. 1744), the History of the Royal Academy (*Der Königlichen Akademie der Aufschriften und schönen Wissenschaften zu Paris ausführliche Schriften*, trans. 1753–54), the complete correspondence of Maupertuis, König and Voltaire (trans. 1753) and numerous plays, prose pieces, satires and educational treatises, many later published under his name.[18] She was extensively involved in all of her husband's monumental works, such as his *Deutsche Sprachkunst* (German Linguistics, 1749), for which she did the etymological research and which she proofread numerous times, and his *Deutsche Schaubühne*, for which she produced thirteen original plays and translations — none of its volumes contain fewer than two dramas written or translated by Luise Gottsched. For this project, she furnished him with *Das Gespenst mit der Trommel* (The Ghost with the Drum, a translation of Destouches' *Le Tambour Nocturne*), a translation of Voltaire's drama *Alzire; Der Verschwender* (The Spendthrift, translated from Destouches' *Le Dissipateur*), and *Der poetische Dorfjunker* (The Poetical Village Fop, translated from Destouches' *La Fausse Agnes*), all in 1741. In 1742, she translated *Der Menschenfeind* (The Misanthrope, from Molière's *Le Misanthrope*) and *Die Widerwillige* (The Stubborn Girl, from Dufresny's *L'esprit de Contradiction*). The year 1744 saw the translation of Alexander Pope's *The Rape of the Lock*, published as *Der Lockenraub*, and three original plays: *Die ungleiche Heirath* (The Mésalliance), *Die Hausfranzösinn* (The French Housekeeper), and *Panthea*, her only tragedy, today commonly belittled as her weakest dramatic effort.[19] The following year, she published *Das Testament* (The Last Will), today commonly considered her best play,[20] and her one-act comedy *Der Witzling* (The Witling). In her "free hours," she wrote reviews and satires, occasional poetry and other translations, another commissioned drama (*Der beste Fürst* [The Best Ruler], 1755), and did odd jobs for her husband (such as copying the Goldast manuscript — one folio! — for his personal use). She ran her husband's household "silently and in the most orderly manner" ("ohne Geräusch aufs ordentlichste," as he confessed in "Leben"), catalogued and labeled his entire library and corresponded with other scholars in his name, when he was "too overwhelmed with other projects" ("wenn ich mit Geschäfften zu sehr überhäufet war"; "Leben").

Luise Gottsched was acknowledged for only a minuscule portion of her writing, most of which was published anonymously or subsumed under her husband's work. She was highly critical of erudite women: she ridiculed Laura Bassi for receiving her doctorate, refused a place in Leipzig's renowned *Deutsche Gesellschaft* (German Society), reportedly because the famous poet Christiane Mariane von Ziegler was also a member, and rejected a request by the ostentatiously feminist author Sidonia Hedwig Zäunemann to correspond with her. Despite the fact that most of her works were not attributed to her and despite her critical attitude towards other accomplished women, Luise Gottsched acquired national fame as Germany's most erudite woman and even participated in public scholarly discussions in 1749. Largely due to her fame, the Gottscheds were frequently singled out for honors and invitations by the aristocracy, most of which, strangely enough, came at a time when Johann Christoph's poetological theories were already falling into disrepute in literary circles. The pinnacle of these honors was reached when the Gottscheds were granted an audience by Maria Theresia, Empress of Austria, an occasion which is lovingly described in one of Luise Gottsched's letters and extensively quoted in Johann Christoph's description of her life.

Chronic illnesses, about which she started to complain in letters as early as 1740, constitute the second distinguishing feature of her biography, and they are frequently blamed on the first: her ceaseless, intense and lifelong literary activity in her husband's service. In 1752, on one of the many journeys which she undertook to repair her ruined health, she met Dorothea Henriette von Runckel and formed a close friendship with her, corresponding with Runckel until her death ten years later. For the last two years of her life, Luise Gottsched was a physical wreck, but continued to work on her husband's projects, by his own admission unwillingly. In 1760, her collaboration on the translation of Bielfeld's *Lehrbegriff der Staatskunst* (Theory of Statesmanship) was "the last thing I could still persuade her to do" — her husband had already arranged for a publication date that winter, and time was running short. So Luise Gottsched "was once more, in the winter of 1760, found willing"[21] — although she was already incapable of writing herself and had to dictate the translation.

The final two years of Luise Gottsched's life are marked by near-constant complaints about overwork and exhaustion, her failing health, and her frequently expressed desire for death. She could no longer eat or drink without difficulty, suffered from fainting spells and was frequently bled. During the last six months of her life, she was unable to leave the house. She died after repeated strokes, blind and partially paralyzed, on June 26, 1762, at the age of barely forty-nine.

A Woman *or* an Author: Paradox and Paradigm

This, in essence, is Luise Gottsched's life as we know it, a life story compiled of various more or less credible biographical sources, begin-

ning of course with her husband's. But this story is significant beyond
the fact that it represents an accumulation of the only recorded facts
about her life still available, for two reasons. One is that the information thus presented to the reader is invariably subjected to a gendered
interpretation. The second is that readers tend to perceive Gottsched's
life not just as the life of an Enlightenment woman author, but as that
of *the* Enlightenment woman author, the "embodiment" or "prototype,"
as she is often called[22] — a move that simultaneously increases her relative significance as a literary figure and generalizes her life as paradigmatic for the life of any female writer of the age. The fact that Luise
Gottsched is often viewed as paradigmatic for Enlightenment women
authors, as unusual but nonetheless representative, tells us nothing about
the lives of other women writers of the age, but much about the desires
and expectations of later readers and scholars. These expectations, which
become especially significant in view of the *symbolic* value of Luise
Gottsched's life, amount to the same as the expectation that underlies
its introductory anecdote: like Gottsched's mother, the reader is expecting a boy who could later turn out to be an author. As was the case
with her parents, the disappointment of this expectation is subtly expressed in manipulations of the biographical material. There is *no* biographical work on Luise Gottsched in which the fact that she turned
out to be a girl, later a woman author, is not the central point, the
point that determines not only the final assessment of her life and position as a literary figure, but also the interpretation of her literature. The
reader's initial expectation of an "author," evoked in the anecdote of
her parents' expectation of a boy and reiterated in the emphasis on the
unusualness of her education, fame, and symbolic significance, is answered in most biographies with an accumulation of evidence that it
was, nonetheless, a girl.

Because most accounts perceive authorship and femininity as oppo-
sites in terms, the fact that Gottsched was a woman *and* an author constitutes a paradox, one that is answered by endless reiterations of two
related statements: Luise Gottsched may have been a "real" woman,
but (therefore) she was not a "real" author. As assertions of her femininity serve, for example, the fact that most of her literary role models
and most of her own heroines were women (Schreiber 60, Hanstein I,
142); her purported despair about her own childlessness (Ploetz;
Schlenther 66 and 80); her virtues as a housekeeper (Crüger lxxvi); her
supposed lack of literary ambition (Hanstein I, 129); her lifelong and
complete subordination to her husband (Sanders, "Kleiner Umweg"
170); her fear of appearing "pedantic" because of her erudition

(Schlenther 26; Sanders, "Kleiner Umweg" 174); her hostility towards other erudite women;[23] and her hypochondria, constant illness, and physical weakness. Scholars and critics have cited the following as evidence for the fact that she was no real author: her lack of "originality" (usually understood to indicate her extensive activities as a translator or the fact that she adhered to her husband's poetics[24]); the vulgarity for which her comedies are harshly criticized (and which is seen as inexplicable in light of the author's gender; cf. Richel, *Luise Gottsched* 65–8; Crüger 253–4; Köster 95); the idea that her female characters can be read as images of the author;[25] the assumption that most of her writing was inspired by personal motives;[26] the statement that she was most successful in the portrayal of lower class women and children (Schlenther 208); and the judgment that while she wrote passable comedies (viewed as light entertainment), she utterly failed at the "serious" genre tragedy. Despite the fact that Luise Gottsched was the most famous "woman author" of the age, she is usually not read as an "author" at all, but rather as a precursor for other, male, authors:

> This childless woman was capable of portraying a child, and that is symbolic of her entire art.
> She herself lived in a childlike age. She witnessed the dawn of a great literary era. The year 1744, in which *The French Housekeeper* appeared, also marks the appearance of Lessing and Klopstock.
> Goethe is born half a decade later. This developing art of the greats follows the bustling activity of our heroine [Luise Gottsched, S. K.] just as the firm tread of a man slowly emerges from the four-legged crawling and groping of a child.[27]

Because femininity and authorship are commonly viewed as antithetical in scholarly literature, the statement that Luise Gottsched was not a real "author" is intricately bound up, indeed identical with, her feminization (or, in this case, her infantilization) in scholarship. In this respect, Luise Gottsched's biography can indeed be read as paradigmatic for that of any eighteenth-century "woman author," because this alternative, in her and other cases, leads to an irresolvable paradox. Luise Gottsched was not a real author: she was a woman. Conversely: Luise Gottsched *was* an author, or at least a "woman author," even the most renowned "woman author" of her age, but was she a "real woman"? If she was, her femininity becomes a kind of consolation prize, the single thing at which Gottsched succeeded: "She was thoroughly feminine despite the fact that she devoted her whole life to writing."[28] Elsewhere, the reader is invited to expect an author *or* a woman and is doubly disappointed:

If we once again visualize the image of this lonely woman, the more familiar image of another spontaneously enters our recollection: a woman who also had to contend with a difficult spouse, but who, at the same time that Maria Theresia somewhat crudely jested with our Gottschedin, had just given her Wolfgang [Goethe, S. K.] to the world. It was the lot of Frau Rath of the Hirschgraben in Frankfurt to pass on to a son and cherish in him all of her cheerfulness and joy of improvisation, her entire poetic nature and her own good sense. In this enjoyment she grew old and happy. Frau Gottsched, on the other hand, was compelled to be herself, at all costs, an "illustrious Sappho," as the Countess Bentinck called her, and thus "poor Sappho," as she termed herself, was undone (Schlenther 81–2).

Schlenther's account, the earliest book-length study of the author and as such highly influential, set the tone for many later accounts in several implied statements. He reiterates the alternatives (Luise Gottsched could either have been an author, or she could have given birth to one), states her real purpose in life (Luise Gottsched could never have been a real author, so she *should* have given birth to one), and implies that the author herself saw things in much the same way: she was "compelled" to be an author, she was made "lonely," "undone" by her ambitions and her childlessness — poor Sappho. Lonely and disappointed Luise Gottsched is contrasted with cheerful and sensible Frau Rat Goethe, who did fulfill her feminine destiny, made absolutely no pretensions to authorship herself, and thus gained the respect of the world as well as the opportunity to live a vicarious poetic existence through her famous son.

The significance of these interpretations lies in the symbolic and paradigmatic quality attributed to Luise Gottsched's life in virtually every work on her. Her life does not stand alone, but is representative of the lives, abilities, successes and failures of that century's women authors. Thus, the point of most Gottsched biographies is threefold: to state that her claims to real authorship were ultimately disappointed, to present this claim as a vain hope and its disappointment as a foregone conclusion due to the author's gender, and thus to extend the point to apply to women authors in general:

> [Johann Christoph] Gottsched, barely able to differentiate between the duties of man and woman, educated her to be an erudite woman, following the ideal that he had outlined earlier in *Die vernünftigen Tadlerinnen*. And her burning ambition accommodated his wishes. She accepted the duties imposed upon her with pride and fulfilled them for decades with ever the same eagerness, even at the price of her own eyesight. Not until the end of her life . . . did she seem to re-

alize that at least in the domain of scholarly pursuits and poetic inspiration, women's capabilities are far beneath those of men (Köster 94).

The picture that emerges of the author in literature on her is either one of an ambitious writer who laid claims to male erudition and authorship that are inevitably (and gleefully) disappointed, or one of a "feminine," obedient and unambitious housewife who wanted nothing more than children, but was instead pressed into lifelong service on her husband's "learned galleys."

To this day, there is no book-length account and very few shorter works on Luise Gottsched that make any reference to evidence in her letters that could cast doubt upon these two canonized views of the female "prototype" for Enlightenment women authors. While it would be highly problematic to take her letters as the basis for an "alternative biography," for reasons that shall be explained later (chapter 2), the letters do make reference to aspects of the author's life and works that were later edited out to arrive at one of the two now-dominant life stories. To cite the three most obvious instances: first, precious few of the works on Luise Gottsched make reference to her repeated postponement of her wedding. Those that do explain her evasions and hesitations either with her mother's wish to find her a better match (Reichel 726–7) or with her fear of poverty and lack of dowry (Schreiber 44). Nobody has ever provided any evidence for either of these speculations, or dared to state what might be the most obvious explanation: that she may not have wished to marry Johann Christoph at all, had no choice in the matter, and sought to delay the inevitable as long as possible. Second, until Magdalene Heuser's rediscovery of Gottsched's ten-year-long relationship with Dorothea Henriette von Runckel (cf. "Das beständige Angedencken"), that association was completely ignored in scholarly literature, although it clearly formed the emotional center of the last ten years of the author's life. Finally, interpretations of Gottsched's works altogether are rare; interpretations of her works as anything more than demonstrations of her husband's poetics are virtually unheard of, and the author's own assessment of *Panthea* as her best and favorite drama has yet to incite anything but perplexity in any commentator. And so it is that Luise Gottsched's letters, which are nonetheless frequently cited as evidence of the two interpretations outlined above, stand in strange contrast to both.

Rereading Luise Gottsched's letters, then, seems necessary not only to rediscover aspects of her life and work that have been neglected and obscured, but also to learn something about the history of her recep-

tion: to find out *which* aspects of her life have been obscured, and why.
Nonetheless, reading and interpreting letters is a highly problematic undertaking, particularly letters by women, and particularly letters authored
in the eighteenth century, the "century of the letter."[29] Should we read
these letters as "history" (that is, as a collection of facts that can be
mined and used as a guarantee of authenticity for the biography we create) or as "literature" (that is, as an aesthetic text in which the author
fictionalizes her own life)? Should we consider these letters "intimate"
(since they were written to persons close to the author and thematize,
as scholarship tells us, mostly friendship and love[30]) or "open" (since
many were written for perusal by third persons in addition to the addressee, since some were even introduced into literary salons and read in
public, and since we know that letter writing developed into a literary
artform in eighteenth-century discourse[31])? These decisions are not
merely interpretive, but very often also editorial, which means that they
have, in many cases, pre-empted differing readings of the same letters
and led to an endless reiteration of life stories that show little variation
over the centuries. Given the scholarly disinterest in women's lives and
literature until the advent of feminist literary scholarship in the 1970s,
traditionally minded scholars were only motivated to preserve and study
letters by women at all if the recipient was one of the century's "great"
men. In many of these rare cases, his side of the correspondence sur-
vived to be reprinted in countless editions, while her side of the exchange was lost — the most famous case being the disappearance of
Charlotte von Stein's letters to Goethe. In cases where letters by the
female correspondent are still available in print, they have almost always
been edited for content, with passages judged too personal, domestic,
mundane and historically or culturally uninteresting edited out by the
(usually male) editor (French 29–30). What this means is that most
editions of women's letters still available are already pre-interpreted, or,
to use French's term, "historicized." This historicization has, as French
rightly claims, obscured major portions of many women's lives and
"conditioned analysis in secondary literature" (19).

    Luise Gottsched's letters are, to some extent, an example of this
process of historicization, but they are also unusual in several respects.
For one thing, we have *only* her side of her correspondence with her
"great man," indeed a highly unusual situation that later repeats itself
in the correspondence between Dorothea Henriette von Runckel and
Johann Christoph Gottsched — of which only Runckel's side is still
extant.[32] Even more unusual is the fact that Gottsched's letters were
edited not by a man (although her husband repeatedly applied for this

position), but by her friend Runckel, and that Gottsched herself exercised considerable control over this process by refusing her husband the right to editorship and conferring it on Runckel. This may indicate that Gottsched's letters were historicized with a different purpose in mind, one that might not correspond to the agenda with which letters by women are commonly edited and read. It does *not* mean that her letters escaped historicization: there is, in fact, incontrovertible evidence that Runckel took extraordinary editorial liberties with Gottsched's letters, liberties well in excess of the usual editorial interventions (cf. chapter 2). As is almost universally the case, the originals are lost and cannot be consulted for differing viewpoints from those expressed through Runckel's edition.[33]

Finally, Gottsched's letters constitute the first published correspondence between female friends, which in itself makes them a unique document because it accords the friendship with another woman a significance that the editor could not possibly have expected to resonate in the reader. Dorothea Henriette von Runckel's introductory remarks to each volume clearly reflect this dichotomy between reader expectations and the motivations behind her own project. They reveal an awareness that unlike editors of letters by male "greats," that is, in cases where the subject matter would naturally excite a high degree of interest in the reader, Runckel could expect no such interest in her subject, despite Gottsched's fame. The editor is thus put into a position of having to justify her edition. The first two volumes are therefore presented to the reader not as volumes of letters by the author Luise Adelgunde Gottsched, but as letters by the "prototype" Luise Adelgunde Gottsched: the reader's interest is presumed to be not in Gottsched's life, but in the exemplariness of her epistolary style, which Runckel holds up as a model for future female letter-writers.

> Germans are often charged to write good letters in German, and due to the lack of good original letters in our language, women are asked to read translations and school their style on them. Most of these, and the best of them, are love stories that cause irreparable harm to young persons. Their hearts are corrupted, and their style will always be unnatural, as long as they seek to imitate these models. I have sought to remedy this ill by publishing a collection that will not leave a harmful impression on anyone. Our Gottsched teaches appropriate style to everyone while writing about various subjects, and without providing explicit rules. She gives each letter and each matter she writes about its own expression, and her natural, informal style shines through everything. Besides, these letters

> are extraordinarily valuable because they are true originals that were
> written to persons both still alive and now deceased.[34]

Runckel's edition of Gottsched's letters, according to this rationale, is
not intended to be a testimony of the author's life, but a moral and
stylistic epistolary school for women. In this emphasis, Runckel echoes
almost precisely the demands that Gellert had made of exemplary
women's letters in his *Praktische Abhandlung von dem guten Ge-*
schmacke in Briefen (1751, Practical Treatise Concerning Good Taste
in Letters), in which he praised women's letters for their naturalness
and simplicity (cf. also the discussion in French 56–7). Like Gellert,
Runckel conflates the "natural" stylistic simplicity with the authenticity
of the letters; the fact that the same letters that are here made to assume
a public function originally constituted a personal correspondence paradoxically heightens their value in this public forum. Runckel accom-
plishes several feats in her introduction that later became standard in
interpretations of Gottsched's life: she accents Gottsched's standing as
a "prototype," as exemplary for other women, while de-emphasizing her
significance as an individual and, paradoxically, as an author. In addition to the obvious implication that the value of these letters lies in
their reception and use by the reader and that their origin is rather beside the point, casting the letters as personal correspondence (by indicating that the letters were not originally intended for publication) further
de-emphasizes Gottsched's authorship. Elsewhere, Gottsched's authorship
is more directly denied in Runckel's foregrounding of Gottsched's
"femininity" at the expense of her authorship: setting the tone for
much later scholarship, Runckel leads the reader to expect a "woman"
instead of an "author."

> If you do not find in these letters the original author, the astute critic,
> the exalted poet in the strictest sense of all of these qualities, you will
> nonetheless not misjudge in them the tender daughter, the virtuous
> wife, the most loyal friend, the Christian, and the philosopher.[35]

Only in Runckel's introduction to the third volume is the reader invited
to expect an author as originator of the letters, perhaps because the
success of the first two volumes, published the previous year, had convinced the editor that Gottsched's letters might indeed be deemed significant by readers as testimony to the author's life and work. In this
third foreword, Gottsched's authorship is admitted in an (albeit incomplete) list of her works. Her individuality is acknowledged in a brief
characterization that, far from the earlier presentation of the author as

the epitomization of every feminine virtue, presents her as a rather androgynous figure. Here she appears as

> A happy combination of masculine seriousness, steadfastness and resolution with the gentleness, reserve and modesty that constitute the greatest assets of the female sex . . . . She proudly commanded a body of knowledge that is rarely found in women and of which some aspects are almost never even suspected, much less demanded, of them.[36]

In this last foreword, Runckel makes no reference whatever to her initial moral/didactic justification of the edition. On the contrary: she now claims that the purpose of the edition is "to renew and preserve the memory of my immortalized friend."[37]

Essentially, what this amounts to is that the editor, the first person to read and interpret these letters, the person on whose "historicization" of these letters we must rely because almost all originals are long gone, offers the reader two different ways of approaching Gottsched's letters. The first approach would be to read them as an "authentic" correspondence that should be read for its aesthetic and educational value, in which case the reader would be invited to ignore as insignificant the fact that Luise Gottsched was an author, that these are *her* letters, and that they could shed light on contentious or neglected aspects of her life. The second interpretive attitude suggested by the editor would be to read the letters as testimony to Gottsched's life, work and personality, which would presume an explicit interest in Luise Gottsched on the part of the reader, an interest presumably grounded in her accomplishments as an author. Gottsched's letters are presented on different occasions as both aesthetic and biographical/historical, as both paradigmatic and specific, as illustrative of that particular author's life and as a phenomenon completely detached from the author — without explanation for or even explicit reference to the remarkable contradictions among the three forewords.

Given the highly gendered context in which paradigmatic letter writing and schooling of epistolary style were viewed in the eighteenth century, one could exaggerate the dichotomy with which Runckel presents her readers as that between femininity and authorship. While both "the original author, the astute critic, the exalted poet" and "the tender daughter, the virtuous wife" appear in these letters, Runckel's introductions clearly present these readings as alternatives. Gottsched's letters can be read either as a work *for women* or as a work *by the author*. If the purpose of the collected letters is purely didactic (the schooling of women's epistolary style), then it is the reader rather than Gottsched herself who is the focus of the text. In this case, Gottsched becomes a writing "woman" whose authorship is unspecific and insignificant and whose "femininity" is compromised by even this secondary kind of creativity and therefore constantly reasserted. Conversely, the historical and biographical value of the edition and its purpose as testimony to Gottsched's life and accomplishments clearly invites the reader to expect an "author" whose life and correspondence are significant for the sake of her authorship alone. What is highly unusual in Runckel's edition is that, unlike all other editors of women's letters, she presents this conflict without resolving it, essentially leaving the reader alone to contend with the conflicting expectations of a "woman" or an "author" from her introductory remarks.

My own reading of Luise Gottsched's letters is motivated by both aspects that Runckel addressed in her forewords: by an explicit interest in Luise Gottsched as an author, and by an interest in Luise Gottsched as an author-figure around whom a discourse of paradoxes formed even during her lifetime. This discourse casts her as simultaneously paradigmatic *and* unique, and it has conditioned interpretations of Gottsched's life and work ever since. As in previous scholarship, my reading of the letters is already partially determined by the motivation behind the investigation. Although I have, in this reading, a specific interest in Gottsched's life and works, it is impossible, as I shall explain later, to rely on the usefulness of these letters as a source of information about that life, or to postulate that Gottsched's letters are a more direct, hence more reliable source of information than any subsequent interpretation of this material. Nonetheless, the letters will play a pivotal role in my investigation, because of the peculiar interaction between gender conformity (for example, Gottsched's subservience to her husband and her hostility towards erudite women) and gender nonconformity (Gottsched's childlessness, her literary ambitions, and her relationships with both her husband and Runckel). The interplay between these apparent contradictions is highly apparent in the letters, but entirely absent in later interpretations.

The creation of the figure of Gottsched as an author begins not with her first biographer, but in her letters — either with her own self-presentation and self-fictionalization in her letters or with Runckel's editorial construction of Gottsched as author. Following French's lead, my reading presupposes what Montrose has called the "historicity of texts" (that every text arises from a specific cultural and social climate) as well as the "textuality of history": the impossibility of gaining "access to an 'authentic' past, unmediated by the texts we use to interpret that past and by the process by which those texts have been compiled, preserved, and effaced" (French 19). My goal, then, is not to arrive at an "authentic" version of Luise Gottsched's life, an account whose claims to authenticity would have to rest on an unreflective reliance on that which has been "compiled and preserved." Rather, my primary interest is in that which has been "effaced" in previous scholarship, because these omissions raise questions. What, if anything, can these bibliographic events tell us about Luise Gottsched's life, her writing, and her self-image as an author? Why did previous researchers see the need to edit Gottsched's life at these particular junctures? To what extent is this editing process related to the creation of the "prototype" Enlightenment woman author? And what does it tell us about reader expectations, of Luise Gottsched in particular and about women and authorship in general?

Notes

[1] An antiquated term for pregnancy commonly used in the eighteenth century.

[2] The story of the bonnet and the headsize first appears in Johann Christoph Gottsched's "Leben" (Life) of his wife, published the year after her death, and is later repeated in Hanstein I, 114 and Robinson 115–6, among many others.

[3] Quoted in Spender 29.

[4] Cf. Kord, *Sich einen Namen machen* chapters 1 and 7; in particular 17–30 with regard to anonymity and pseudonyms and 156–64 on the near-universality of the assumption that the author is necessarily male in book reviews. With regard to pseudonyms, cf. also Hahn and Kittler 132–34.

[5] "Der Eine Name"; the term was coined by Barbara Hahn; cf. Hahn 8–10.

[6] For some eighteenth- and nineteenth-century examples, cf. Kord, *Sich einen Namen machen*, 156–64.

[7] Perhaps the most glaring, but by no means unusual example is Doris Maurer's 240–page-biography of Charlotte von Stein, in which she actually completely avoided mention of three of the author's plays and limited her discussion of the fourth to three pages (164–7). In biographical accounts on Gottsched, there can be little doubt that her works were of little concern to her biographers, beginning with her husband's initial accounts of her life ("Nachricht"; "Leben") and Runckel's introduction to her letters and culminating in some life-stories that are either entirely free of discussion of her works (Ploetz) or accord that discussion minimal space (most notably Schlenther's highly influential work on her).

[8] On Amalie von Sachsen, cf. Anna Jameson's introduction to her own translation of Amalie's plays and Kallin's reception history of the author. For an

account of Ebner-Eschenbach's variable reviews, cf. Goodman, *Dis/Closures* 166. Similar patterns hold for many other eighteenth- and nineteenth-century women authors (cf. Kord, *Sich einen Namen machen* 158–64).

[9] Cf. the many sources cited in Kord, *Sich einen Namen machen* 157 (note 1). Peter C. Pfeiffer has contrasted the usual glorification of Ebner-Eschenbach as "the good woman of Zdißlawitz" with the fact that critics have always attributed cerebral qualities to her when trying to defend her ability to write in "masculine" genres (68).

[10] Marie von Ebner-Eschenbach authored twenty-one dramas and wrote only in that genre for almost thirty years, but she is canonized as an author of stories and some biographical material (which she did not start writing until 1875 and which comprise only about half of her work). Ebner-Eschenbach and Droste-Hülshoff have both been the victims of so-called "complete" editions of their works that did not include a single one of their plays. Cf. Kord, *Ein Blick* 258–67.

[11] Cf. the discussion and examples in Kord, *Sich einen Namen machen,* 157–8.

[12] Among many others Sanders, "Ein kleiner Umweg" 174; Buchwald 434.

[13] For example in Robinson 120; Richel, *Luise Gottsched* 13; Schlenther 10; Kerth/Russell xii.

[14] Buchwald 434. Unless otherwise noted, all translations from this or other documents or secondary sources are mine. The original German is provided only for primary literature, original documents and letters. German secondary sources are cited in translation only.

[15] For example Richel, *Luise Gottsched* 14; Schlenther 22–3; Sanders, "The Virtuous Woman" 54. Köster's critical interpretation of this relationship: "The most loyal helpmate in this case was to become the master's 'skillful friend,' his wife Luise Adelgunde Viktoria, née Kulmus, an unusual woman for her time. Gottsched, barely able to differentiate between the duties of man and woman, educated her to be an erudite woman, following the ideal that he had outlined earlier in *Die vernünftigen Tadlerinnen* [The Reasonable Female Critics, Johann Christoph Gottsched's influential moral weekly published in 1725–6; S. K.]" (94).

[16] "Er suchte sie dadurch, mehr und mehr in dem Geschmacke an den Wissenschaften und freyen Künsten zu befestigen: zu welchem Ende er sie dann allmählich mit allerley deutschen und französischen Büchern, die ihrer Fähigkeit gemäß waren, versorgete" ("Leben," unpaginated). Throughout the document, Johann Christoph Gottsched speaks of himself in the third person.

[17] "Hauptsächlich machte ich dabey auf meine fleißige und arbeitsame Gattin Rechnung, die theils zu dieser Arbeit alle Lust und Fähigkeit hatte, theils ihre Nebenstunden nicht besser anwenden konnte" (Johann Christoph Gottsched, "Leben").

[18] For a complete list of her works, cf. Kord, *Ein Blick*, 281–82 and 372–4 and Sanders, "Ein kleiner Umweg."

[19] For example in Kerth/Russell xxv. Most assessments of the play appear vituperative beyond mere criticism; cf., e.g., Richel, who considers "Frau Gottsched's one tragedy . . . little more than painful evidence that her talent lay with the comic genre" (*Luise Gottsched*, 52; cf. also 104–5); Robinson, who takes the play as proof "that this 'Sappho,' as her friends liked to call her, was wholly devoid of poetic talent" (121); or Waniek, who sums up his highly contemptuous remarks on the play with his statement that Johann Christoph Gottsched's "skillful friend had indeed turned out to be the least skillful tragedian of all affiliates of the *Deutsche Schaubühne*" (400–1).

[20] Cf., e. g., Crüger's introduction to his reprint of *The Last Will*, in which he calls it "the most stomacheable of her works" (*Joh. Christoph Gottsched*, 253); Schlenther, who considers the play as evidence of "progress" in Luise Gottsched's "dramatic development," 189; Richel, *Luise Gottsched* 38 and 44–5.

[21] "Das einzige, wozu ich sie noch bewegen konnte . . . . Sie ließ sich auch dießmal im Winter 1760 willig finden . . ." (Johann Christoph Gottsched, "Leben").

[22] Cf. Becker-Cantarino, "Outsiders" 149 and Schreiber 41–2.

[23] Cf., e. g., Schlenther 26 and Hanstein I, 118–9. Traditionally, her first drama *Die Pietisterey* has been read as a scathing critique of erudite women and as a clear demonstration that the author considered her own erudition exceptional for women. (Cf., e. g., Sanders, "Kleiner Umweg" 185–6).

[24] Cf., e. g., Richel, *Luise Gottsched* 49–50 and 189; Hanstein I, 152; Brüggemann, *Bürgerliche Gemeinschaftskultur* 17.

[25] The simple equation between author and character is frequently supported only by the fact that all of Gottsched's main characters are women and that some of them carry her first name (Luischen in *Pietism* and *The French Housekeeper*). Other interpretations tend to view the many reasonable women characters, who comment on the action rather than participate in it, as the drama's "voice of Reason" and mouthpiece for the authorial "message."

[26] Both *Die Hausfranzösinn* and *Die ungleiche Heirath* were supposedly written as illustrations for advice she gave to correspondents in letters, one advocating German governesses over their French counterparts, the other advising against a socially incompatible marriage (cf., e. g., Schlenther 39). Because of its prominent foregrounding of marital fidelity, Gottsched's only tragedy *Panthea* is at times read as the author's sublimation of her husband's infidelities (Schlenther 62–3 and 183). Reading Gottsched's heroines as self-portraits of the author and establishing a link between her life and literature constitutes the most prevalent interpretive tradition with regard to Gottsched's dramas (cf., for example, Bohm and Kerth/Russell xxx). To identify the author with

her characters or reduce the work to the biographical context is an interpretive move applied to women's literature as a matter of course, but very rarely to men's. In an interpretive context in which one of the defining characteristics of "high" art is its complete separation from life (cf. Bürger, *Leben Schreiben*), such an interpretation deprives the woman author of the two most significant elements that make an "author": on the one hand, a vocation to authorship that can be seen as transcending the personal; on the other, the grounding of her work in the *Gelehrsamkeit*, the erudition that provides the scholarly and philosophical motivation for writing and that remained a defining characteristic of authorship throughout much of the eighteenth century, when creative writers were frequently identical with scholarly authors in philosophy, theology or poetics.

[27] Schlenther 208; very similarly in Hanstein I, 146–7.

[28] Schreiber 43; analogous Ploetz: "It is true that she became famous through her works, but she was admired for her human, her feminine dignity. . . . Certainly, she was an intellectual, but nonetheless she remained a woman" (12).

[29] So styled in much scholarship because of the "naturalness" of epistolary style developed in the eighteenth century (as opposed to the formalistic letters of earlier centuries) and because of the frequency of correspondence, which diminished greatly in the nineteenth century due to the improvement of transportation systems and the invention of the postcard. Cf. the sources cited in French 37–8.

[30] Cf. Rasch, Mauser/Becker-Cantarino, and the discussion in French 32 and 53–4.

[31] Cf. Gellert's *Praktische Abhandlung* and his *Gedanken von einem guten deutschen Briefe* (1741, Thoughts on a Good German Letter), which were seminal for the development of women's epistolary style as an artform, as well as Ebrecht et. al., 21–7, 56–98, 112–7 and French 51–60.

[32] Runckel's letters to Johann Christoph Gottsched have meanwhile been published in Magdalene Heuser's article "Die Sprache meines Geschlechts."

[33] The speculation I have heard from librarians and archivists in Leipzig and Dresden with respect to the disappearance of Gottsched's original letters is that they were transferred to Runckel's hometown Dresden after Gottsched's death, where they remained as part of Runckel's effects after her death in 1800 and were subsequently destroyed in the firebombing of Dresden in 1944. But the original letters were lost long before then, because Schlenther was unable to trace them in 1886 (cf. his remarks on p. 229).

[34] "Man fordert von den Deutschen sie sollen gute deutsche Briefe schreiben, und aus Mangel guter Originalbriefe in unserer Sprache, empfiehlet man dem Frauenzimmer Uebersetzungen zu lesen, um ihren Styl darnach zu bilden. Die meisten, und die besten darvon, sind Liebesgeschichten, woraus jungen Personen unbeschreiblich viel Nachtheil zuwächst. Ihr Herz wird verderbt,

und ihr Styl wird immer unnatürlich seyn, wenn sie ihren Vorbildern nachzu-ahmen suchen. Diesem Uebel habe ich abzuhelfen gewünscht, und eine Sammlung liefern wollen, die nirgends einen schädlichen Eindruck machen wird. Unsere Gottsched lehrt, ohne Regeln darüber zu geben, bey mannig-faltigen Gegenständen, den, einem jeden angemessenen Styl. Jeden Brief, und jeder Sache, darüber sie schreibt, giebt sie eine eigene Wendung, und das natürliche, das ungezwungene, leuchtet durchgängig hervor. Diese Briefe ha-ben noch den vorzüglichen Werth, daß es wirklich Originale, und theils an noch lebende, theils an verstorbene Personen geschrieben sind" (Runckel, "Vorbericht" to Gottsched, *Briefe* I, no pagination).

[35] "Findet man auch in diesen Briefen nicht die originelle Schriftstellerin, die scharfsinnige Kunstrichterin, die erhabenste Dichterin in der strengsten Be-deutung dieser Vorzüge: so wird man doch die zärtliche Tochter, die tu-gendhafte Ehegattin, die treuste Freundin, die Christin, die Philosophin darinnen nicht verkennen" (Runckel, "Vorbericht" to Gottsched, *Briefe* II, no pagination).

[36] "Eine glückliche Mischung von dem Ernste, der Standhaftigkeit und Ent-schlossenheit des männlichen Geschlechts mit der Sanftmuth, Zurückhaltung und Bescheidenheit, die die größte Zierde des unsrigen ausmachen . . . . Sie konnte auf Kenntnisse stolz seyn, die bey Frauenzimmern so selten angetrof-fen und deren einige fast niemals vermuthet, geschweige denn verlangt wer-den" (Runckel, "Vorbericht" to Gottsched, *Briefe* III, no pagination).

[37] "Das Andenken meiner verewigten Freundin zu erneuern und zu erhalten" ("Vorbericht" to Gottsched, *Briefe* III).

2: Originality: Contaminated Letters and Textual Hierarchies

"... these letters are extraordinarily valuable because they are true originals ..."

— From Runckel's "Vorbericht"
to her edition of Luise Gottsched's letters

The Text as Original: Historicizing "Authenticity"

ORIGINALITY, AUTHENTICITY, AND AUTHORSHIP in the eighteenth century in general, but for women in particular, are complex concepts. Nonetheless, virtually all interpretations of either eighteenth-century literature or of women's literature make certain a priori assumptions about all three of these concepts, most notably about authorship. Since the nineteenth century, interpretation of texts has traditionally conceptualized authorship in at least two ways: it has assumed the "authenticity" of the text, and it has privileged "original" authors over "epigonal" authors. "Originality," initially cast in this role during the Storm and Stress movement, is to this day usually viewed as a prerequisite for real authorship so crucial that some categories of writers (translators, adapters, imitators) are frequently excluded from the concept of authorship altogether. Yet the eighteenth-century project of "literature," which is today interpreted using these criteria, viewed itself as an undertaking in flux. "Literature" in the German national context did not yet exist; it was to be created by the importation of exemplary texts from other nations that did have a "great" national literature, most notably the French. "Exemplary" in this case did not indicate "superlative" but rather "prototypical": these texts were viewed not so much as texts to be revered, but as texts to be emulated. And the process of emulation was a liberal one: it began with translations, for which the French prototypes served loosely as the "original" and ended — or so it was hoped — with the creation of a German national canon of texts, for which the entire French national literature, embodied in these single texts, served as conceptual model.

In order to interpret eighteenth-century translations, then (or, for that matter, "original" literature), concepts of originality and authorship need to be rethought: they can no longer function in a context that posits them antithetical to translations. Luise Gottsched as a translator has been universally and harshly criticized for deviating from her original texts (cf. Vulliod; Richel, *Luise Gottsched*, 65–84), because such deviations were viewed as indicating a lack of linguistic skill, textual knowledge or awareness of cultural context. In short, the text she produced was read as a flawed translation rather than as a new original. In the eighteenth century, however, the text that furnished the basis for the translation served as no more than a template; contemporaries would have considered the translator who transferred the text into the German context most ingeniously and most completely — and this task involved substantial changes to the original — the most successful. Consider, for example, Richel's criticism of Luise Gottsched's translations:

> While the Destouches translations can by no means be regarded as failures, they are lacking in what might best be termed polish. They are faithful enough to their originals; but often a nuance, an effective turn of phrase in the French becomes clumsy or even mangled in the German rendition . . . . Frau Gottsched is more deserving of criticism when she invariably supplies considerably more coarse or excessive terms for the sarcastic or angry epithets found in the French texts . . . . In general, then, a comparison of the French and German texts shows that wherever the German version departs from the model, it proves inferior. (Richel, *Luise Gottsched*, 65-7)

In Richel's assessment, in which she reiterates many of Vulliod's earlier comments, the greatest failing of Luise Gottsched's translations appears to be her deviations from the originals: her critique takes place within a conceptual hierarchy of texts in which the translation is invariably inferior to the original and in which the best translation is therefore the one that reproduces the original as faithfully as possible. But the changes the translator made would not only have been tolerated by eighteenth-century readers, they would have stood as a sign of the translator's success in transferring the French text to the German context and, in strange and stark contrast to today's interpretive methodology, as testimony to the translator's genius. Consider Runckel's remarks on Gottsched's translations:

> How many demonstrations of her skill has she not placed before the world in her many translations from the French and the English? . . .

Often, when she found something in the texts she translated that seemed vulgar to her, she skillfully changed it, so as to avoid giving offense.[1]

The other strange contrast that emerges in these interpretations is Richel's criticism of Gottsched's "considerably more excessive" vocabulary vis-à-vis the more moderate originals versus Runckel's statement that Gottsched modified the vulgar original in her translation — but more of that later. The point I wish to emphasize here is that Richel bases her criticism of Gottsched's translations on a conceptual category that would have been dismissed out of hand by eighteenth-century readers: on an authenticity and authority of text, on the text's right to remain the "original," that is, unchanged in the translation. Eighteenth-century translators showed no such reverence for the original: very often, the original is not even mentioned in publications of translations. Vague attributions like "adapted from the French" or "translated from Destouches" are the norm. Eighteenth-century texts were public domain, intellectually as well as legally: before the institution of copyright in the late nineteenth century, published works could be plagiarized, reworked, performed, adapted or translated without reimbursing authors or even asking their permission. Authors had no legal recourse against appropriations of their work. It is quite possible that before the institution of *legal* copyright, there was little sense of what Germans today call *geistiges Eigentum,* intellectual ownership. Texts simply were not "owned" in a manner that would support Richel's allegations that Gottsched perverted the original.

The Text as Template: Editorial Interventions

To take this situation seriously — merely to consider the possibility that eighteenth-century authors and editors did not have the same reverence for the authenticity of the text — has severe consequences for any attempt at textual interpretation or biographical writing that takes as its subject any author of the age. If Luise Gottsched saw fit to change originals substantially in the translation, if this practice was universally accepted as evidence of the translator's skill and praised as part of what was seen as a potentially national project, then there can be no guarantee for the "authenticity" of any eighteenth-century text that exists today only in mediated form — that is, texts that are only extant today as translations or editions. One of the texts to which that statement applies is Luise Gottsched's own letters, most of which exist today only in Runckel's edition (and in Kording's 1999 edition, which follows

Runckel's faithfully). And it is indeed strange that the authenticity of these letters, which have after all been praised for their "naturalness" for two hundred years (an indication that readers do indeed attribute to them a kind of "authentic" expression), has been questioned only once: by Magdalene Heuser in her report on her proposed re-edition of Luise Gottsched's letters.

Heuser has done precisely the kind of work that tends to overturn interpretations that seemed unquestionably valid for centuries, the only kind of work that can give us access to the mostly obscure lives and texts of early women: archival work — the unglamorous work of searching, counting, collecting, selecting, comparing, and transcribing. Her archival research yields the following results: there are 224 published letters by Luise Gottsched, of which 66 were written to Johann Christoph Gottsched, 95 to Runckel, 63 to third persons ("Neuedition" 322). The archives of the Bibliotheca Albertina in Leipzig and the Gesamthochschulbibliothek in Kassel possess 52 original letters by Luise Gottsched, addressed to neither Johann Christoph Gottsched nor Runckel, of which 46 were not included in Runckel's edition. Five of the remaining original letters in Leipzig that Runckel did include in her edition were written to Ernst Christoph Count von Manteuffel (1676–1749); the sixth, housed in the archives at the Gesamthochschulbibliothek Kassel, is addressed to Gottsched's sister-in-law in Kassel. A comparison of these six originals with their printed counterparts in Runckel's edition reveals extensive editorial liberties taken by the editor. Place names and personal names, which are fully written out in the original, are abbreviated or anonymized in other ways; descriptions of persons and encounters as well as many details are omitted; Gottsched's often rather coarse language is cleaned up. In one instance, Runckel inserted a portion of one of Johann Christoph's letters into a letter by Luise Gottsched ("Neuedition", 324–7). A comparison of one of Gottsched's original letters (as transcribed by Heuser) with the version printed in Runckel's edition indicates conclusively that the letters published by Runckel as Luise Gottsched's letters can no longer be considered "original" letters by Luise Gottsched.

I. Letter from Luise Gottsched to Katharine Friderike Gottsched in Kassel. Original in the GHB Kassel, 2° Ms. hist. litt. 4. Transcribed by Magdalene Heuser. *Hanover, August 7, 1753, Tuesday*	*II. Printed version, as edited by Dorothea Henriette von Runckel. Vol. II, pp. 131–35. One hundred and twenty-fourth letter.* *To Mrs. S.* *Hanover, Aug. 7, 1753.*

Nobly born, highly esteemed Sister,

I would have to be ingratitude itself, if I were to wait any longer to thank you most obligingly for the extremely cordial reception with which you have honored me in your home. As much as I was moved by this even in Kassel, still I cannot deny that in Göttingen, I have experienced the truthfulness of the old proverb: one does not recognize something good until one has lost it. A landlady who obviously lacks common sense, and an in every way disorderly and unsanitary household have reminded me all the more sternly of the loss I have sustained in being deprived of the pleasant and spirited company of my highly esteemed sister and her household, which was as orderly as it was clean. But I do not intend to make either my or your heart heavy nor to renew that sorrow of which you have given me such eloquent testimony in parting, and which I cannot interpret as anything but the sign of generous and affectionate sentiments on your part, to which I recommend myself most heartily in the future.

Rather, I will write you a brief history of my life in Göttingen, and let you be the judge of whether I have improved or changed for the worse. As soon as we arrived in Göttingen beneath a near-constant rain around eight o'clock in the evening, the appearance of my landlady would have evoked the greatest terror in me, if I had not been advised of her appearance by Herr Hofrat Huber, for which I ask you to express my renewed thanks to him on occasion. After a brief meal we laid down in the bedroom assigned to us, in which

Highly esteemed lady,

I would have to be very ungrateful if I did not assure you of the most obliging gratitude for the exceedingly cordial reception with which you have honored me in your home. As much as I was moved by this even in ---: still I cannot deny that thereafter, I have experienced the truthfulness of the old proverb: one does not recognize something good until one has lost it. Innumerable loathsome objects have reminded me of the pleasure which I enjoyed in your house and with your pleasant hospitality. But I do not intend to make either my or your heart heavy nor to renew that sorrow of which you have given me such moving testimony in parting. I have taken these as signs of your affectionate sentiments, to which I recommend myself most heartily in the future.

I will sketch you here a brief history of my continued life; you be the judge as to whether I have improved or changed for the worse.

As soon as we arrived in *** beneath the constant rain around eight o'clock in the evening, we sat down at table. After a brief meal we laid down in the bedroom assigned to us, in which we, due to our great exhaustion, slept through the noise made by the mice. The following nights, I was deprived of sleep by my mortal enemies, which was a most unpleasant experience for me.

we, due to our great exhaustion, slept through the noise caused by the mice, a noise with which these my mortal enemies have kept me awake every night until morning since then. Throughout the days that followed, we have feasted our way through the menus of Göttingen, and if I report to you, dearest sister, that we consumed daily 14 warm meals and extensive desserts and spent six and a half hours per day at table, then you will easily discern that we neither died of starvation nor (as that Swiss man put it) stuffed ourselves on the run. But I can assure you of this much, that this has not prevented me from remembering our pleasant meals in Kassel with regret.

On early Saturday morning the hour that I had wished for for so long finally appeared, the hour in which we continued our journey, and during which I once again had occasion to gratefully remember the loving care accorded me by my highly esteemed sister. For we were served a very agreeable breakfast, but since it was only seven o'clock and we had just taken coffee, we could not eat a single bite of it; and to give us some to take along did not occur to anyone, although this would have come in very handy during our stop at mid-day, where we could not obtain anything beyond aged butter and stinky cheese. We then went on to the road which was bearable at first but finally led us onto DAMNED evil ways. You can imagine who it was who DAMNED it!, but I helped a little in this, because these roads are really made to break wheels, and are yearly made worse, not better, with the aid of 20 000 thalers. Long live Count Brünau! he can really make

Every day of our stay here we have feasted our way through the menus of ***. If I tell you that we have daily eaten fourteen warm meals as well as extensive desserts and that we sat at table for over five hours: you will easily discern that we have not died of starvation. How often, while sitting at these richly laden tables, have I thought back with regret to our meals in ***!

Saturday morning the hour that I had wished for for so long finally appeared: the hour in which we continued our journey. On this occasion, I once again thought back to your loving care. We were served a very agreeable breakfast, but since it was only seven o'clock, we could not eat a single bite of it. It would have served us better at our midday station, where we could get nothing but aged butter and spoiled cheese. The road finally led us onto desperately evil ways. You will be able to guess who became impatient, scolded and complained: I helped as much as I could. These roadways are really made to break wheels. They are yearly made worse, not improved, with the aid of 20 000 thalers. In all cities, we drove through mud as high as our axles, but here in Hanover, paving-stones are valuable. If, at the moment that I am writing this, the Herr Privy Councillor v. M. did not have a certain poet at table and was not in all manner of ways a genteel good roads! but the Hanoverians don't know anything of this, the Hessians don't either; but do not be annoyed, dear Brother! In all cities during our journey, we drove through the mud up to our axles; but here in Hanover, paving-stones are valuable!, and I suppose the mud must be as well: since it is neatly swept together in piles and placed on both sides of the bridge like precious stones, until the falling rains return it to its original position. In short, if, at the moment that I am writing this, Herr Privy Councillor von — Münchhausen did not have a certain poet at table, and if he was not such a genteel gentleman himself; then the Hanoverian roadways might easily be accorded the same honor as those of the Upper Palatinate.[2]

Tomorrow, we will dine respectively with His Excellency the Herr Privy Councillor and Her Excellency — the Frau Privy Councillor von Schwichelt, which I ask you to convey to Her Excellency Frau President von Borcke. All jesting aside, it would be appreciated if Herr Councillor Arkenholz (to whom I ask you to remember me and whom I assure of my particular respect and gratitude) would convey this message on occasion, with an appropriate critical commentary.

Please convey our deepest regards to the indefatigable, industrious, obliging and truthful Herr Reifstein. His generous care accompanied us after we departed, and as recently as the day before yesterday, we drank to his health with his own wine. But here is a very special, great, mighty, precious compliment, which should not at all be confused with the others. It goes to my highly esteemed

gentleman: then the roadways of H--- might easily be accorded the same honor as those of the Upper Palatinate.

Please convey our best regards, mine and that of my dear traveling companion, to the indefatigable, industrious, obliging and truthful Herr R-- -. His generosity has accompanied us after we departed, and we have as recently as yesterday drunk to his health that noble juice of the grape for which we have his kindness to thank. We will acquaint ourselves with all curiosities

Brother and is adorned from top to bottom with expressions of thanks. I do know that my duty would demand that I write to him in person; but at the moment, this is not possible: for in half an hour, the Schwichelts' coach will come to fetch us in order to acquaint us with Herrenhausen and the other curiosities of this locality. I must therefore save this letter for the first hour of leisure that I will have. In the meantime, I am exceedingly obliged to him for his letter to me.

of this locality and also see Herrenhausen.

Farewell, dearest Sister! I embrace you and the little pair with all possible tenderness and remain with the utmost dutifulness

Farewell, dearest friend; I embrace you with all tenderness and remain

Your most noble born Lady's most obedient and most obliged servant Gottsched Hanover, August 7, 1753.

Your most obliged servant Gottsched[3]

Reading these letters side by side gives us an idea about the extent of the liberties Runckel took with Gottsched's letters. They far transcend the usual editorial liberties one might expect, such as the anonymization of places and persons described in the letters (which in contemporary publications was frequently done to protect persons still living). Aside from the fact that quantitatively, Runckel edited out about 50% of the original letter, the following changes seem noteworthy:

•Runckel not only deleted the recipient's personal identity, but also her relationship to the author of the letters. Her printed version leaves no allusion to the familial relationship and none to the personal friendship between the two women. This must have been of particular importance to the editor, because she goes beyond the usual anonymization accorded to other people mentioned in the letters (Herr Reifstein in the original becomes Herr R--- in the printed version) by falsifying the addressee and substituting a fictitious "Frau S." for Katharine Friderike Gottsched. Even assuming "Frau S." to be Runckel's stand-in for "Frau Schwester" (Kording's commentary, 355), the existence of a familial relationship between Katharina and Luise Gottsched is obscured beyond recognizability on the part of the casual reader, removed to the level of a vague allusion that could only be understood by readers who were already aware of the family connection.

•Runckel erases all place names (Kassel, Göttingen, Hanover, with a single exception) as well as all references to distinct persons: Luise Gottsched's brother-in-law, Hofrat Huber, Count Brünau, the Schwichelts, President von Borcke, Arkenholz, Reifstein and "the little pair" (her sister's-in-law children) are deleted from her published version.

•In Runckel's version of the letter, Gottsched's flowery and elegant style is clipped to more concrete and distinct sentences. Conversely, in a single instance, Gottsched's thanks for Reifstein's gift of the wine (in the original: "as recently as the day before yesterday, we drank to his health with his own wine") is made more profuse in the printed version: "we have as recently as yesterday drunk to his health that noble juice of the grape for which we have his kindness to thank." The reasons for these discrepancies are unclear, but they clearly demonstrate that Runckel saw Gottsched's style, her expressions, her turns-of-the-phrase precisely as Gottsched herself would have seen the "originals" of her translations: as little more than a template to be re-worked at the editor's discretion.

•Runckel omits several expressions and entire anecdotes in the original that could have been read as on the margins of propriety, a subject about which the late eighteenth and early nineteenth centuries had much sterner attitudes than the mid-eighteenth, during which Gottsched wrote. This is evidenced in Runckel's substitutions (of "spoiled cheese" in the printed version versus "stinky cheese" in Gottsched's original letter), her omission of Gottsched's relation of the Swiss man's crude remarks in Swiss dialect, and the omission of Gottsched's humorous digression about the value of Hanoverian mud. More significantly, Runckel omits the entire encounter with Gottsched's slovenly landlady. Heuser took this example as an impetus to compare similar omissions of chance encounters in other letters with some of the instances in which equally chance meetings were left intact and concludes that editorial decisions as to whether to print or cut these encounters were most likely governed by the picture Runckel wanted to convey of Gottsched. A chance meeting with a curator of a university, for example, would successfully convey the image of the Gottscheds as a well-known and universally respected couple and was perhaps left intact for that very reason, while a chance encounter with a slovenly landlady could accomplish nothing of the kind and was cut (Heuser, "Neuedition" 326).

•Perhaps most interesting are the two changes Runckel made in Gottsched's references to her husband. One of them corresponds to the general modification of crude expressions: the printed version greatly modifies Johann Christoph's cursing of the roadways, which is packaged in Gottsched's original as an amused allusion to the irritable temper of a man whom the recipient of the letter knows well, as the tone of Gottsched's original clearly implies: "the road . . . finally led us onto DAMNED evil ways. You can imagine who it was who DAMNED it!" In Runckel's printed version, this knowledge on the part of the recipient is edited out; so, for that matter, is the intimacy between author and recipient that would permit the author to make an allusion of this kind. The modification of Johann Christoph's "DAMNED" roads to "desperately evil ways," the act of muting his wild curses to mild-mannered complaints ("You will be able to guess who became impatient, scolded and complained") are undoubtedly designed to change, in the printed version, the impression conveyed of Gottsched's relationship with her husband and her attitudes towards him: the amusement and the tone of resignation are gone entirely from the printed version, as is the sense of Gottsched *sharing* this implied characterization of the man with another woman who knew him well. Equally revealing is one of Runckel's rare additions: where Gottsched in the original simply asks to convey "our deepest regards," Runckel inserts an expression of fondness for Johann Christoph: "mine and that of my dear traveling companion." It is changes of this nature that prompted Heuser to speculate that Johann Christoph Gottsched may have participated in the creation of Runckel's edition of his wife's letters ("Neuedition" 321).

There are of course numerous conclusions to be drawn from Runckel's extensive interventions into Gottsched's writing, the least significant of which concerns the strangely contradictory statements with regard to Gottsched's style that I mentioned earlier. Richel accuses Gottsched of unnecessary and uncalled-for coarseness in her translations, echoing a scholarly tradition of long standing that began with Lessing's harsh criticism of Luise Gottsched's drama *Die Hausfranzösinn*.[4] Conversely, Runckel claims that Gottsched often modified coarse expressions in translation. The explanation for this discrepancy would seem to lie in Runckel's interest in portraying Gottsched as a model of virtue, stylistically and otherwise. Demonstrably, Runckel made these changes herself, modifying Gottsched's expressions wherever they appeared crude to her and thus creating the impression of "sober respectability" that Runckel clearly interpreted as appropriate style for a paragon of virtue (Heuser, "Neuedition" 326).

Textual Bases: On the Search for Biographical Truths

But the consequences for our reading of Luise Gottsched's letters, knowing that they cannot be considered *originals* in any sense of the word, knowing that they have been cut, pasted, changed and contaminated by the editor (at least two were omitted entirely), go far beyond merely clearing up any such minor controversies. For one thing, Runckel's changes clearly indicate that like any eighteenth-century translator, she did not merely see herself as the medium through which Luise Gottsched's letters would be passed on to future readers. Like eighteenth-century translators, she had an authorial agenda that she wished to further through this edition. Her introductory remarks in which she portrays her friend Luise Gottsched as a model letter writer have to be read literally: the important thing about Gottsched's letters was not their "originality" but their potential to serve as models to be emulated, as templates for the writing of others. That is the way in which Runckel used them, and that is the way in which she intended for future letter writers to use them.

For literary historians who have an interest in the lives and works of eighteenth-century women writers, and that means almost invariably feminist literary historians, the consequences of this knowledge are profound. It deprives literary historians of the very factor on which one might base any authoritative statements about the "author's" life and work: the undisputed originality and authenticity of source documents. Feminist scholars are deprived of the equally powerful hope that whereas male editors have demonstrably falsified women's writings, particularly women's writings about themselves, and they have done this both to further their personal agendas and to put forward an ideologically tainted view of women's lives that probably had no basis in reality, the same motivation did (should) not apply to female editors: in short, the hope that female editors could be trusted not to manipulate texts by women in a similar manner. The origins of this hope are understandable: women have only very rarely acted as editors of other women's writings, and they have almost always had a personal stake in the edition. As in the pairing Gottsched-Runckel, many of them were close personal friends. Possibly this personal interest has given rise to feminist hopes that these editors would consider their friends' texts sacrosanct and absolute, that they would refrain from exercising editorial control over the text, thus providing later interpreters with a document that can grant us an unblemished view into the past.

My reading of Luise Gottsched's life, as well as any future work on the author, will have to grapple with Heuser's results. It is now impossible to read Luise Gottsched's letters as originals, as authentic documents that can give us uncontaminated insights into the author's life.[5] Nonetheless, it is equally impossible to disregard them, because they remain the *only* documents about Luise Gottsched's life in whose creation the author herself had a hand. Since there are only six letters that overlap — that is, that are both still extant in the original manuscript and included in Runckel's printed version — we do not have enough material to generalize about what Runckel cut, added, changed or edited, so that Runckel's changes, as well as her reasons and motivations, remain a matter of speculation. Out of this maze of conflicting interests emerge certain methodological mandates for an interpretation based on this contaminated material:

1) Arriving at an authoritative biographical or historical "truth" can no longer be the goal of the investigation. This statement means, for the interpreter, a considerable radicalization of Montrose's aforementioned concept of the "historicization of the text" and the "textuality of history," because it implies that *no* part of history is discernible beyond its own textuality, beyond the manner, that is, in which it has been textualized.

2) Runckel's edition must serve as one of the primary textual bases for an interpretation of Gottsched's life and work due to the lack of other primary source materials. The decision to work with Runckel's edition can rest on one of two interpretive attitudes: the modern one that insists on an originality of the text and on the notion that there is a biographical or historical truth to be recovered, or the eighteenth-century one that reads all texts as essentially equal. This second view would refuse to privilege Gottsched's text as authentic and to read Runckel's changes as contaminations; it would give up all attempts to distinguish between Gottsched's and Runckel's texts, and it would read the fused text as a new original rather than as an inadequate translation. If this seems ethically questionable, it does so only because of our predilection to equate "originality" with "authenticity" and "authenticity" with "truth." New historicists and feminist scholars alike have long pointed out the dubiousness of these claims: no direct line can be drawn from Runckel's "contaminated" edition of Gottsched's letters to Gottsched's life, but even if Gottsched's letters were available in untainted form, would it not be highly questionable methodological practice to draw such a line from these texts to the author's life? Would such an act of reading not assume that Gottsched was willing and able to write her life "history" as it oc-

curred or, more generally, that writers do not "edit" their own texts (and lives) as they write them? The abandonment of our search for biographical authenticity is far from a genuine choice in a situation where our hand is forced by the material situation: as is so often the case with eighteenth-century women writers, there is precious little biographical "truth" left to investigate. There are good intellectual arguments to be made, however, for reading the text produced by Gottsched and Runckel and later published as letters by Luise Gottsched as an "original" text in the eighteenth-century sense.

Briefly, what this decision entails is a willingness on the part of the reader to suspend twentieth-century attitudes about the hierarchy of texts: the "original" cannot be privileged over the translation or edition. The edition or translation does not function as a weak imitation, but as an entirely new text that can be read as cohabited by both the original and the secondary author. As readers of an eighteenth-century translation did not read the translation to find out how close it was to the original, so we, perhaps, should not necessarily read Runckel's edition as falsifications of Gottsched's authentic letters, or at least not exclusively. Although Luise Gottsched did formally confer the editorship of her letters to Runckel, and although she was certainly aware of the liberties editors and translators took with their templates, we should also resist the temptation to rationalize that this may indicate silent permission on Gottsched's part for the editor to change her text at will, because such a statement would bespeak an attempt to do what is now impossible: to recover, however indirectly, Gottsched's "original" text, if not in body, then at least in intentionality.

It is my contention that the only way in which we can productively read the text now entitled *Briefe der Frau Louise Adelgunde Victorie Gottsched*, edited by Dorothea Henriette von Runckel, is to read it not as a *history* of Gottsched's life, but as a *story* for which Gottsched's life loosely served as inspiration. We would read this story not to discern real biographical background, but as a testimony of how the secondary author wanted the primary author's life to appear, to investigate the construction of a life that became the template for subsequent biographies of Luise Gottsched and that also became prototypical for contemporary women authors in general. Such a reading would be perhaps more informative and conscientious than the continued search for authenticity, because the numerous contradictions that pervade different accounts of Luise Gottsched's life and work (vulgar translator or paragon of virtue? ambitious author or industrious helpmate? the most learned woman of her age or the disparager of learned women everywhere?) would not have to be suppressed to arrive at an authoritative biographical "truth." On the contrary, such an act of reading would be productive in the sense that it would permit us to explore the tension between texts by Luise Gottsched edited, directly or indirectly, by her husband (her dramas, most of which were commissioned by him) on the one hand and texts by Luise Gottsched edited by Runckel (Gottsched's letters) on the other. Although none of this can give us undisputably historical insights into her actual life, we are presented with something perhaps even more interesting: two diametrically opposed, indeed warring, presentations of the *image* of Luise Gottsched, the most famous woman writer of her age, by the two people closest to her.[6]

Notes

[1] Runckel, "Vorbericht" to *Briefe*, vol. I, no pagination: "Wie viele Beweise ihrer Geschicklichkeit hat sie der Welt, durch ihre Uebersetzungen aus dem Französischen und Englischen, nicht vor Augen gelegt? . . . Oft, wenn sich in den Schriften, die sie übersetzte, etwas fand, was ihr anstößig zu seyn schien, so wußte sie solches geschickt zu ändern, um kein Aergernis zu geben."

[2] During earlier travels through the Upper Palatinate, Johann Christoph Gottsched had acquired dubious fame by publicly making disparaging remarks about its roadways, an incident that so offended the locals that it led to numerous retaliatory satires on Johann Christoph Gottsched published by local authors. Among these are Aichinger's *Bemühung der Obern Pfalz den Zorn des Herrn Prof. Gottscheds zu besänfftigen* (The Endeavor of the Upper Palatinate to Assuage the Wrath of Herr Professor Gottsched, 1750) as well as the satires *Klag-Lied des Herrn Professor Gottscheds über das rauhe Pfälzer-Land in einer Abschieds-Ode* (Herr Professor Gottsched's Lamentation on the Rough Palatinate Countryside, an Ode of Farewell) and *Der Zorn des Herrn Professor Gottscheds über das rauhe Pfälzer-Land* (Herr Professor Gottsched's Wrath about the Rough Palatinate Countryside), both published anonymously in 1750. Luise Gottsched alludes to this as well as her own assumption that her husband was only prevented from further venting his anger by the company of Privy Councillor von Münchhausen.

[3] *I.* In: Heuser, "Neuedition" 328–31:

"*Transkription nach der Briefhandschrift (GHB Kassel, 2° Ms. hist. litt. 4.*

Louise Adelgunde Victorie Gottsched an Katharine Friderike Gottsched in Kassel Hannover 7. August 1753 Dienstag HOCHEDELGEBOHRNE,

II. In: Heuser, "Neuedition" 333–5:

"*Druck in: Briefe. Th. 2. S. 131–135 (Nr. 124) Hundert und vier und zwanzigster Brief*

An die Frau S. Hannover den 7. Aug. 1753. Hochzuehrende Frau,

Insonders hochgeschätzte Frau Schwester,

Ich müßte die Undankbarkeit selbst seyn, wenn ich länger anstehen wollte, Ihnen für die überaus liebreiche Aufnahme deren Sie mich in Dero Behausung gewürdiget haben, den allerverbindlichsten Dank abzustatten. So lebhaft ich davon bereits in Cassel gerühret worden bin, so kann ich doch nicht leugnen, daß ich in Göttingen die Wahrheit des alten Sprüchworts erfahren: Man erkennet das Gute nicht eher, als bis man es verloren hat. Eine Wirthinn, der es an der gesunden Vernunft fehlet, und eine in allen Stücken unordentliche und schmutzige Haushaltung, haben mich des Verlusts den ich an dem angenehmen und geistreichen Umgange meiner hochgeschätzten Frau Schwester, und an einer so ordentlichen als saubern Haushaltung erlitten, nur desto lebhafter erinnert. Doch, es ist hier meine Absicht nicht, weder mir noch Ihnen das Herz schwer zu machen, und diejenige Betrübniß zu erneuern, davon Sie mir bey meinem Abschiede so deutliche Proben gegeben, die ich nicht anders als Zeugnisse einer großmüthigen und freundschaftsvollen Gesinnung aufnehmen kann, zu welcher ich mich ferner auf das eifrigste empfehle.

Ich will Ihnen vielmehr eine kurze Geschichte meines Lebenslaufes in Göttingen überschreiben, und Dieselben hernach selbst urtheilen lassen, ob ich mich verbessert, oder verschlimmert habe. Sobald wir, unter einem fast beständig anhaltenden Regen in Göttingen, gegen 8. Uhr des Abends angelanget waren, würde die Erscheinung meiner Frau Wirthinn, mich in das äußerste Schrecken gesetzet haben, wenn ich nicht durch den Herrn Hofrath Huber davon wäre benachrichtiget gewesen, wofür ich ihm bey Gelegenheit meine nochmalige Danksagung abzustatten bitte. Nach einer kurzen Mahlzeit legten wir uns in das uns angewiesene Schlafgemach, in welchem wir vor großer Müdigkeit, das Getöse der Mäuse verschliefen, wodurch diese meine Todtfeinde, mich nach diesem alle Nacht bis gegen Morgen vom Schlafe abgehalten haben. Die folgenden Tage haben wir uns durch die Göttingischen Küchenzettel durchgeschmauset, und wenn ich Ihnen, wertheste Frau Schwester melde, daß wir fast täglich 14. warme Essen und einen weitläuftigen Nachsatz verzehrt, dabey aber auch sechstehalb Stunden bey Tische

Ich müste sehr undankbar seyn, wenn ich Ihnen für die überaus liebreiche Aufnahme, deren Sie mich in Ihrem Hause gewürdiget haben, nicht die verbindlichste Erkenntlichkeit versicherte. So lebhaft ich bereits in == davon gerühret worden bin: so kann ich doch nicht leugnen, daß ich nachhero noch die Wahrheit des alten Sprüchworts erfahren: Man erkennet das Gute nicht eher, als bis man es verlohren hat. Unzählige eckelhafte Gegenstände erinnerten mich an das Vergnügen, welches ich in Ihrem Hause und bey Ihrer angenehmen Bewirthung genossen habe. Doch es ist nicht meine Absicht, mir oder Ihnen das Herz schwer zu machen, und die Betrübniß zu erneuern, davon Sie bey meinem Abschiede so rührende Proben gegeben haben. Ich habe diese als Zeugnisse Ihrer freundschaftlichen Gesinnung angenommen, welcher ich mich auch ferner auf das eifrigste empfehle.

Ich will Ihnen hier eine kurze Geschichte meiner Lebensart entwerfen; urtheilen Sie selbst, ob ich mich verbessert oder verschlimmert habe.

Sobald wir unter anhaltenden Regen in *** gegen 8 Uhr des Abends angelanget waren, setzten wir uns zu Tische. Nach einer kurzen Mahlzeit, legten wir uns in das uns angewiesene Schlafgemach, in welchem wir vor großer Müdigkeit, das Getöse der Mäuse verschliefen. Die folgenden Nächte wurde ich von meinen Todfeinden, bis gegen Morgen vom Schlaf abgehalten, eine Sache die mir höchst unangenehm gewesen ist. Alle Tage unsers Aufenthalts haben wir uns durch die ***er Küchenzeddel durchgeschmaußet. Wenn ich Ihnen sage, daß wir fast täglich vierzehn warme Speisen und einen weitläufigen Nachsatz gehabt, dabey aber auch über fünf Stunden bey Tische gesessen: so werden Sie leicht schlüßen, daß wir nicht Hungers gestorben sind. Wie oft habe ich an diesen reich besetzten Tafeln, an die ***ischen Mahlzeiten mit Wehmuth zurücke gedacht!

gesessen, so werden Sie leicht die Rechnung
machen, daß wir, weder Hungers gestorben,
noch (wie jener Schweizer sagete) uff der
Puscht g'fressa haben. So viel aber kann ich
versichern, daß sie mich nicht abgehalten
haben, an die angenehmen Caßler-
Mahlzeiten, oft mit Wehmut zurück zu
denken.

Sonnabends früh erschien endlich die von
mir so lang gewünschte Stunde, da wir
unsern Stab weiter setzeten, und wobey ich
abermal Gelegenheit hatte, an die liebreiche
Fürsorge meiner hochgeschätzten Frau
Schwester, mit dankbarem Gemüthe zu
denken. Denn es ward uns zwar ein sehr
artiges Frühstück aufgetragen; allein da es
erst sieben Uhr war, und wir nur eben erst
Caffee getrunken hatten, konnten wir keinen
Bissen davon genießen; das Mitgeben aber
fiel keinem Menschen ein, so sehr es uns auf
der Mittags-Station zu statten gekommen
wäre, allwo wir nichts bekommen konnten,
als alte Butter und stinkenden Käse. Wir
kamen denn auf die Landstraße, welche
anfangs noch so ziemlich war, endlich aber
uns auf verFLUOCHTE böse Wege führete.
Sie können denken wer darüber
GEFLUOCHT hat! doch habe ich ein wenig
dazu geholfen, denn sie sind ordentlich zum
Räderbrechen gemacht, und werden jährlich
mit 20000. Thalern, nicht verbessert, sondern
verbösert. Es lebe der Graf Brünau! der kann
Wege machen! aber die Hannoveraner
verstehen gar nichts davon: auch die Hessen
nicht; aber werden Sie nur nicht böse Herr
Bruder! In allen Städten unterwegens, sind
wir im Kothe gefahren bis über die Achsen;
aber hier in Hannover ist das Pflaster
kostbar! und der Koth muß es wohl auch
seyn: denn er wird in Häufchen zusammen
gekehret, und liegt an beyden Seiten der
Brücke, wie die Edelsteine, bis ihn ein
herabfallender Platzregen wieder an Ort und
Stelle bringt. Kurz, wenn den Augenblick da
ich dieses schreibe, der Herr geheime Rath
von — Münchhausen nicht einen gewissen
Dichter zur Tafel hätte, und an sich selbst ein
so gnädiger Herr wäre; so könnte den
Hanöverischen Wegen leicht mit den
Oberpfälzischen einerley Ehre widerfahren.
Morgen speisen wir beyderseits, bey des
Herrn geheimen Raths und der — Frau
geheimen Räthinn von Schwichelt Excellenz,
welches ich der Fr. Präsidentinn von *Borcke*
Excellenz zu melden bitte. Scherz À PART,
es wäre schön, wenn der Herr Rath

Sonnabends früh, erschien endlich die von
mir so lange gewünschte Stunde, da wir
unsern Stab weiter setzten. Hier dachte ich
ebenfalls an Ihre liebreiche Fürsorge
zurücke. Es ward uns zwar ein sehr artiges
Frühstück aufgetragen, allein da es erst
sieben Uhr war, konnten wir keinen Bissen
davon genüssen. Es würde uns besser auf der
Mittagsstation zu statten gekommen seyn,
wo wir nichts als alte Butter und verdorbnen
Käse bekommen konnten. Die Landstraße
führte uns endlich auf verzweifelte böse
Wege. Sie können errathen, wer darüber
ungedultig ward, schimpfte und schmählte:
ich habe treulich geholfen. Diese Wege sind
ordentlich zum Räderbrechen gemacht. Sie
werden jährlich mit 20,000 Thlr. nicht
verbessert, sondern verschlimmert. In allen
Städten sind wir bis über die Achsen im
Kothe gefahren, aber hier in Hannover ist das
Pflaster kostbar. Wenn in dem Augenblicke,
da ich dieses schreibe, der Herr Geh. R. v.
M. nicht einen gewissen Dichter zur Tafel
hätte, und in allen Stücken ein so gnädiger
Herr wäre: so könnte den H=== Wegen, mit
den Oberpfälzischen leicht einerley Ehre
wiederfahren.

Arkenholz (dem ich mich ergebenst zu
empfehlen und ihn meiner ausnehmenden
Hochachtung und Erkenntlichkeit zu
versichern bitte) diese Nachricht bey
Gelegenheit, mit einer gehörigen kritischen
Anmerkung an den Mann brächte.

Dem unermüdeten, fleissigen, dienstfertigen und redlichen Herrn Reifstein, bitten wir uns beyde nochmals auf das geflissenste zu empfehlen. Seine freygebige Fürsorge hat uns sogar bis auf den Weg begleitet, und wir haben noch vorgestern, seine Gesundheit aus seinem eigenen Weine getrunken. Aber nun kömmt ein ganz besonderes, großes, mächtiges, kostbares Compliment, so mit den andern gar nicht verwechselt werden muß. Es ist an den hochgeschätzten Herrn Bruder, und über und über mit Danksagungen verbrämet. Ich weis wohl, daß es meine Schuldigkeit erfoderte, selbst an ihn zu schreiben; aber jetzt ist es nicht möglich: denn in einer halben Stunde, holet uns die Schwicheltische EQUIPAGE ab, um uns Herrenhausen, und die andern Merkwürdigkeiten hiesiges Ortes bekannt zu machen. Ich muß es also bis zu der ersten Stunde versparen, die ich müssig haben werde. Indessen bin ich Demselben für das mir übermachte Schreiben ergebenst verbunden.	Den unermüdeten, fleißigen, dienstfertigen und redlichen Herrn R== bitten wir beyde, ich und mein lieber Reisegefährte, uns auf das beste zu empfehlen. Seine Freygebigkeit hat uns sogar auf dem Wege begleitet, und wir haben noch gestern auf sein Wohl, den edlen Rebensaft getrunken, den wir seiner Güte zu danken hatten. Wir werden uns alle Merkwürdigkeiten hiesiges Orts bekannt machen und auch Herrnhausen sehen.
Leben Sie wohl, theureste Frau Schwester! ich umarme Dieselben und das kleine Paar, mit aller möglichen Zärtlichkeit, und bin mit der vollkommensten Verpflichtung	Leben Sie wohl, liebste Freundin; ich umarme Sie mit aller Zärtlichkeit und bin
Eurer HOCHEDELBOHRNEN ganz ergebenste u. verbundenste Dienerinn Gottsched Hannover den 7. August 1753.	Ihre verbundenste Dienerin Gottsched

Gottsched's original rendition of the Swiss expression *uff der Puscht g'fressa* is intranslatable. The allusion here is to the often hurried meals while changing horses at postal stations.

[4]   From Lessing's review of a performance of Gottsched's *Hausfranzösinn* in Hamburg, June 10, 1767: "This drama is one of the six originals with which the German nation was graced, with [Johann Christoph] Gottsched as midwife, in the fifth volume of his *German Stage*. It is said that it was here and there performed successfully when it was still new. The goal was to see what kind of applause it would receive in this day and age, and it received as much as it merited: none whatsoever. *The Last Will*, by the same author, is at least something, but *The French Housekeeper* is nothing at all. Less than nothing:

for it is not only low and flat and cold, but on top of that dirty, disgusting, and offensive in the extreme. It is inconceivable to me how a lady was capable of writing such filth" (224).

[5] Kording's 1999 edition of Luise Gottsched's letters (*Louise Gottsched — mit der Feder in der Hand*) mentions Heuser's article in her commentary (339), but disregards Heuser's conclusions and all documentation indicating that Gottsched's letters were substantially altered by Runckel. Notwithstanding this evidence, Kording's commentary attempts to minimize Runckel's editorial intervention (cf., e. g., 318, 341, 343, 353). In "Zu dieser Ausgabe," Kording states (376) that Runckel made only negligible changes (an assumption already invalidated by Heuser) and only to a few letters (an unverifiable conjecture, in view of the fact that most of Gottsched's hand-written originals are no longer extant, and an unreasonable supposition in view of the fact that the six hand-written letters still available in archives that appear in Runckel's edition all were published in substantially altered form). Whether Kording's edition was conceptualized as a scholarly edition remains unclear from the editor's comments: Kording's afterword described it as a "Leseausgabe," lays claim to bibliographic and scholarly reliability ("wissenschaftlicher Anspruch") but simultaneously admits that the hand-written originals were not consulted (377). The extent to which the editor has chosen to disregard the severe problems with regard to the authorial provenance of the letters is apparent in her comment that she has not modernized Gottsched's spelling in order to avoid compromising the "authenticity" of the letters and obscuring "Louise's methodical usage of language" (376). Kording's edition is an achievement in that it is the first to make Luise Gottsched's letters, as edited by Runckel, available to a broader reading public, but it is misleading and unreliable in terms of its capricious and selective use of recent scholarship. Its misrepresentation of Luise Gottsched's letters as unproblematic, authentic and original can only be upheld by its avoidance of any response to, indeed any mention of, Heuser's conclusions and the archival evidence she presented (377). Because of these doubts with regard to the scholarly reliability of the new edition, I will quote from Runckel's original edition throughout my discussion.

[6] Gaby Pailer, one of the few scholars who has approached Runckel's letter edition with a critical eye as to their ability to tell us the authentic story of Luise Gottsched's life, makes this exact point when she views both Johann Christoph's biography and Runckel's edition of Gottsched's letters as diametrically opposed biographical constructions (48, 53–4). Pailer's interpretation of Johann Christoph's biography as an obvious construction of Gottsched's life and Runckel's edition as a "counter-construction" in direct response to his text (57) assumes no greater degree of biographical or historical credibility for Runckel's edition than it does for Johann Christoph's biography. Both constructions, Pailer concludes, clearly influenced later scholarship on the author (60).

3: Negotiations: Letters to Johann Christoph Gottsched

Vacillations: The Mentor and the Lover

DOROTHEA HENRIETTE VON RUNCKEL described Luise Kulmus's letters to her fiancé Johann Christoph Gottsched as completely free of "amorous weaknesses."[1] Whether young Luise Kulmus indeed felt so casually towards her suitor or whether Runckel later edited her letters to reflect this cool poise, the letters as they were published in Runckel's edition were not written to a lover, but to a mentor and teacher. The first lesson Luise Kulmus took from her suitor was "instruction on how to become a virtuous woman"; in that same letter, she requests his mentorship in intellectual matters as well. Whereas virtue, as she describes it, is achieved intuitively by the heart, "Other accomplishments are more difficult to obtain. They require intellectual talents and abilities. I have, at times, and very shyly and fearfully, risked a glance into the realm of scholarly learning, but I have not advanced very far. You have often caused me to wish that you could be my mentor."[2] In return for his mentorship, which would permit her entry into the realm of "learning," seventeen-year-old Kulmus professed her willingness, perhaps not entirely seriously, to acknowledge his intellectual superiority, constantly, ostentatiously, and demurely. Only once did he have to scold her for writing in French before she switched to German, accompanying her decision with profuse thanks to her mentor for teaching her to appreciate the "masculine beauty of my mother tongue" ("die männliche Schönheit meiner Muttersprache," *Briefe* I, 8). "You will censure me, and your censure will improve me. I take it that such is your intention?"[3] There is every indication in these early letters that Kulmus viewed Johann Christoph Gottsched, who had already gained national fame as the author of *Versuch einer Critischen Dichtkunst* (*Critical Poetics*) and *Der sterbende Cato* (*Dying Cato*), not as a potential suitor but as a paternal teacher, a literary role model on the same plane as other writers she did not know personally, such as the French essayist Anne-Thérèse Marquise de Lambert (1647–1733), whom she called an "incomparable mother" ("unvergleichliche Mutter," *Briefe* I, 6). That she initially viewed the relationship with him as a purely intellectual one, or tried to keep it on that level, is also indicated, for example, by the fact that she categorically rejected all of his gifts with the exception of books (*Briefe* I, 9). And indeed, she had good reason to expect no more than a lifelong platonic epistolary mentorship, if other contemporary correspondences (for example, between Caroline Lucius and Gellert or between Anna Luisa Karsch and Gleim) are any indication.

The tone of the relationship changed shortly after the death of Luise Kulmus's father in October 1731. Johann Christoph Gottsched must have proposed marriage to her as soon as decently possible thereafter, in his second letter after her father's death, on the heels of his condolences in the first. Considering Luise Kulmus's extremely precarious position after her father's death, which must have left her and her mother penniless and desperate to marry Luise off just to have her "provided for," her ambivalent reaction to Johann Christoph's marriage proposal is highly remarkable.

> The good opinion which you have formed of me has much that is flattering for me, and your choice honors me. How happy would I be if my achievements gave me any right to it. Your approval is the sole source of my worth, and I would be proud of it, if I was not humbled by my own convictions. I only ask for one thing: permit my period of mourning to end undisturbed before I think of happier days. I consider it my duty not to lessen the respect for my father in death that I owed him in life; and I can no less shorten my heart's grief than decorum allows me to change the color of my dress. Permit me to suspend a joy which I owe, to a great extent, to the deceased, until time has conquered my grief and permits me to exchange it for the sadness over my loss. This delay is the smallest sacrifice that I owe to my father's memory.[4]

Luise Kulmus's remarks in this letter have always been read as a mere postponement of the wedding, that is, as a de facto acceptance of her suitor's proposal, perhaps because Runckel, in one of her rare annotations to the letters, deftly steers the reader's inclinations in that direction. "The Herr Professor already wanted to consummate the union at that time," Runckel explains,[5] reading the "joy" that Kulmus wants suspended in her letter as the potential wedding. In so doing, Runckel effectively buries the other possible interpretation of Kulmus's "joy" as her correspondence with Johann Christoph. In that case her letter, far from indicating an acceptance of his proposal, would hint at a desire for more distance — substantially more distance, if not a complete separation, if she did indeed mean that she wanted to suspend their correspondence for an entire year (the traditional period of mourning). That she answers his marriage proposal with this request must be read, at the very least, as an expression of grave doubt on her part. As radical and unlikely as it might appear, given her completely despondent social situation, this interpretation seems the most likely, for three reasons. First, it was her father who granted the two permission to exchange letters, so that Kulmus literally owed this "joy" to the deceased. Second, there is no indication whatsoever in subsequent letters for the next three years that Kulmus considered herself engaged to Johann Christoph Gottsched. Third, Kulmus's request to curb their correspondence or suspend it entirely recurs frequently in subsequent years.

Visions: Death and the Lover

Luise Kulmus's early letters to Johann Christoph Gottsched, written during the time now commonly interpreted as their "engagement," are startling in their incessant vacillation between two potential relationships with the recipient, the mentorship on the one hand and the love relationship on the other. Kulmus's treatment of complex and broader themes expresses both of these relationships indirectly: the mentorship in her discussions of contemporary literature, her remarks on other erudite women and her assessment of her own early writing; the love relationship in more personal themes such as their various visualizations of each other as partners, diseases, visions of death, and death wishes. Kulmus first mentions a desire to die on the occasion of her father's death, a move that is important in that she answers her suitor's marriage proposal, albeit indirectly, with the threat of her permanent removal from his grasp. "Would that I could soon follow him [her father, S. K.] into the blessed abode, where he perhaps, even now, awaits me with paternal joy! This is my only wish for the present."[6]

The same scenario repeated itself in more elaborate form when her mother died in 1734. The letter in which she reports on her mother's death is filled with death wishes, death fantasies and reports on a sickness that nearly killed Kulmus herself after her mother's death. It is, on the other hand, completely free of what one might reasonably expect — an admission of her despondency and fear of the future, or of an acknowledgment that her entire future now depended on her suitor. She begins with the indirect threat to dissolve the relationship ("I want to relate to you the final days of the deceased, because during her last hours, I myself was at death's door. By a hair's breadth you would have lost me as well, and in me your most loyal friend."[7]) and continues with a graphic description of the disease which befell her and the simultaneous dangers of falling bombs and the pending invasion of Danzig, all of which serve to underscore this threat. This letter, written on June 5, 1734, is also the first letter to Johann Christoph Gottsched in which Luise Kulmus acknowledges that she considers them an engaged couple, but she does so negatively. In her fantasy death and *dissolution* of the relationship she even, in a grotesque reversal of social realities, "provides" for *him*:

> During the hours in which my disease had reached its pinnacle, in which life and death warred within me, so to speak, I was consumed by thoughts of death. I lay there and quietly expected the hour of my dissolution. In these moments, I remembered you, my best friend, and my heart became ever more uneasy with this remembrance. I pleaded with God, earnestly and in tears, to send you a bride once more who, if possible, loved you as tenderly as I, and who possessed all the material goods that you deserve and that I lack.
> . . . I still expected to die, and wished not to be separated from my beloved mother even in death, but now I had to experience this separation.[8]

Whether or not the death wish uttered on the occasion of both her parents' deaths is to be read literally, there can be little question that Kulmus here plays out an alternative fantasy, one that perhaps amounts not so much to her own dissolution as to that of her relationship with Johann Christoph Gottsched. Her frank reminder that he was about to marry a penniless woman and might do better elsewhere might have constituted a veiled allusion that she would not object if he rescinded his proposal — a feat of great daring, given a financial situation that effectively deprived her of choice in the matter.

Another major point of negotiation in this relationship is the thematic complex of visualizing the partner, both positively (in the miniature portraits traditionally exchanged between lovers) and negatively (in visions of disease and deformation). Given that pictures of the other constituted an emotionally charged gift, it is interesting how Kulmus negotiates this issue in her letters. From her letters it becomes abundantly clear that the impetus for exchanging pictures came, once again, from Johann Christoph. On December 15, 1731, she accepts the gift of his picture with an ambiguous commentary: "Your picture will please me very much: I will often converse with it and share all the laments with it that I cannot tell the original."[9] But in her next letter, dated

January 9, 1732, in which she acknowledges receipt of his picture, she almost flippantly refuses to return the favor.

> You ask that I should send you a copy of my face in return and surmise that I must have changed very much in two years. Of that change, my mirror tells me nothing. My length has increased by a quarter cubit; but since I cannot find a painter who could, even if he were the greatest artist alive, show you this change in a portrait, I cannot bring myself to send you my imperfect picture.[10]

If it is true that Kulmus was unsure of the relationship, that she vacillated between a potential mentorship and a possible engagement, her refusal makes sense. More consequentially than we can imagine today, a picture was worth a thousand words. During the Storm and Stress era, pictures were sighed over and drenched with tears, but even during the Enlightenment, a picture constituted a substitute presence and, moreover, a semi-public admission of the nature of the relationship: a picture could be shown to others, with the presentation of the relationship left to the discretion of the one who showed it. It is likely that both Johann Christoph Gottsched and Luise Kulmus saw her picture as a visible signal and clarification to both themselves and outsiders of their attachment, as an end to the oscillation between mentorship and love. Hence, perhaps, Luise Kulmus's renewed refusal when Johann Christoph repeated his request in October 1732; hence her final concession to his wishes only after their engagement was formalized in 1734 (*Briefe* I, 92).

On one occasion, the visualization of the other assumes a different tone in the correspondence: Johann Christoph Gottsched, apprised that Luise Kulmus was penniless and had moreover been completely disfigured by smallpox, immediately wrote to her, demanding that she confirm or deny these rumors. Kulmus readily admitted to the state of her finances, reminding him that she had frequently pointed this out to him in previous letters. Her answer to the second charge reads as follows:

> Concerning the second [aspersion] with regard to my health: I have never looked more sickly and deformed than at my father's death and six months thereafter . . . . You did not come to Danzig to seek out beautiful faces and beautiful bodies; you would have had those nearer in Saxony. Or if you had demanded such here, you would not have chosen me. Even supposing I had had the smallpox; supposing that it had disfigured me very badly; I would still have trusted in your steadfastness to the extent that you could have read an exact description of my scarred face without disgust. I think I would have counted the scars in order to give you a precise report.[11]

In response to her suitor's visualization of her scarred face, Luise Kulmus attempts to envision a love relationship with him. Her vision simultaneously states her expectations of such a relationship and alludes to her awareness that these expectations had already been disappointed in his letter. It is perhaps this dilemma that led to the near-constant renegotiations of the relationship on her part, most prominently expressed in her attempts to curb the correspondence and in her evasive responses to all of his attempts to define the relationship.

Virtues: Negotiating Enlightenment Discourse

Kulmus's negotiations most frequently make use of the Enlightenment discourse of feminine virtue, a discourse which her suitor took it upon himself to teach her in their correspondence and which she had formally agreed to accept: "instruction on how to become a virtuous woman." Feminine "virtue" expressed itself above all in submission and obedience — a submission which took, as its extreme expression, the form of gratitude for chastisement:

> I owe you more thanks for your last letter than you perhaps realize. In it, you have called me back from a path on which my forwardness would have led me too far astray. You have shown me how easily our sex forgets its weakness, and how often it dares challenge its master; how it seeks to find fault with those with whose permission we rise to a level to which we could never aspire without their help. I am startled at my own boldness and I promise you never again to forget myself to that extent. Everything that you in your goodness have sent me I will utilize for the increase of my knowledge, and I will ask you, my mentor, for your opinion about every dubious passage.[12]

On the one hand, Kulmus's employment of this discourse seems to place her firmly under his control and displays a tone of humiliating submissiveness that is distasteful to modern readers, and this is undoubtedly one reason why scholarship has proven so utterly incapable of reading Luise Kulmus, later Luise Gottsched, as anything but his loyal "helpmate." But conversely, the Enlightenment discourse of feminine "virtue" with its inherent double standard afforded Kulmus splendid opportunities to subvert his arguments in the service of her own alternative vision of the relationship. Obedience, for example, was due not only her mentor/suitor, but also her family, and indeed, as she once pointed out to him, her future obedience to a husband could be measured by her present obedience towards her family:

But what an injustice you do me when you assume my earlier letter [in which she had announced that she was no longer permitted to write to him, S. K.] to be a declaration of my wishes instead of that which I owe to my family's instructions! What would you think of a person who showed herself recalcitrant in her mother's home and did not utterly submit her wishes to those of her mother? Would you not assume that this person would also, in the future, turn into a recalcitrant wife? how unjust, then, are your complaints? You call me cruel, you accuse me of having forgotten my promise - - - [13]

Kulmus's repeated attempts to create more distance in the relationship are ostentatiously substantiated in her filial duty but clearly rooted in her ambivalence, as occasionally expressed in allusions that he might end up marrying someone else (*Briefe* I, 45) and in her answers to what must have been stern requests for clarification of the relationship from him. In one such letter, written on October 29, 1732, she assures him that although her mother was not principally *opposed* to their marriage (a matter of his choice, not hers, as she subtly points out), mother and daughter alike were determined to leave all such matters to "Providence and Virtue" (*Briefe* I, 42).

> You see, then, that my mother is not opposed to your choice. Nonetheless, under the present circumstances, I see our union as taking place far, far in the future. May Providence interpose to help ease a decision that will be long delayed without its aid! I hope everything from your goodness. Do I not write you long letters? Does this not literally mean that I am your obedient servant?
> Kulmus[14]

Such delay tactics and passive resistance are perhaps the distinguishing features of the entire correspondence. In the name of filial duty and religious piety, Luise Kulmus pleaded for a curbing or suspension of the correspondence, curtly informing him that she would no longer be able to respond to his letters and postponing the wedding numerous times. Whenever she was supposed to set out to join him in Leipzig, renewed obstacles to such a long journey regularly presented themselves — her own frailty or illness, her mother's death, confusion about her finances, or bureaucratic hindrances (*Briefe* I, 115–6). What made this passive resistance possible was recourse to two concepts central to the Enlightenment discourse of feminine virtue: her filial duty of obedience and the Enlightenment virtues of "patience," "equanimity" and "faith in Providence" (*Briefe* I, 2, 18, 77–8, 83, 87, 97–100, 121, 123) which she constantly invoked to counter his increasingly angry and accusatory letters. One example representative of many, written in August 1734 after setting the wedding date:

> My angry friend!
> This moment I have received a letter from you which has dismayed me in the extreme. Jest and solemnity, love and coldness are so artificially entwined in it that I don't know what to think. Nothing but the unavoidable circumstances, which keep me here longer than I would wish, are the cause of your displeasure . . . . But how can you attack my heart so severely and accuse it of being pleased at the delay which circumstances demand? How insulting would this suspicion be, were I not to take your ardor for a tender impatience which is extremely flattering to me. Is it my fault that Fate, from the very beginning of our acquaintance, has placed many obstacles to its continuation in our path, and that to surmount them, time and much, much patience was necessary? Spare me, dearest friend, the accusation of coldness, or teach me the art of bearing it with equanimity.[15]

By employing the rhetoric of the Enlightenment, which centered on *philosophische Gelassenheit* (philosophical equanimity), Luise Kulmus conformed to the teachings of her *mentor* Johann Christoph Gottsched while keeping her potential *lover* Johann Christoph at bay. She claimed once that she owed the "patience" which so thoroughly unnerved her suitor to his own philosophical writings (*Briefe* I, 99). Kulmus's tactic, which essentially consisted in playing off her mentor against her lover, allowed her to stoically bear his constant accusations, reasonably counter his oft-expressed demands for more emotional demonstrativeness on her part, and calmly sabotage the wedding as long as humanly possible. Because her world view, in accordance with his own teachings, was rooted in fact, she could refuse to join in Johann Christoph's fantasies of their future life together: "I am too philosophical to wish for the impossible."[16] She firmly placed the married life he envisioned in the realm of the improbable, even "the impossible." At a time when he made concrete wedding plans, she left it up to "Providence" to end their separation. And at a time when he embarked on a search for a joint residence, her perfunctory good luck wishes remained rather unspecific as to whether or not these plans would include her. One of her scenarios even implies his moving to Leipzig alone, accompanied merely by her fondest "wishes" (*Briefe* I, 65–7).

One of the more interesting, and frequently recurring, motifs in Luise Kulmus's correspondence is the request for reassurance and approval with which she customarily closes her letters. In direct contrast to her vacillations elsewhere between the mentorship and love relationship, these pleas are without exception directed at her potential lover; indeed they are the *only* part of the correspondence that can clearly be said to presume an intimate attachment between the two. These quests for his approval most frequently take the form of a question: "Sind Sie nun zufrieden?" ("Are you happy now?"), a recurring ending that appears highly evocative, as well as purely rhetorical. The fact that the question is so often repeated would indicate that it has not sufficiently been answered in intervening letters, that it cannot be answered, or that the purpose of asking the question is not to receive an answer. Kulmus asks the question while pointing to facets in her behavior that *should* make him happy (but perhaps do not), and she almost always takes this question as an occasion to end the letter, often abruptly.

> I uncover before you my heart's most secret thoughts, the largest part of which is directed at you. Are you happy with this straightforwardness? Yours, Kulmus[17]

> Do I not write you very long letters? and does this not mean literally that I am your obedient servant?
>
> Kulmus[18]

> . . . often I wish that you might love me less than I love you, so as not to suffer as much as I do. Tell me whether this is indeed a cold-hearted, indifferent love, as you have so often termed my feelings?[19]

> May Heaven grant that I will always be as assured of the incessant duration of your tender love as I feel that my heart will always be loyal and devoted to you. Are you now happy with all of these assurances? Will you continue to complain about my silence?[20]

In this fashion, her final question takes on a placating quality: the question serves as an expression of Luise Kulmus's appeasement politics and of her sacrifice of time, effort and feeling to the angry God of Love.

A Little Detour: Negotiating Authorship

In her other relationship with Johann Christoph, the mentorship, Kulmus seems to have been a great deal more comfortable. In the course of this relationship, she commented on readings he had sent her, elaborated on her own projects, critiqued her own writing, and debated the limits of scholarly learning and female erudition. For the first time, she was able to exercise her talents as a literary critic (she discussed his tragedy *Cato* tactfully and supportively; *Briefe* I, 79–80) and satirical writer (witness her witty and sarcastic critique on the writings of others through-out the correspondence) and to explore her own intellectual goals. Her mentor's general ideas on female erudition, which undoubtedly greatly influenced her own, form the basis of these goals, but they are also de-fined by the example of contemporary intellectual women, most notably Kulmus's two most famous contemporaries, Laura Bassi and Christiana Mariana von Ziegler. Laura Bassi (1713–80), the first woman to receive her doctorate (Ph.D. in physics, Bologna 1732), also became the first female professor to lecture at a university; Christiana Mariana von Ziegler (1695–1760) was the first female poet laureate, one of Johann Christoph Gottsched's own protegées and the first woman to gain admission into the famed German Society in Leipzig. Both women became the touch-stones for Luise Kulmus's theoretical discussion of the permissibility of female erudition, a thought process that every woman of the age with an interest in learning had to undergo. Kulmus's commentary on Bassi's accomplishment, which traditional scholarship has read as a se-vere judgment on Bassi's unfeminine ambition, strikes me instead as ironically aware of the absurd situation in which Bassi presumably found herself upon graduation:

> How do you like Donna Laura Bassi who has recently received her doctorate at Bologna? I presume that when this young doctor reads at college, she will in her first lessons attract more spectators than listen-ers for the rest of her career.[21]

Kulmus's remarks on Ziegler are a great deal more harsh, perhaps because this woman was the more direct model for her own career. Johann Christoph Gottsched clearly intended for Luise Kulmus to mirror Ziegler's career more or less exactly (he asked her to submit translations and poetry for publication, requested her permission to suggest her for membership in the German Society, and even sought to bring her into direct contact with Ziegler). Kulmus's reaction has usually been read as a sign of her conservatism and opposition to scholarly women in gen-eral, and understandably so, given that she couches her reaction in very general terms:

> Frau von Z[iegler] is right to deem her admission into the German So-ciety as highly as if she had received a doctorate from any university. But surely, you must think me very bold if you presume me capable of aspiring to similar honors. No, this idea shall never enter my head. I will permit my sex to take a little detour; only where we lose sight of our limitations we end up in a labyrinth and lose the guiding light of our weak reason which was supposed to bring us to a happy ending. I

will beware of ever being carried away by this current. For this reason
I assure you that I never wish to see my name among those of the
members of the German Society.[22]

Kulmus's comments can be read in several ways: as implied censure
of an ambitious and accomplished woman (scholars traditionally have
taken great delight in giving this twist to her remarks about both Bassi
and Ziegler, and in emphasizing the enmity between Kulmus and
Ziegler); secondly (and more personally), as a statement of Kulmus's
own goals in that regard; thirdly (and more generally), as a broader prescriptive statement as to what kinds of intellectual accomplishments she
considers permissible and justifiable for the entire sex. What most of
these interpretations traditionally overlook is the context in which these
remarks are made: one of negotiation, the context in which the entire correspondence between Johann Christoph Gottsched and Luise Kulmus
takes place. Kulmus wrote this letter not to her lover, but to her mentor,
and as numerous facets in her letters indicate, that was manifestly the
part of the relationship that she was interested in upholding. She wrote
it as a pupil who had already been harshly censored several times; all of
these instances of rebuke from her mentor followed upon Kulmus's expressions of her own ambition and initiative (cf., for example, *Briefe* I,
7–8 and 25–6). It is no wonder that she takes an entirely different tone
here, one of submission and deference that ostentatiously reinstates him
in his position of superiority. She does so, however, while flatly refusing
his plans for her advancement and career: she indicates that while she
accepts and appreciates his mentorship, she has no interest in becoming
his protegée in the same sense as Ziegler. It is important to realize that
this constitutes a refusal of his expressed wishes, a refusal that is couched,
as is the case in negotiations elsewhere in her letters, in the Enlightenment discourse of prescriptive and restrictive femininity. For that reason, I find the dominant interpretation in both traditional and feminist
research — that Kulmus chastised intellectual ambition in women and
refused it for herself — highly questionable. Given the context of negotiation in which Kulmus writes, her tactic of passive resistance and her
tone of self-irony, the trite imagery she employs (the guiding light, the
confusing labyrinth, the little detour, the dangerous current) and the
all-too-obvious message (the necessity of reigning in unruly women
before they stray from the path of feminine virtue and lose their way in
the dangerous maze of intellectual activity) are too evocative of the worst
contemporary clichés to be taken entirely seriously.

Kulmus's initial refusal to permit her mentor to determine her intellectual life expresses itself repeatedly in her attempts to retain some control over her own writing and publishing. In 1734, he requested her permission to let him publish her letters, a permission emphatically refused by Kulmus ("All I ask of you is this: prevent the printing of these letters, or delay it until after my death") and somewhat smugly annotated by Runckel: "This task was left to me."[23] Another realm of negotiation for control of her own writing emerges in Kulmus's descriptions of the relationship between writing and feeling. There are clear indications that Johann Christoph Gottsched, from very early on, sought to regulate both. He operated on the assumption that poetry was the medium best suited for the expression of intense emotions, an assumption very much in keeping with contemporary literary tradition. (Poems were the preferred medium for public wedding felicitations, declarations of love and obituaries, particularly obituaries written by the surviving spouse.) Kulmus, on the other hand, repeatedly professed both her own skepticism towards this medium and her hesitancy to view it as an adequate expression of emotion. On August 23, 1732, she listlessly reported to Johann Christoph that she had begun the poetic lamentation for her father, apparently commissioned by him:

> I have made a start on the poetic lamentation on my father's death, but have not gotten very far in it. Here is the beginning:
>
>> Glorified elder, the day has started,
>> That you this world and me departed,
>> The day I have feared all along.
>> The hour in which your spirit rose
>> Has been the worst of all of those
>> That I lived through my whole life long.
>
> I will say it again: intense grief can be felt, just like all other intense emotions, but never described.[24]

It is highly debatable whether this poem is a sign of literary ineptitude, as its author claims. Perhaps the very fact that Kulmus — a competent and expressive writer in her letters and translations — resorts to clichéd phraseology, trite meters, and weary rhymes in her poem indicates another point of negotiation: an instance of passive resistance that spared her the necessity of refusing his commission directly. Johann Christoph's attempts to turn Kulmus into a poet, one whose writing derives its originality from the authenticity of her emotions expressed in personal documents (letters or poems), failed in the face of Kulmus's insistence on distinguishing between writing and emotion. Her attempts to establish an inherent dichotomy between real feelings and their expressibility through the literary medium subverted his agenda. Here and elsewhere in the correspondence, Kulmus defined literature in general and poetry in particular as fiction to which no claim of biographical authenticity should be made. Her own most earnest and intimate feelings find no expression in the literary realm but the tritest platitudes imaginable. Just as real emotions are inexpressible through literature, literary skill in expressing emotions can be seen as an indictment of their authenticity. Witness her sarcastic commentary on a poem written as an obituary on the poet's lover:

> The poem which tender bridegroom S. wrote commemorating his beloved I read out of pure curiosity; I wanted to know if this is an occasion on which one can write as much as one really feels. But Heavens! what all the good man said, I believe: much more than he could have felt. If he finds a second and a third bride, he will sing as beautifully and tenderly as he mournfully cooed and moaned on this occasion. A poet is after all an inexhaustible man: truth and falsehood flow from the same fountain, and the saying that a poet is never happy except in fiction is infallible.[25]

Kulmus's remarks on the authenticity of feelings and their inexpressibility in writing explain the cautious tone of her own letters, described by Runckel as free from "amorous weaknesses" and by Johann Christoph, with increasing reproachfulness as the correspondence wore on, as coldhearted and indifferent. It seems clear that Kulmus's letters were read in a different spirit than they had been written: their author viewed them as a personal correspondence in which a complex relationship was being negotiated. Their recipient regarded them as a correspondence between lovers that could later be published as an exemplary collection — exactly as Runckel did publish it forty years later. In such a publication, Kulmus's succinct style, her wry irony, her well-roundedness in literary matters, her exemplary faith in Enlightenment concepts such as Virtue and Reason balanced by her sensitive poetry of mourning and occasional expressions of passion – in short, her unusual talent — could stand simultaneously as a monument to their love and to his mentorship. It would appear that one partner in the correspondence was trying to negotiate the relationship, while the other was, even at this early date, negotiating the production of texts. As we have seen, Kulmus repeatedly boycotted this project by refusing Johann Christoph permission to publish her texts and by furthermore refusing to *produce* publishable texts. His requests that she translate her feelings into literature invariably resulted in lethargic platitudes, and in her personal correspondence with him she firmly refused to enter into any kind of emotional discourse: "No, I do not wish to be Euridice and you shall not be my Orpheus."[26]

In 1735, Kulmus had run out of obstacles and prepared to receive her lover, who had come to pick her up from Danzig to accompany her back to Leipzig as his bride. At this point, when the relationship had clearly progressed beyond the friendship and mentorship she had envisioned, she defined it as a "philosophical love," promising him a thrifty housekeeper. The letter, completely bare of the loving impatience which one could reasonably expect, reads like an accountant's report: it is filled with minute detail about where and how she planned to save money in the arrangement of their wedding and the establishment of their joint household (*Briefe* I, 213–4). And even at this late date, she insisted on some autonomy over her works: when he commissioned from her a translation of the history of the baths of Thermopylae, she instead chose to translate Madame de Gomez's *Triumph of Eloquence*, begging him to forgive her "this little stubbornness" ("Vergeben Sie mir immer diesen kleinen Eigensinn," *Briefe* I, 163). Shortly before his arrival, she calmly counters his wrath about the fact that she had burned all of her works, including her translation of Madame de Lafayette's famous novel *La Princesse de Cleves*: "I thought I was doing you a favor in destroying this waste paper, which is why I lit this bonfire. Could you permit a person so close to you to bring such very insignificant writings before the world?"[27] It was the last time that Kulmus exercised such control over her writing and publishing.

Her marriage, as she described it diplomatically in letters to third parties, found her comfortably installed in Leipzig ("daß ich mich in dem vortreflichen Leipzig wohl, sehr wohl befinde"), content in the knowledge that she had "made the most fortunate and best choice in my marriage" ("in meiner Ehe die glücklichste und beste Wahl getroffen habe," *Briefe* I, 224). Rather dispassionately, she describes her early married life:

> I am healthy, cheerful, and quite happy, according to my inclinations. Our activities are as uniform as our thoughts. We read a lot; we remark on every beautiful passage; we often divide our opinions for appearance's sake and dispute a sentence just to see whether the opinions that we have formed of our reading materials are justified.[28]

This passage indicates that in marriage, the mentor-relationship continued: the feigned arguments Gottsched describes here attest to the fact that her husband tutored her in rhetoric. Shortly thereafter, she reports that she was now taking formal lessons in Latin in order to be able to read ancient Roman writers: "My Gottsched wishes . . ." ("Mein Gottsched wünscht," *Briefe* I, 230). Most of her letters from the early days of her marriage report on scholarly projects and translations, undertaken at his behest or with his support. In one letter, she neutrally comments on her childlessness, clearly indicating that a child would mean the end of her intellectual activities: "I am working a lot and learning even more. I am practicing music and would like to continue with composition if at all possible. I would be prevented from doing all of this if I had a child, for I would spend all my time on it."[29] Her first complaints about her failing health appear in a letter written in 1740, after only five years of marriage. In this letter, she describes her daily life precisely as she had five years earlier: as "uniform" and work intensive (*Briefe* I, 258). The letter ends with her first correlation of her physical weakness with her intellectual activity, a theme that was to recur many times in her correspondence with Runckel years later:

> I am spending the largest part of my life doing work that is anomalous for most of my sex; and my health would perhaps be better if I had more exercise and more pleasant diversions. This from my physician, whom I have at times questioned about the frailty of my body. My own inclination tells me, however, that the occupation with whatever answers my inclinations and satisfies my spirit cannot be detrimental to my health. I will follow this inclination so long as my machine has not become entirely defunct.[30]

This letter stands out in the correspondence for the simple reason that it is the *only* letter in which she ever professed satisfaction in her professional role. For the emotional and intellectual satisfaction she derived from writing, Gottsched calmly accepted the fact that such activities were considered an anomaly for her "sex," rejecting — along the way — the contemporary stereotype that linked women's intellectual activities with their inevitable physical decay. It is an unusual statement from a woman who had yet to do the bulk of her writing, and who complained about overwork in countless other letters, placing the blame for her constant overwork squarely on her husband. From a journey to Dresden, she reported her initial hope "that one could rest here from all the overload of work; but I soon found out that people who are so used to keeping busy as my friend [her husband, S. K.] find ways of satisfying their inclinations anywhere."[31] Upon her return from this journey, the workload mounted:

All the repose that we experienced in Dresden has been transformed into an uninterrupted chain of work. From early morning until late at night there are only a few hours to spend on the most necessary requirements of life. I force myself to remember the multiple past kindnesses I received in Dresden to be able to face up to the present difficulties of a scholarly lifestyle. But this is my fate, and I will submit to it with equanimity. It was my wish, and since Providence has fulfilled it in richer measure than I ever believed possible, I do not wish to complain, but fulfill my destiny to the best of my ability.[32]

Her first death wish appears in a letter addressed to an unnamed female recipient, written in April 1743 — eight years into her marriage, nineteen years before her death, and still a full year before she wrote any of the dramas for which she would subsequently become famous.

Prophecy and Manipulation: Runckel as Editor

The relationship between Luise Kulmus and Johann Christoph Gottsched has always been perceived in scholarship as cool, cerebral, unromantic, or at best, echoing Kulmus's kinder term, as "philosophical" — unusually so in scholarly perception, even allowing for the fact that this correspondence took place in the age of "reasonable matches." Scholars have uniformly marveled at the emotional coldness permeating Kulmus's letters and her steadfast refusal to give in to Johann Christoph's demands for more emotional expressiveness. At times, a great deal of blame is attached to these observations (Reichel, for example, speculated bitterly that Kulmus and her mother were engaged in a sinister plot to renege on the marriage promise as soon as a richer suitor could be found for Kulmus; 726–7). All of this is based exclusively on Kulmus's side of the correspondence with her future husband during the time spanning her "engagement" and early marriage, as edited by Dorothea Henriette von Runckel. There can be no question that there is an intense negotiation in progress in the correspondence, and that the letters more than allude to the acute differences between Johann Christoph's and Kulmus's respective expectations and interpretations of their relationship. A highly complex and difficult relationship is being portrayed in this correspondence. The question that arises, given that Runckel took extraordinary editorial liberties with her material, is by whom. Was this "philosophical" love story as it appears in the letters authored by Gottsched or by the editor? While it is impossible to determine precisely who wrote what, we do have some indications — from Runckel's introductions, but more clearly from her annotations – of where the editor wanted to steer readers' interpretations.

Runckel's editorial interventions clearly suggest that she was heavily engaged in the preservation of an image, for the most part that of Johann Christoph Gottsched, at times also Kulmus's. (As I have already established, she portrayed Kulmus as a paragon of virtue for supposedly "cleansing" her translations of vulgar language and maintained this image by cleaning up coarse expressions in Kulmus's letters.) In the first volume of the correspondence, Runckel annotated the text twenty-eight times. Many of these explanatory notes are truly editorial in today's sense: Runckel explains allusions in the letters, clears up personal identities, points to publications that resulted from projects being discussed in the letters, or lists sources for works by Luise Gottsched. In other annotations, Runckel assumes a prophetic voice. When Kulmus insisted that she would never agree to become a member of the German Society, Runckel confirms in her annotation that she remained firm in her resolve (note on p. 27); when Kulmus expressed her hope that Johann Christoph's future wife, "whoever she may be," would die before her husband, Runckel informs us that she did indeed precede him by four years ("sie sey wer sie wolle," and note on p. 45); when Kulmus pleaded with Johann Christoph not to publish her letters, Runckel, stating the obvious, declares that she, not Johann Christoph, was ultimately entrusted with this task (note on p. 126). These annotations transcend what we would today consider an editorial function in the sense that they treat the letters as a story, as "fiction" in Kulmus's sense, by alluding to the ending of the story of which readers unfamiliar with Luise Gottsched's biography are as yet unaware.

Runckel's annotations of most significance here concern interventions between the letters and the reader's interpretations. In each case, the note is intended to transform the reader's view of the relationship between Luise and Johann Christoph from one of a cold and unromantic exchange to one of a more pronounced emotionality. A first example is the instance cited above, where in a one sentence note Runckel transforms Kulmus's possible intention to break off her correspondence with Johann Christoph into a mere postponement of their wedding. In a second instance, Runckel took a fairly innocuous remark in one of Kulmus's letters — that Glycera owed much of her impressive knowledge to Menander — as an opportunity to print a poem written by Kulmus and dedicated to Johann Christoph, in which Kulmus thanks her mentor profusely for his twofold gift of instruction and love — "as evidence that our Kulmus owed a large portion of her erudition to her friend."[33] So far as we know, neither of these editorial interventions comprise outright falsifications of the letters, but they do illustrate the editor's interest in presenting the relationship between Kulmus and Johann Christoph Gottsched as an amicable one and demonstrate her attempts to forestall potentially differing interpretations.

A third instance of Runckel's intervention is possibly the most consequential because it involves editorial omission as well as commission. Kulmus had apparently heard of her fiancé's infidelity, probably in April 1732; she must have written to him, requesting clarification, and received an answer. Neither of these letters is included in the correspondence; the only trace left of the entire affair appears in Luise Kulmus's subsequent letter of abject apology to him for ever having harbored such suspicions — discreetly annotated by Runckel: "A certain unfounded rumor had tempted our Kulmus to voice complaints that she later regretted."[34] The primary goal behind Runckel's editorial decisions in this instance was first to shield Johann Christoph's reputation — so much so that Heuser speculated that he may have collaborated with Runckel in preparing the edition ("Neuedition" 321) — and second to evoke the image of a harmonious relationship between the two. For one thing, Runckel minimizes the reader's exposure to Johann Christoph's infidelity by omitting the letter in which Kulmus must have directly addressed the issue. For another, she claims that the rumor was unfounded, that is, she uses her prophetic voice by forecasting an ending as omniscient narrator of the story (offering a conclusion that appears dubious at best, considering the frequency with which similar suspicions later recur).

Runckel's role as editor can, in the final analysis, be described as threefold: she acted simultaneously as an editor of *biographical material* in her purely explanatory notes, as an editor of *fiction* in her prophetic and/or forecasting annotations, and as an editor of *biographical fiction*. In this final and most consequential of her editorial roles, she was engaged not in editing the letters, but editing the lives that are described in them, in mitigating, embellishing, and creating a very specific image of her heroine Luise Kulmus as well as of Kulmus's relationship with her mentor for posterity. This image portrays Luise Kulmus as a virtuous and completely subservient helpmate to her mentor/husband and the relationship between them as cautious and unemotional, but undeniably harmonious.

Two facts about this image are of decisive importance: one is that, along with Johann Christoph's biography of his wife, the letters as edited by Runckel furnished the basis for future scholarship on Luise Gottsched. Second, while this image is explicitly Runckel's in her introductions and annotations, we have no way of knowing precisely where and how she edited it into the letters, and this indiscernibility of the editor's hand further complicates the fact that Runckel's portrayal of Gottsched is frequently incongruous with statements in the letters themselves. To cite just one example, despite her frequent complaints about overwork, Luise Kulmus steadfastly denied that there could be a direct correlation between her physical weakness and her intellectual activity. Runckel, on the other hand, rather pointedly stated in her foreword that Kulmus worked "inexhaustibly" ("unermüdlich"), to the detriment of her "frail body" ("schwächlicher Körper"), which seemed hardly capable to bear the "burden of scholarly activity" ("[die] Last gelehrter Beschäftigungen"; "Vorbericht" to *Briefe* I, no pagination). Again, two interpretations are possible: either Luise Kulmus was complaining about the burdens of a scholarly lifestyle per se, that is, she saw this lifestyle as inherently incompatible with her femininity, here circumscribed as "feminine" (physical) weakness. This is, in essence, the interpretation encouraged by the editor and favored by virtually every scholar who has written about Luise Gottsched to date. The other is that Luise Gottsched's objection concerned not the *quality* of the work, but its *quantity* — read literally, the letters reveal nothing but an unwillingness to being worked incessantly, always on projects not of her own choosing, and at least occasionally on projects that she may have had little or no interest in.

Similar inconsistencies, as I have attempted to show, permeate the entire correspondence. The image handed down to us of Luise Gottsched as a subservient "helpmate" to her husband without literary ambitions of her own and uncompromising objections to learned women certainly appears more consistently in Runckel's introductions and annotations than in the letters themselves. Juxtaposed against Runckel's image of Gottsched as subservient helpmate, the letters themselves reveal a woman who desired "instruction" enough to attempt a negotiation of what proved to be a highly complex relationship, and who did so by skillful manipulation of the dominant philosophical discourse governing her "sex" and — ironically — of Johann Christoph Gottsched's own philosophical premises. Awareness of these dissimilarities presents the reader with a choice: One can choose to read them as the last traces of Luise Gottsched's own "voice," of her part of the co-authorship of the letters, and as the sum total of biographical "truth" not created by Runckel. One can alternatively choose to adopt a fundamental doubt about the apparent reliability of historical "truth" and assume that a notion of "truth" has been inextricably woven into the text and its interpretive history. In making this assumption, my reading of Luise Gottsched's letters and her literature is less interested in uncovering biographical facts than in opening new interpretive possibilities for her literature. In the absence of a recoverable biographical truth, such interpretations can only be strengthened by a refusal to ignore dissimilarities, as scholars invariably have, by an attempt to read for dissimilarities as well as confirmation, and by a commitment to include that which has been effaced as well as that which has been preserved.

Notes

[1] "… ohne in verliebte Schwachheiten zu verfallen"; Runckel, "Vorbericht" to Gottsched, *Briefe* I, no pagination.

[2] Luise Kulmus to Johann Christoph Gottsched, September 20, 1730: "eine Vorschrift wie ein tugendhaftes Frauenzimmer seyn soll . . . . Andere Vorzüge zu erlangen ist weit schwerer. Darzu werden Talente und Fähigkeiten des Geistes erfordert. Sehr schüchtern und furchtsam habe ich zuweilen einen Blick in das Reich der Wissenschaften gewaget, aber ich bin noch nicht weit darinnen gekommen. Sie haben schon oft den Wunsch bey mir erreget, daß Sie mein Mentor . . . seyn möchten." (*Briefe* I, 4–5)

[3] Letter to Johann Christoph Gottsched, October 27, 1730: "Sie werden mich tadeln, und dieser Tadel wird mich bessern. Dieses ist doch Ihre Absicht?" (*Briefe* I, 7)

[4] "Die vortheilhafte Meynung, so Sie von mir gefaßt, hat ungemein viel schmeichelhaftes für mich, und Ihre Wahl macht mir Ehre. Wie glücklich wäre ich, wenn mich meine Verdienste darzu berechtigten. Ihr Beyfall macht meinen einzigen Werth aus, und ich würde stolz darauf, wenn ich nicht von meiner eigenen Ueberzeugung gedemüthiget würde. Eins bitte ich Sie H. H. lassen Sie meine Trauer ungestört zu Ende gehen, ehe ich an vergnügte Tage gedenke. Ich rechne es mir zur Pflicht, gegen meinen Vater auch im Tode die Ehrfurcht nicht zu mindern, die ich ihm im Leben schuldig war; und ich kann die Trauer meines Herzens eben so wenig verkürzen, als es der Wohlstand erlaubt, die Farbe der Kleider zu verändern. Erlauben Sie mir immer, eine Freude, zu welcher der Verstorbene mir großen theils selbst geholfen, so lange auszusetzen, bis die Zeit meinen Schmerz besieget und mir gestattet, dieselbe mit der Traurigkeit über meinen Verlust zu verwechseln. Es ist dieser Aufschub das geringste Opfer, das ich dem Andenken meines Vaters schuldig bin." (*Briefe* I, 12–3)

[5] "Der Herr Professor wollte schon damals seine Verbindung schlüssen." (13)

[6] "Möchte ich ihn doch bald in die seeligen Wohnungen folgen, wo er mich vielleicht schon mit väterlicher Freude erwartet! Dieses ist jetzt mein einziger Wunsch." (*Briefe* I, 11–2)

[7] "Ich will Ihnen die letzten Tage der Verstorbenen erzählen, denn in ihren letzten Stunden bin ich selbst am Rande des Grabes gewesen. Es hätte nicht viel gefehlt, so hätten Sie auch mich, und in mir Ihre treuste Freundin verloren." (*Briefe* I, 104)

[8] "In den Stunden, da meine Krankheit aufs höchste gestiegen war, und so zu sagen, Tod und Leben mit einander kämpften, war ich mit lauter Sterbensgedanken beschäftiget. Ich lag, und erwartete meine Auflösung im Stillen. In diesen Augenblicken fielen Sie, mein bester Freund, mir ein, und mein Herz wurde bey dieser Erinnerung noch beklemmter. Ich bat Gott flehentlich und mit Thränen, er möchte Ihnen wieder eine Braut zuführen, welche, wo es möglich, Sie so zärtlich liebte als ich, und alle Glücksgüter besäße, die Sie verdienen, und mir mangeln.

... Ich erwartete immer noch den Tod, und wünschte von meiner geliebten Mutter auch im Sterben nicht getrennt zu seyn, aber jetzt muste ich diese Trennung erfahren" (*Briefe* I, 106–8).

[9] "Ihr Bild wird mir sehr angenehm seyn: ich werde mich oft mit demselben unterhalten, und ihm alles klagen, was ich dem Originale nicht sagen kann." (*Briefe* I, 13)

[10] "Sie verlangen, daß ich Ihnen auch eine Copey von meinem Gesichte schicken soll, und vermuthen, daß ich mich in zwey Jahren sehr verändert haben würde. Davon sagt mir mein Spiegel nichts. Meine Länge hat einen Zusatz von einer Viertel Elle bekommen; weil ich aber keinen Mahler finden kann, der Ihnen diese Veränderung (wäre es auch der größte Meister) auf dem Bilde zeigen kann, so kann ich mich nicht entschließen, Ihnen mein unvollkommenes Gesicht zu schicken." (*Briefe* I, 15)

[11] "Was den zweyten wegen meiner Gesundheit betrift; so habe ich niemals kränklicher und entstellter ausgesehen, als bey meines Vaters Tode, und 6 Monate hernach. ... Sie waren nicht nach Danzig gekommen, schöne Gesichter und schöne Körper zu suchen; diese hatten Sie in Sachsen näher. Oder hätten Sie diese auch hier verlangt, so würde Ihre Wahl nicht auf mich gefallen seyn. Gesetzt auch, daß ich die Blattern gehabt hätte; gesetzt, daß mich diese sehr übel zugerichtet; so hätte ich Ihrer Standhaftigkeit doch so viel zugetrauet, daß Sie die treue Beschreibung meines narbigen Gesichts ohne widrigen Eindruck würden gelesen haben. Ich glaube, ich hätte die Gruben gezählet, um Ihnen alles genau zu melden." (*Briefe* I, 129–30)

[12] "Ich bin Ihnen für Ihr letztes Schreiben mehr Dank schuldig, als Sie vielleicht vermuthen. Sie haben mich dadurch von einer Bahn zurücke gerufen, darauf mich mein Vorwitz zu weit würde geführet haben. Sie haben mir gezeiget, wie leicht unser Geschlecht seine Schwäche vergißt, und wie oft es sich

unterfängt seinen Meister zu tadeln; Wie es an denjenigen Fehler zu suchen sich bemüht, mit deren Erlaubniß wir uns zu einer Stufe erheben, dahin wir ohne ihre Hülfe uns nicht wagen dürften. Ich erschrack über meine Kühnheit und verspreche Ihnen mich niemals wieder so sehr zu vergessen. Alles was Sie mir mit so vieler Gutheit überschicken, will ich zur Vermehrung meiner Kenntnisse mir zu Nutze machen, und bey zweifelhaften Stellen will ich Sie mein Mentor um Ihr Urtheil bitten." (*Briefe* I, 25–6)

[13] "Aber welch Unrecht thun Sie mir, wenn Sie mein voriges Schreiben für eine Erklärung meines Willens, nicht aber für das annehmen, was ich der Vorschrift meiner Anverwandten schuldig bin? Was würden Sie von einer Person halten, die in dem Hause Ihrer Mutter sich derselben widerspenstig erzeigte, und dieser nicht ihren ganzen Willen aufopferte? Würden Sie nicht vermuthen, daß diese Person in Zukunft auch eine widerspenstige Frau seyn würde? wie unbillig sind also Ihre Verweise? Sie nennen mich grausam, Sie beschuldigen mich meines Versprechens vergessen zu haben - - -" (*Briefe* I, 52–3)

[14] "Sie sehen also, daß Sie die Stimme meiner Mutter bey Ihrer Wahl nicht wider sich haben. Gleichwohl sehe ich bey den jetzigen Umständen unsre Verbindung noch weit hinausgesetzt. Möchte nur die Vorsehung sich ins Mittel schlagen, und den Entschluß erleichtern helfen, der ohne ihren Beystand noch länger verzögert wird. Ich hoffe alles von Ihrer Güte. Schreibe ich Ihnen nicht lange Briefe? heißt dieses nicht buchstäblich, ich bin Ihre gehorsame Dienerin?
Kulmus" (*Briefe* I, 42)

[15] "Mein erzürnter Freund!
Diesen Augenblick erhalte ich ein Schreiben von Ihnen, worüber ich ungemein bestürzt bin. Scherz und Ernst, Liebe und Kaltsinn finde ich darinnen so künstlich vermischt, daß ich nicht weis, was ich denken soll. Nichts als die unvermeidlichen Umstände, die mich länger, als ich wünsche, hier aufhalten, sind die Ursache Ihres Unwillens. . . . Aber wie können Sie mein Herz so empfindlich angreifen, und es beschuldigen, daß ihm der Aufschub, den die Umstände erfordern, lieb wäre? Wie beleidigend wäre dieser Verdacht, wenn ich Ihren Eifer nicht für eine zärtliche Ungedult ansähe, die so schmeichelhaft für mich ist. Ist es denn meine Schuld, daß das Schicksal gleich im Anfange unserer Bekanntschaft so viel Hindernisse ihrem Fortgange im Weg gelegt, zu deren Ueberwindung Zeit, und viel, viel Gedult erfordert wurde? Verschonen Sie mich, bester Freund, mit dem Vorwurf des Kaltsinns, oder lehren Sie mich die Kunst, ihn mit Gelassenheit zu ertragen." (*Briefe* I, 120–1)

[16] "Denn unmögliche Dinge zu wünschen, bin ich wirklich zu philosophisch." (*Briefe* I, 65)

[17] "Ich entdecke Ihnen die verborgensten Gedanken meines Herzens, davon der meiste Theil auf Sie gerichtet ist. Sind Sie mit dieser Aufrichtigkeit zufrieden? Von Ihrer
Kulmus" (*Briefe* I, 36)

[18] "Schreibe ich nicht sehr lange Briefe? und heißt dieses nicht buchstäblich, daß ich Ihre gehorsame Dienerin bin?

Kulmus" (*Briefe* I, 127; cf. also the identical ending on October 29, 1732; *Briefe* I, 42.)

[19] "[. . .] oft wünsche ich, daß Sie mich weniger lieben möchten, als ich Sie liebe, um nicht so viel zu leiden, als ich leide. Sagen Sie einmal, ob dieses eine kaltsinnige, gleichgültige Liebe ist, wie Sie so oft die meinige nennen?" (*Briefe* I, 134)

[20] "Gebe doch der Himmel, daß ich immer von der ununterbrochenen Dauer Ihrer zärtlichen Liebe so gewiß versichert seyn möge, als ich in mir selbst fühle, daß Ihnen mein Herz lebenslang treu und ergeben seyn wird. Sind sie nun mit allen Versicherungen zufrieden? Werden Sie noch über mein Stillschweigen klagen?" (*Briefe* I, 149–50)

[21] "Wie gefällt Ihnen *Donna Laura Bassi*, welche neulich den Doctorhut in Bologna erhalten? Ich vermuthe, daß wenn dieser junge Doctor Collegia lesen wird, solcher in den ersten Stunden mehr Zuschauer, als in der Folge Zuhörer bekommen möchte." (*Briefe* I, 22; emphasis original)

[22] "Die Frau von Z. kann mit Recht die Aufnahme in die deutsche Gesellschaft eben so hoch schätzen, als wenn sie von irgend einer Academie den Doctorhut erhalten hätte. Aber gewiß, Sie halten mich für sehr verwegen, wenn Sie mir zutrauen, an dergleichen Ehre zu denken. Nein, dieser Einfall soll nicht bey mir aufkommen. Ich erlaube meinem Geschlechte einen kleinen Umweg zu nehmen; allein, wo wir unsere Grenzen aus dem Gesichte verlieren, so gerathen wir in ein Labyrinth, und verlieren den Leitfaden unserer schwachen Vernunft, die uns doch glücklich ans Ende bringen sollte. Ich will mich hüten von dem Strom hingerissen zu werden. Aus diesem Grunde versichere ich Sie, daß ich meinen Nahmen nie unter den Mitgliedern der deutschen Gesellschaft wissen will." (*Briefe* I, 26–7)

[23] "Alles, was ich Sie bitte, ist dieses: Verhindern Sie den Druck dieser Briefe, oder verschieben ihn, bis nach meinem Tode"; Runckel's annotation: "Diese Besorgung war mir vorbehalten." (*Briefe* I, 126)

[24] "Der Anfang zum Trauergedichte auf meines Vaters Tod ist wohl gemacht, aber ich bin noch nicht weit darinnen gekommen. Hier ist er:

Verklärter Greiß, der Tag, der Tag ist kommen,
Da du der Welt und mir entnommen;
Der Tag, vor dem ich längst gebebt.
Die Stunde, da dein Geist genesen,
Ist mir die schrecklichste gewesen,
Die ich in meinem Lauf erlebt.

Ich bleibe darbey, ein heftiger Schmerz läßt sich so wie alle heftige Gemüthsbewegungen wohl empfinden, aber nicht beschreiben." (*Briefe* I, 31–2)

[25] "Das Gedicht, welches der zärtliche Bräutigam S. auf seine verstorbene Geliebte gemacht, habe ich aus bloßer Neugier gelesen; ich wollte wissen, ob dieses eine Sache sey, darüber man so viel schreiben könne, als man wirklich empfindet. Aber, Himmel! was hat der gute Mann alles gesagt, ich glaube viel mehr, als er empfand. Findet er vielleicht eine zweyte und eine dritte Braut, so wird er eben so schön und zärtlich singen, als er bey jener Gelegenheit gegirret und geklaget hat. Ein Poet ist doch ein unerschöpflicher Mann, es quillt Wahres und Falsches aus einem Brunnen, und das Sprüchwort ist untrüglich: Le Poëte n'est jamais heureux qu'en fiction." (*Briefe* I, 134–5)

[26] "Nein ich mag keine Euridice und Sie sollen nicht mein Orpheus seyn." (*Briefe* I, 74)

Orpheus and Eurydice stand as a testimony to emotional intensity among Greek antiquity's lovers and as symbols to the concept of love-beyond-death. The famed singer Orpheus loved Eurydice so much that when she died, he went into the underworld to plead with Hades to return her to him. Hades granted his wish, on the condition that Orpheus not turn around to gaze upon Death's realm until they had left it entirely. Orpheus, fearful of losing Eurydice again, turned around too early and watched her recede back into the realm of Death. He subsequently went insane and was torn to pieces by Maenads during a bacchic orgy. Kulmus commented on this highly emotional story dryly: "Orpheus' journey . . . seems rather improbable to me." ("Orpheus Reise . . . kommt mir nicht recht wahrscheinlich vor." *Briefe* I, 73)

[27] "Ich glaubte Ihnen selbst einen Gefallen durch die Vernichtung dieser Maculatur zu erzeigen, und darum habe ich dis Freudenfeuer angezündet. Wäre es wohl erlaubt, daß eine Person, die Ihnen so eigen zugehörte, als ich, der Welt solche sehr geringe Schriften lieferte?" (*Briefe* I, 216)

[28] "Ich bin gesund, vergnügt, und recht, nach meiner Neigung, glücklich. Unsere Beschäftigung sind, so wie unsere Gedanken, immer gleichförmig. Wir lesen sehr viel; wir machen über jede schöne Stelle unsere Betrachtung; wir theilen oft zum Schein unsere Meynung, und bestreiten einen Satz, bloß um zu sehen, ob die Meynungen gegründet sind, die wir von unseren Schriften fassen." (*Briefe* I, 227–8)

[29] "Ich arbeite viel, und lerne noch mehr. Ich übe mich in der Musik, und möchte wo es möglich, mich in der Composition festesetzen. An allen diesen würde ich verhindert werden, wenn ich ein Kind hätte, denn auf dieses würde ich meine ganze Zeit verwenden." (*Briefe* I, 233–4)

[30] "[Ich] verwende . . . den größten Theil meines Lebens auf Arbeiten, die vielen meines Geschlechts ganz fremd sind; und meine Gesundheit würde vielleicht besser seyn, wenn ich mehr Bewegung und angenehmere Zerstreuung hätte. Dies sagt mein Arzt, den ich über die Schwächlichkeit meines Körpers zuweilen um Rath frage. Mein eigner Trieb hingegen sagt mir, daß die Beschäftigung mit allem, was meine Neigung befriediget, und meinen

Geist zufrieden stellt, meiner Gesundheit nicht schädlich seyn kann. Diesen Trieb will ich folgen so lange meine Maschine nicht ganz baufällig wird." (*Briefe* I, 259–60)

[31] "Ich glaubte, hier könnte man sich von allen überhäuften Arbeiten erholen; ich erfahre aber, wer so gewohnt ist sich zu beschäftigen wie mein Freund, der findet aller Orten seine Neigung zu befriedigen." (*Briefe* I, 272)

[32] "Alle Muße, die wir in Dresden gehabt, hat sich in eine ununterbrochene Kette von Arbeit verwandelt. Vom frühen Morgen bis in die späte Nacht, sind wenig Stunden übrig, auf die nothwendigsten Bedürfnisse des Lebens zu wenden. Ich muß an das vergangene, und in Dresden auf so vielfältige Art erhaltene Gute zurückdenken, um mich über die gegenwärtigen Beschwerlichkeiten eines gelehrten Lebenswandels zufrieden zu stellen. Doch es ist mein Schicksal, diesen will ich mich mit Gelassenheit unterwerfen. Es ist mein Wunsch gewesen, und da ihn die Vorsehung in reichern Maaße, als ich jemals geglaubet, erfüllet hat, will ich nicht murren, sondern nach allen Kräften meinen Beruf gleichfalls erfüllen." (*Briefe* I, 275–6)

[33] Runckel's note: "As evidence that our Kulmus owed a large portion of her erudition to her friend I will offer the following verse which she composed in the year 1737:
My Gottsched, you alone
And that you loved me shall be my laurel crown.
The fact that you have taught, that you've instructed me
Shall be my song of praise writ for posterity.
Whoe'er has such a master won't die in obscurity:
Although the pupil be unworthy of eternity."
"Zum Beweis, daß unsere Kulmus ihrem Freund einen großen Theil ihres Wissens dankte, dienen folgende Zeilen, welche sie im Jahr 1737. verfertiget:
Mein Gottsched! Du allein
Und daß Du mich geliebt, dies soll mein Lorber seyn.
Daß Du mich hast gelehrt, daß Du mich unterwiesen,
Das sey der Nachwelt noch durch manches Blatt gepriesen.
Wer solchen Meister hat, da stirbt der Schüler nicht,
Wenn ihm gleich das Verdienst der Ewigkeit gebricht." (note to *Briefe* I, 154) The same poem was quoted by Johann Christoph Gottsched in his biography of his wife, published the year after her death ('Leben," unpaginated; cf. discussion in chapter 8).

[34] "Ein gewisses ungegründetes Gerüchte hatte unsre Kulmus zu Klagen bewogen, die sie hernach bereuete." (Runckel's note to *Briefe* I, 17)

4: Ailing Women and Bartered Brides: Comedies

LUISE GOTTSCHED IS KNOWN TO CRITICS TODAY primarily as an author of comedies (rather than as a satirist, translator or epistolary writer), despite the fact that she spent almost her entire life writing letters, satires and translations, whereas all of her comedies, with the exception of *Pietism in Petticoats* in 1736, were produced within three short years, from 1743 to 1745. Because these years coincide with her husband's project *The German Stage*, which featured all of her plays but *Pietism*, and because her plays correspond formally to the rules laid down in her husband's *Critical Poetics* (Bryan/Richel 193), her comedies have been read as mere *Auftragsarbeiten*, as commissioned works written in the service of her husband's poetic reform.[1] Taken by itself, that fact is indisputable, but what seems worthy of debate is the implication behind the statement: that commissioned works and works of aesthetic value are incompatible. According to Veronica Richel, "Luise Gottsched's comedies cannot be accounted works of art" in the minds of modern readers (*Luise Gottsched*, 22), because "art" is bound to the laws of originality, which presuppose the poet's autonomy and with it the complete absence of exterior or ulterior motives. Whereas a true "artist," literary and otherwise, produces to satisfy an inner need and calling, Luise Gottsched qualifies at best as an "occasional" author despite her lifelong activity as a writer and her quantitatively enormous output, and as a derivative author in her husband's service, even as "an author against her will" (Bovenschen 137). Exterior and ulterior motives, such as a commission or a direct connection between life and work, are read as sure signs of triviality. Thus, the fact that her husband commissioned virtually all of Gottsched's plays and the fact that biographical connections, however tenuous, can usually be drawn to her dramas,[2] have served Gottsched ill in the estimation of posthumous critics. Most scholarly assessments of Luise Gottsched's comedies suffer from the conditioned response that defines her dramatic writing as occasioned by exterior forces and hence inferior — a scholarly tradition riddled not only with biases, but also with inaccuracies. To claim, for example, that Luise Gottsched "was basking, at that very time [in the early 1740s, S. K.], in the fame she had gained as a comedy author with her *Pietisterey*" (Waniek 339), is not only to ignore historical fact (Gott-sched's authorship of the play was not uncovered until after her death), but also to reiterate, in patronizingly judgmental phraseology, the pur-ported incompatibility of "women" and "authors." The incompatibility is invoked here with an implied contrast between the unappreciated genius (who would not have the opportunity, let alone the inclination, to "bask") and the successful author of trivial literature ("comedy author").

This consideration of genre is another aspect that has led to the overwhelming trivialization of Luise Gottsched's authorship in schol-arly writing. Comedy has always been considered the inferior dramatic genre, an assessment that has changed little since Gottsched's day. It was the supposed vulgarity and lasciviousness of comedies performed by contemporary travelling troupes that drew the bulk of Johann Christoph Gottsched's criticism and initially inspired his reforms. Later, tragedies by Lessing, Goethe, Schiller, and Kleist became virtually syn-onymous with dramatic "art" in Germany, while comedies played a negligible role in the works of all major male playwrights of the age. (Neither Goethe's nor Schiller's canonized work includes a single com-edy, Schiller did not write any, and Lessing and Kleist wrote only few comedies in comparison with their extensive output in other dramatic genres.) What is actually a near-mechanical response based on a now-established genre hierarchy often passes for aesthetic judgment in mod-ern criticism: "comedy does not attain the caliber of tragedy, despite all verbal offensives" (Steinmetz, *Das deutsche Drama* 53). The two re-lated facts about genre and gender worth noting here are that comedy from the eighteenth century on has been almost universally perceived as aesthetically inferior to tragedy, and that eighteenth- and nineteenth-century comedy was a woman's genre. Between 1720 and 1900, women authored approximately one thousand comedies but only 86 tragedies (Kord, *Ein Blick* 93). Statistically, there exists a distinct genre- and gender-specific discrepancy in the writing habits of eighteenth-century "women," who wrote primarily comedies, as opposed to those of eight-eenth-century "authors" (men), who wrote predominantly poetological treatises and tragedies. The generalization holds true for the Gott-scheds: "if the dignified Herr Professor could not or would not frater-nize with the comedy, his skillful friend [Luise Gottsched; S. K.] was supposed to serve in this capacity" (Waniek 210). While Luise "served" as a comic writer, her husband, rising above the comic rabble, went on to "higher" things — tragedy, poetology, philosophy.

Gottsched's five comedies, all published between 1736 and 1747, include *Die Pietisterey im Fischbein-Rocke* (Pietism in Petticoats, anonymously, 1736) and, following seven dramatic translations, her plays for Johann Christoph's *The German Stage: Die ungleiche Heirath* (The Mésalliance, 1743), *Die Hausfranzösinn, oder die Mamsell* (The French Housekeeper, 1744), *Das Testament* (The Last Will, 1745) and the one-act-comedy *Der Witzling* (The Witling, anonymously, 1747). With the exception of the last one, all plays and most of her translations seem to have been at least moderately successful on the stage, including stages over which her husband exercised influence (such as Karoline Neuber's troupe) as well as others. The impact of *Pietism in Petticoats* was spectacular and nationwide (Consentius), and there is evidence that it was performed in Gottsched's hometown Danzig (Linke 26), despite the author's anonymity (which meant that the play could not capitalize on the fact that it had been authored by a local) and the controversial nature of the play. Devrient lists performances for all plays but *Pietism* and *The Witling* between 1743 and 1757 (*Schönemann* 19, 49, 90, 168, 182, 189; *Schönemannsche Truppe* 12–56); apparently, almost all of Gottsched's plays and most of her translations were regularly performed by Schönemann's troupe. While Karoline Neuber, who, as Johann Christoph Gottsched's protegée and primary vehicle for his theatrical reform, may have felt a certain obligation to perform plays by his wife, there is no evidence that Johann Friedrich Schönemann, Neuber's strongest competitor, felt similarly obliged. The constant presence of Luise Gottsched's plays in his repertoire and in those of other troupes as well as the fact that her plays were performed until well into the 1770s (Schlenther 222) stand in contradiction to the frequent assessment of her dramatic writing as dated.[3]

Luise Gottsched's reception as an author in her own time is fairly difficult to establish because her later reception obscures the one by her contemporaries, but there can be no question that she was nationally famous. The next generation of writers knew her as Germany's most famous erudite woman: in a letter to Sophie von LaRoche, written in 1751, Christoph Martin Wieland cites her in the same breath as the Marquise de Chatelet and Laura Bassi.[4] In large measure, this fame must have been due to her plays. The sensational impact of her first play *Pietism* was not connected with her name until after her death, but her later plays firmly established her reputation as a playwright on a national scale. Invitations by the aristocracy to the Gottscheds were at times accompanied by performances of Luise Gottsched's plays in her honor. Even Lessing's vituperative reviews of Luise Gottsched's plays in the late 1760s stand as testimony to the recognizability of her name and her enduring fame as a playwright among contemporaries: Lessing was demonstrably attempting to diminish her influence, along with that of her husband, to make room for the new National Theater.

As scholars have endlessly reiterated, all of Gottsched's plays, most notably those written for inclusion in *The German Stage*, adhere strictly to her husband's poetics. They are all five-act plays except *The Witling*; there is a strict division of scenes; a discernible moral principle serves as the point of each play's departure. Gottsched strictly observes Johann Christoph's demands for verisimilitude and division of social classes, with the tragedy reserved for the nobility and comedy for the bourgeoisie and the lower classes; there is characterization by type; and specific vices are ridiculed for the spectator's edification and moral improvement.[5] Undeniably, then, Gottsched's plays can serve as illustrations of her husband's poetics; at least four of her original plays and most of her translations were probably initially written as exemplifications of his theories in *Critical Poetics*. But this fact does not mean that there are no evasions or modifications of her husband's poetics in her plays, nor does it mean that her plays cannot be regarded as independent works.[6] As I have attempted to show earlier, Gottsched's letters seem to indicate significant deviations in her poetological thinking from that of her husband. It is this aspect of her work, that which has been "effaced" (French 19) in subsequent scholarship, that will be at the center of my investigation.

Character Constellations: Flawed Families, Diminutive Daughters, Reasonable Female Critics

In Johann Christoph Gottsched's poetics, comedy "is nothing other than the imitation of a vice" to be ridiculed for the viewer's edification and amusement ("Die Comödie ist nichts anders, als ein [*sic*] Nachahmung einer lasterhaften Handlung"; "Von Comödien" 348). The fact that vice is at the center of comedy already presupposes Johann Christoph's two central prohibitions regarding the characters of comedy: that they be neither members of the upper classes[7] nor complex characters.[8] Neither of these prescriptions is entirely observed in Luise Gottsched's comedies: in one, members of the aristocracy do appear as the butt of the satire (*The Mésalliance*). Indeed, class *difference*, which her husband's poetics casts as a thematic complex to be avoided at all costs, is occasionally thematized in Luise Gottsched's plays (in different ways in *Pietism*, *The Mésalliance*, *The French Housekeeper*, and *The Last Will*). In several of her plays, complex characters appear alongside the types recommended in her husband's poetics. Usually, Gottsched's character constellation suggests not the *Typenkomödie* envisioned by her husband, but the semi-tragic sentimental comedies authored by the next generation of women writers in the late 1700s and early 1800s (cf. section 4 of this chapter). If Johann Christoph Gottsched's poetics viewed comedy's purpose as the ridicule of Vice, Luise Gottsched's character constellation hints at the opposite theme: the Virtue-in-Distress motif popular in women's sentimental comedies as of approximately 1770. Although the actual character appears only once, in *Pietism in Petticoats*, the Virtue-in-Distress theme is everywhere implied, either in plot devices (forced marriages) or in character constellations such as incomplete families. Most of the families in Gottsched's plays consist of only one parent or guardian, at times a distant relative or someone entirely unrelated. *Pietism*'s daughter-in-distress is left to her mother's tender mercies until her father's return at the end of the play, the children in *The French Housekeeper* are raised by a widowed father, those in *The Last Will* by their aunt, and Lottchen in *The Witling* by an unrelated guardian appointed by her dead father. The vices that Johann Christoph Gottsched placed at the center of the comedy do play a part in these dramas, but they are, in all but one case, of secondary importance compared to the central issue: the domestic disaster occasioned by these vices and the disturbance caused in the relationship between parent(s) and child(ren) and in the authority structure of the family. In many cases, the single-parent family leads to a changed authority structure, a more precarious position for the daughter, and domestic chaos. Rarely does this situation result in an increase in self-determination on the part of the daughter — a constant theme in women's comedies from the early nineteenth century on.[9]

Readers familiar with the tradition of foolish or absent mothers in late-eighteenth-century plays by men, from Lessing's Claudia Galotti to Schiller's Frau Millerin,[10] will not find this model prefigured in Gottsched's character constellations. Her comedies blame neither the domestic disarray that usually ensues in the play on an unreasonable female parent or guardian, nor do they imply that such disaster could have been averted under the management of a more rational pater familias. Both female (*Pietism*) and male (*The Witling*) authority figures propose forced or unreasonable marriages for their charges: the domestic chaos in *The French Housekeeper* is blamed squarely on the indecisiveness and credulousness of the family's father, and the only parental figure in Gottsched's plays that can be considered at all competent is a woman — Frau von Tiefenborn in *The Last Will*. The only complete family in Gottsched's plays ("complete" in the sense that it includes both a mother and a father) is also the one that exercises the least amount of influence over their child (the Ahnenstolzes in *The Mésalliance*). In the economy of Gottsched's families, unusually enough, parental competence seems unrelated either to the constitution of the family (single-parent, or "complete," or one headed by guardians rather than biological parents) or, for that matter, to the parent's gender.

What does seem to be at issue in Gottsched's plays is the measure of parental authority: in all of her comedies, the well-being of the family and the happiness of the child or charge is endangered by either too much control (*Pietism, The Witling*) or not enough (*The Mésalliance, The French Housekeeper, The Last Will*). Parental control is exercised, with varying degrees of success, mostly over daughters and, less notably, also over sons in two areas: education (of both daughters and sons, in *Pietism, The French Housekeeper, The Last Will*) and marriage (of daughters, in *Pietism, The Mésalliance, The Witling*). Daughters at times are named in the diminutive (Luis*chen* and Dor*chen* in *Pietism*, Luis*chen* and Hann*chen* in *The French Housekeeper*, and Lott*chen* in *The Witling*), a designation that cannot be completely explained by their ages (of the daughters above, all but Hannchen are intended to be of marriageable age). Nor does the diminutive serve unilaterally as an implied characterization of the daughter as childlike or helpless: both Luischen in *The French Housekeeper* and Lottchen in *The Witling* demonstrate a high degree of verve, spirit and intelligence and exercise, as heads of their guardians' households, a modicum of authority. The difference between daughters who are named in the diminutive and those who are not (Philippine in *The Mésalliance* or Caroline and Amalie in *The Last Will*) may indeed be related to the degree of self-determination accorded them within the family. Whereas Philippine, Amalie and Caroline are, to a great extent, portrayed as mistresses of their fate (all three are relatively free to choose or reject husbands, for example), the Luischens and Lottchens are made diminutive in that they are reduced to a state of utter dependence on parental decisions: they are diminished — de nomine and de facto. The diminutive describes less the character's constitution than her surroundings and situation; it indicates not so much how the playwright devised the daughters as how other characters in the play perceive the daughters. The palpable tension in the characterization of Luise Gottsched's comic figures often emerges from this discrepancy between the potential of the character and its perception by others. Even that most subservient of Gottsched's diminutive daughters, Luischen in *Pietism in Petticoats*, is not unaware of the ironies inherent in utter powerlessness, elevated to the status of divine dispensation by Magister Scheinfromm in the following scene:

HERR SCHEINFROMM. Oh, *Mademoiselle*! Since the Fall of our first parents — note that! — our nature has been so corrupt that everything it loves and does is sin.

FRÄULEIN LUISCHEN. Then what must one do?

HERR SCHEINFROMM. Through its conquering strength, Grace must make itself the unlimited ruler of our will and guide it unperceived to the good. Then — give heed! — we're led by a heavenly bond that we can't resist. Otherwise, sensual desire necessarily drives us to evil through lack of this Grace.

FRÄULEIN LUISCHEN. Well, sir! That is precisely the condition in which I find myself.

HERR SCHEINFROMM. How is that?

FRÄULEIN LUISCHEN. I do not yet have the Grace to conquer my inclination; I am still moved by earthly desire.

HERR SCHEINFROMM. How do you know that you don't have Grace?

FRÄULEIN LUISCHEN. Because it doesn't move me, I don't have it. I am waiting for it.

HERR SCHEINFROMM. Indeed! But one must endeavor . . . .

FRÄULEIN LUISCHEN. How can I endeavor without the assistance of Grace? I'm waiting for it.

HERR SCHEINFROMM. What? You wish to be so cool and persist in a matter to which your Mama is opposed?

FRÄULEIN LUISCHEN. I'm waiting for Grace.

HERR SCHEINFROMM. You must ask our dear Lord for it.

FRÄULEIN LUISCHEN. How can I if Grace doesn't move me to prayer?

HERR SCHEINFROMM. In truth, you sin greatly by persisting in a passion which is not the work of Divine Compassion!

FRÄULEIN LUISCHEN. Say, rather, that I am unfortunate. For how can I sin if I have no guilt? I'm waiting for Grace.

HERR SCHEINFROMM. You are very disobedient to your Mama.

FRÄULEIN LUISCHEN. What can I do about that? As soon as I have Grace, I will obey her. But because this is your teaching,

> sir, do explain that to her so that she will have compassion
> for my disobedience.
>
> HERR SCHEINFROMM. What? Then you want your Mama to bring you
> to obedience through force?
>
> FRÄULEIN LUISCHEN. Oh, she can certainly force me! But Grace alone
> changes our hearts. I'm waiting for it.[11]

This scene makes three important points about diminutive daughters: their intellectual potential transcends their assigned roles; that same potential is artificially restrained (and for no honorable purpose); and, most significantly, theirs is the power of subversion from within — the subversion that takes Scheinfromm's paralyzing philosophy at face value and immobilizes his intention along with one's own capacity for action. What Luischen does in this scene is to play out the paradox of the diminution of daughters: rather than refusing her assigned part, she thwarts Scheinfromm's purpose by *overplaying* it — an act of will, verve and intelligence, not to mention an awareness of the paradox that far transcends that of Scheinfromm and other manipulators in the drama.

Finally, the most unusual aspect of Luise Gottsched's characterization technique, and the one that clearly corresponds least to her husband's dramatic rules, is the inclusion of complex characters in most of her comedies: characters who cannot, as per her husband's recommendation, be reduced to a single characteristic ("Von Comödien" 354). Gottsched's complex characters are always female, they are always presented as role models for other women — in the audience as well as in the play — and they are somewhat anomalous in that they do not so much participate in the play's action as comment on it. Luise Gottsched's Reasonable Female Critics (Amalia in *The Mésalliance*, Luischen in *The French Housekeeper*, Caroline in *The Last Will*, and Lottchen in *The Witling*) are an institution unto itself, unique in contemporary comedy writing — a mixture between the chorus of ancient Greek tragedy and the shrewd maidservant of eighteenth-century comedy. But Gottsched's Reasonable Female Critics transcend both: like the chorus they provide a running commentary on the action, and like the maidservant their ironic asides are responsible for a great deal of the humor. They furthermore provide a foil and contrast not only to the representatives of the Vice attacked in the play, but also — implicitly — to Virtue and its helpless laments.[12] The Reasonable Female Critics in Gottsched's comedies combine the maidservant's lighthearted freedom of speech with moral claims to bourgeois virtue, and they differ from the Greek chorus in that they usually have some ability to influence the play's outcome — an ability they frequently choose not to exercise. Gottsched's Reasonable Female Critics, with their interpretations and mediations of the plot, illustrate what Sanders has described as Gottsched's central dilemma: how could an intelligent, well-educated woman assert herself without rebelling against the dictates of feminine virtue? (*Virtuous Woman* 57) Gottsched leaves this question purposefully open: her Reasonable Female Critics are the only women who succeed in this moral balancing act, and they can do so only by remaining outside of the play's action. The "inside" of the drama is reserved for the helplessness of Virtue and the machinations of Vice — a world of extremes and typifications, a climate forbidding of gradations or complexities, a realm in which the differentiation between self-assertion and rebellion cannot be expressed.

Plot Essentials: Ailing Women

The themes of Gottsched's comedies cover a broad spectrum: a young girl is saved from an arranged marriage to a religious hypocrite; a young bourgeois is rescued from his own unreasonable ambition to marry into the aristocracy; a father discovers the havoc wreaked upon his family by the rule of unscrupulous and villainous French servants; an aunt tests the character of her wards by playing the hypochondriac; a young girl is saved from a marriage to an arrogant scholarly fop. The vices under attack are as varied as the themes, among them religious hypocrisy, bourgeois ambition and noble haughtiness, "French" falseness and ingratitude, greed, and the stupidity and overbearing attitude attributed to some scholars. Gottsched's comedies thus reiterate the standard concerns of Enlightenment didactic dramaturgy, and it is partly this eternal sameness of method coupled with her ostentatious adherence to her husband's poetics that has prevented scholars from reading these plays as "works of art." In addition to a mere refusal to consider Gottsched's plays *art*, however, there is a strict refusal to read them as *works*, and that may be due less to the eternal sameness of methodology than to the eternal variation of themes. To consider Luise Gottsched's comedies "her work" would require thinking of her dramas as expressions of the author's world-view. This would in turn require that the reader assume that the author had an overriding concern that was not, or not necessarily, congruent with her husband's. Such a concern would most often emerge in recurring motifs, questions, or issues, that is, recurring "original" elements that transcend Johann Christoph's mandates for good comedy.

One recurring independent motif in most of Luise Gottsched's comedies, and the one I would therefore place at the center of her work, is the theme of diseased or frail femininity, a factor in three of five comedies, *Pietism, The Mésalliance,* and *The Last Will.* In each play, the issue of female weakness or disease is presented in connection with the central theme: usually parental authority or, more precisely, the extent of female parental authority. Not coincidentally, female disease is thematized only in those plays in which parental authority rests with the mother or aunt, and it is these women who are beset by illnesses.

What is most striking about the treatment of this theme is that *none* of these diseases is presented as real: all feminine ailments in Gottsched's plays are either imagined (*Pietism; The Mésalliance*) or simulated (*The Last Will*). Gottsched's female authority figures are thus capable of running the household, at least physically, but they deprive themselves of all ability and authority to do so with the help of fabricated weaknesses. Luischen's mother in *Pietism,* turned fervent Pietist by the ministrations of the hypocritical Magister Scheinfromm, certainly loses all credibility with the audience when she faints at the mention of Lutheran theologians and recovers at the fervent invocation of Pietist notables and theo-babble:

FRAU GLAUBELEICHT [*faints*]. Oh, Cathrine! Catch me! Oh! — Oh! I'm dying!

CATHRINE. Good Lord! Why did you use those names! You might better have invoked Beelzebub and his angels. I'll have the poor woman dead in my arms.

HERR WACKERMANN. What is this? At the mention of Fecht and Wernsdorff she faints?

CATHRINE. Certainly! She always does. This is already the third time.

HERR WACKERMANN. I had no idea! Give her some smelling salts! You have some there.

CATHRINE. Oh, that won't help at all. I know the medicine she needs. Shout along with me! [*She shouts.*] Arnold! Petersen! Lange! Gichtel! Francke! Tauler! Grace! Born Again! The Inner Spark! Spiritual Unction! — Come on! Please join in the shouting!

HERR WACKERMANN. I think you're insane.

CATHRINE. No, no, Colonel, you see she's coming around. [*She shouts.*] Grace! The Inner Man! Saint Jacob Böhme! Look! Look! She's recovering.[13]

More significant than all the obvious conclusions with regard to Frau Glaubeleicht's foolishness and her unfitness as a parent is her act of *self-deprivation*, the fact that she *abdicates* both her credibility on stage and her authority over her daughter, at least in the spectator's view. The spectator of *Pietism* is presented with two utterly helpless women: Luischen cannot defend herself against the authority exercised over her by her mother without compromising her role as a model of feminine virtue. Conversely, her mother cannot exercise this authority within the bounds of the genre, since a forced marriage would inevitably end in a tragedy. The generic conflict is resolved first through ridiculing the character of the mother on stage and second through a high degree of self-referentiality within the comedy.[14] By "self-referentiality" I mean passages in which the play calls attention to its own genre, but in such a way as to point out the limitations forced upon the play by its genre. "Comedy" in these scenes is never perceived as a source of amusement, but as a highly ambivalent matter; the term itself is used with a great deal of sarcasm. Examples are the scene in which Herr Wackermann announces his intention to attend a theological meeting of Pietistic women instead of, as originally planned, seeing "a comedy at the theater,"[15] or Herr Liebmann's comment when he hears his love maligned by Pietist doctrine: "Is this where we're supposed to laugh?"[16] This kind of self-referentiality serves to express the same sentiment as the ridiculing of the diseased mothers on stage, the women with only nominal authority that they cannot properly exercise: a primary ambivalence towards the comic genre, an ambivalence possibly rooted in the knowledge that traditional "comedy" *subsists,* primarily or entirely, on women's weakness, ridiculousness, and utter helplessness.

In *The Mésalliance*, Frau von Ahnenstolz's multiple diseases are usually read as signs of her noble heritage; the near-unanimous conclusion is that Gottsched's point here is a not-so-subtle critique of "sick" aristocracy and an implicit contrast with the "healthy" bourgeoisie, personified in forthright Herr Wilibald. While this interpretation finds some support in occasional scenes in which aristocratic frailty is contrasted with the "clumsy, coarse" health of the "common people" (cf. *Pietism* 79; 93), there are two facets that cast doubt on this reading. Gottsched's lifelong and well-documented veneration for the aristocracy is one, and the other is the fact that in the play frailty is again identified with femininity rather than social standing. The disease that scholars have seen as a distinctive attribute of the aristocracy spares all aristocratic men (Herr von Ahnenstolz, Herr von Wildholz and Herr von Zierfeld) and plagues solely the Lady of the Manor, Frau von Ahnenstolz. As in the previous play, the disease besets exclusively women, specifically the woman who is potentially in a position of authority (the mother figure); and the disease is again self-inflicted. In a parallel scene to the one cited above, Frau von Ahnenstolz threatens to faint at the mention of her rival's name:

> FRAU VON AHNENSTOLZ. Oh! Oh! Don't mention that woman's name to me! That name pierces my heart like an arrow! You might irritate my polyp and suffocate me immediately.
>
> HERR VON WILDHOLZ. Heaven forbid! I didn't know that My Lady also had a polyp. But, dear lady, just consider . . . .
>
> FRAU VON AHNENSTOLZ. Consider? Do you believe that I have the strength to consider anything? Thinking exhausts all my energy; and ever since I've had the *malum hypochondriacum*, I must protect myself from all thinking as from the plague.[17]

This scene reveals more clearly than any other the effect of the disease: to prevent the woman in authority from "thinking," from making use of her facilities for reason and intellect and, above all, of her decision-making capacity. The relationship between dramatic treatment of the theme and viewer reaction is fairly complex here. The audience is invited to view Frau von Ahnenstolz's fashionable hypochondria as ridiculous and exaggerated, but within the play female hypochondria is universally encouraged and approved. Women who are completely incapacitated, intellectually ("Thinking exhausts all my energy") and physically (Frau von Ahnenstolz: "I suffer every illness imaginable and can undertake no physical activity without risking my life"[18]), serve as models: their physical and mental debility is generalized as the *condition des femmes*. "I'm quite sure that no other woman in the world has ever better represented the attributes of the weaker sex." (Herr von Wildholz on Frau von Ahnenstolz[19]) The viewer's amusement at the *particulars*, the endless lists of Frau von Ahnenstolz's diseases and her unprovoked fainting spells throughout the play, does not invalidate the *generalization* ("the weaker sex") or the implied exemplariness of Frau von Ahnenstolz's behavior.[20] Only the conclusion that women are seen as *ideally* frail and weak can, for example, explain daughter Philippine's otherwise bizarre claim to uphold "the honor of the sex" with a severe headache.[21]

The Last Will is the first comedy that explores what happens if women refuse to conform to this ideal. Frau von Tiefenborn's tactic is to dissemble and resemble the ideal: on the surface she tests her wards' gratitude and affection for her, but more significantly, it seems, she claims for herself the life of which they are trying to deprive her. The play is characterized by a tension unusual in Gottsched's plays, because it is the first to portray an alternative to female authority undermined by feminine frailty. While Amalie and Herr von Kaltenborn, in their attempt to influence their aunt Frau von Tiefenborn to write her last will, spend much of the play trying to put her in her place (that is, on her deathbed), Frau von Tiefenborn herself and her third niece Caroline are engaged in a different project: to restore to her health, life, and — not least of all — the authority to dispose of her person and property as she sees fit. This reverse process shows a striking parallel to earlier plays in its treatment of (un)reality: of consequence to the outcome of the play is not what is real, but what is perceived as real by characters in the drama. Just as Frau Glaubeleicht and Frau von Ahnenstolz are deprived of all capacity or justification to act by a disease they *do not have*, Frau von Tiefenborn's pretended illness helps her secure rights *she already has*. Reality in *The Last Will* is malleable: both Herr von Kaltenborn and Amalie, although aware of Frau von Tiefenborn's state of perfect health, firmly believe in the same power of psychosomatic suggestion that the spectator has already witnessed at work in *Pietism* and *The Mésalliance*. Their goal is not initially to turn Frau von Tiefenborn into a sick or dying woman, but merely to suggest to her that she is sick and dying — not to turn her into a patient, but to turn her into a *hypochondriac*, the precise image of frail femininity ridiculed in the earlier plays.

To force Frau von Tiefenborn into this weakness and thus to abdicate her authority, the siblings fabricate an illness that all characters in the play, the doctor, patient, family members and potential heirs, know does not exist. This deception works on several levels. Amalie and Kaltenborn attempt to suggest to their aunt that she is deathly ill; Frau von Tiefenborn, with the aid of her doctor Hippokras, acts the hypochondriac to test their loyalty, while Caroline, the play's Reasonable Female Critic, attempts to disabuse Frau von Tiefenborn of her hypochondria without betraying her siblings directly. This constellation depicts the authority structure as intact, because the authority figure, Frau von Tiefenborn, is the initiator of the comedy's plot and simultaneously the only person who knows the entire truth. The "comedy" of the earlier plays, in which the audience got their laughs at the hypochondriac's expense, is once removed here to a play-within-a-play, authored and performed by Frau von Tiefenborn. She plays the hypochondriac to perfection, with Dr. Hippokras as her prompter and Caroline and Amalie as the audience who interject their very different interpretations of the "play":

DR. HIPPOKRAS. Your humble servant, gracious lady. I hope Your Ladyship finds herself better disposed today than yesterday.

FRAU VON TIEFENBORN. If only I did, Doctor! I spent a quite miserable night . . . . It's true, isn't it? My pulse is quite weak and irregular?

FRÄULEIN AMALIE. Indeed, our aunt looks quite terrible today!

FRAU VON TIEFENBORN. Well now, I don't ever look terrible . . . .

FRÄULEIN AMALIE. Oh, I just meant to say "pale" . . . "poorly." [*Flatteringly.*] One who was so beautiful in youth as Your Ladyship was can certainly never look terrible. [*She gestures to her sister.*]

FRÄULEIN CAROLINE. Without trying to flatter our aunt with her former beauty, I can truly say that she doesn't look at all sick to me. You must have slept quite well.

FRAU VON TIEFENBORN . . . . Well, Doctor, what do you say?

DR. HIPPOKRAS [*thoughtfully.*] The pulse . . . the pulse is . . . a bit fast.

FRAU VON TIEFENBORN [*sickly.*] I had a very bad night.

DR. HIPPOKRAS. Oh? You had a bad night? [*CAROLINE shakes her head.*]

DR. HIPPOKRAS. Did you also suffer anxieties?

FRAU VON TIEFENBORN. Yes, frightful ones!

DR. HIPPOKRAS. Oh? So Your Ladyship suffered anxieties? Did you eat anything last night?

FRAU VON TIEFENBORN. A little something. But I wasn't really hungry.

FRÄULEIN CAROLINE. Well, you certainly must be able to control your appetite. To devour a partridge and a half, not to mention the main course? And all that while fighting a loss of appetite? [*She shakes her head.*]

FRÄULEIN AMALIE [*motions to her sister.*] I observed quite clearly that our aunt left almost everything lying on her plate.

FRAU VON TIEFENBORN. Oh, what I ate didn't amount to a thing![22]

Hypochondria, in this play-within-a-play, assumes the status of the absurd rather than merely the ridiculous. The play's bizarre humor hinges upon the characters' — *every* character's — awareness that this is much ado about nothing and upon their stolid determination to pretend otherwise, illustrated in their earnest and endless discussions of an imaginary disease that nobody believes in.

The only other scene in which Frau von Tiefenborn's condition is analyzed at such length concerns not her physical health but her mental disposition. At issue in this second scene are her decision-making powers, her ability to be "mistress in my own home."[23] When Kaltenborn and Amalie bribe the stablehands to pretend all the horses are sick in order to prevent their aunt from leaving the house, Frau von Tiefenborn acts precisely the part expected of her: that of the hapless widow at the mercy of others. "Oh, what a tormented woman a widow is! In such matters, which are men's work, she has to rely on whatever her servants say. Oh, what a proper stable my late husband kept! If he were to see this! (*She cries.*)"[24] That there are alternatives to this despondency is aptly demonstrated by Caroline, who, showing absolutely no hesitation to do "men's work," immediately offers to go to the stable, threaten the coachman with dismissal and thus to "make your horses well with a single word."[25] The perfect parallelism of this scene with the first shows once again the real issue at the bottom of the imaginary physical disease. The sole purpose and effect of the disease is to deprive the woman in authority of her capacity to make decisions and thus to render her dependent. It is important to remember despite the surrounding characters' near-unanimous approval and praise of the ailing women that the disease is, in all three plays, *imaginary* and that it is therefore theoretically possible for the hypochondriac to influence the outcome. Frau von Tiefenborn does just this by marrying instead of dying and leaving her wealth to her niece Amalie so she can marry, thus taking Caroline's advice from Scene II: "If I were in her place, I would marry again and enjoy my wealth properly."[26] Frau von Tiefenborn is the only female authority figure who does not give in to the suggestion of feminine frailty and the only one who manages to engineer the ending of her own comedy. It is perhaps not surprising, then, that of all of Luise Gottsched's comedies, *The Last Will* is the only one in which the generic Happy Ending (marriage) coincides with a Happy Ending generated by the play's narrative.

Not for Love and Not for Money:
Happy Endings Beyond Marriage[27]

As is the case for fairy tales, the Happy Ending is a generic requirement of comedy, which means that in most (not all) cases, the entire play hinges largely on its ending. The attributes that Bausinger singles out as defining the Happy Ending of fairy tales apply to comedies as well. In both cases, the narrative is largely pre-determined by the outcome; both genres commonly describe a love story in which initial obstacles are overcome and which ends with the lovers' union; both genres attempt to portray the possibility of a permanent and conflict-free state of happiness; and both genres imply a convergence of happiness and morals — the Enlightenment theme of Virtue Rewarded (cf. Bausinger; Kord, "All's Well" 181). The difference is one of genre and tone: the fairy tale is a narrative genre and one that presupposes the reader's complete suspension of disbelief; it is thus limited neither by the rules of probability nor by the logistics of performance. Whereas in fairy tales, the means of bringing about the Happy Ending are practically limitless, the comedic Happy Ending is usually engineered by recourse to reconciliation and marriage.

Another notable difference between the comedic Happy Ending and that of fairy tales is their varied receptions: the Happy Ending of comedy has often been regarded with a discomfort, voiced by authors and critics alike, that has not plagued readers of fairy tales in the same manner.[28] In comedy, the Happy Ending assumes a significance equivalent to the entire play: it pronounces judgment on the play.

> . . . the ending becomes the touchstone for aesthetic accomplishment. It is here that the author must demonstrate whether he [*sic*] can resolve the entanglements in a way that makes sense or whether he just hacks through the knot, whether he can solve the conflicts in a convincing equilibrium or merely by a phoney reconciliation, in other words: whether his solution will endure beyond the moment of comedy-cleanup (Hinck 126).

What this indicates is that unlike in fairy tales, where hacking through the knot is always acceptable, the Happy Ending of comedy must be believable: the resolution must make sense and leave the viewer with an impression of permanence capable of carrying him or her past the climactic — and slightly ludicrous — moment of conclusion. Given the fact that the ending is predetermined by the genre, that the viewer knows it is coming and is counting firmly on it, it seems that what is required of the author is that s/he make the inevitable appear plausible. Unlike the fairy tale ending, the Happy Ending of comedy is a contradiction in terms: on the generic level, the outcome is predetermined, while on the narrative level, the author must bring this ending about in a realistic manner. S/he must uphold the apparent relevance of factors that are rendered pointless by the fatalism of the ending: alternatives, coincidences, human intervention, and individual choice.

Luise Gottsched is one of the few comedy authors of the century who granted the narrative structure of her own comedies predominance over generic demands. That the identification of happiness with marriage at the end of comedy was already a generic requirement in contemporary comedies is clearly apparent from her husband's comment in *Critical Poetics:*

> This subject is already so trite that I don't understand why people have not tired of it long ago. It seems to me the same when all dramas end with weddings. Is there nothing else in the world than marriage that could provide us with a Happy Ending?[29]

Luise Gottsched's comedies answer this objection by eliminating the identification of "happiness" with "marriage." Marriage in her comedies is presented as a purely financial transaction; her characters are motivated to marry not by love but by greed. Consequently, what provides us with a Happy Ending to her comedies is usually not a wedding, but the *prevention* of one. All Reasonable Female Critics in her plays voice their determination to remain unmarried; conversely, women characters who are eager to marry are usually saddled with character flaws, such as greed and treachery (Amalie in *The Last Will* and Dorchen in *Pietism*). In *Pietism in Petticoats*, the plot revolves less around Luischen's marriage to Herr Liebmann than around the prevention of her arranged marriage to Herr von Muckersdorff. When the wedding to Herr Liebmann does take place, it is limited to a few lines and presented as a mercenary transaction rather than a love match: "The contract has been ready for two years; we only need to sign it."[30] In *The Mésalliance*, Philippine is subject to her parents' wishes, which force her into a marriage with the despised but rich bourgeois Herr Wilibald, whereas Amalia, the play's Reasonable Female Critic and stepsister to Frau von Ahnenstolz, is not subject to any authority and uses her influence to prevent the wedding. Both Amalia and Philippine emphasize repeatedly that money is the sole reason for this wedding (87). Philippine even presents such egotism as the sole possible reason for marriage: "Every one has his own reasons for getting married; and these are always based on self-interest, whatever shape that may take."[31] Self-interest, in this case, is financial on both sides: Wilibald wishes to acquire a certificate of nobility through this marriage, whereas the Ahnenstolzes, a family of impoverished aristocrats, enter into this alliance with a rich bourgeois suitor solely to pay their debts. Marriage is presented as a financial transaction in which the father (current owner) sells to the groom (future owner) a bride at a more or less exorbitant price, and this conception of marriage is a foregone conclusion to everyone in the play. Amalia's impulse to prevent the marriage between Wilibald and Philippine is inspired by two fears: that Wilibald's money "is going to buy him everlasting misfortune"[32] and that he could "purchase the bride at too high a price,"[33] a fear that is confirmed when Wilibald is presented with the price-tag (107–9). When Amalia warns Wilibald of his future unhappiness she clearly implies that even if he were to marry among the bourgeois she would not consider this a love match, but merely a more reasonable transaction: "for all your great wealth, with which among your own sort you could have chosen the most perfect woman at home and abroad, you have purchased . . . only reproaches . . . and ridicule . . . ."[34]

If marriage is ever considered anything other than a financial transaction, it is presented not as Happiness, but as a series of domestic disputes. Philippine vows to terrorize her husband in marriage with her hypochondria: "I'll see to it that I become even worse than my mother" (129; "so will ich sehen, daß ich es noch ärger mache, als meine Mutter," *Die Lustspiele* I, 108). Both Ahnenstolz parents view such altercations as characteristic of marriage itself. Observing a quarrel between Wilibald and Philippine, Frau von Ahnenstolz remarks: "Why are you quarreling so? It's just as though you were already married";[35] Herr von Ahnenstolz comments in a similar vein: "You good children are starting too soon! After the wedding you'll have time enough for disagreements."[36]

The play ends with Amalia unveiling the secret courtship between Zierfeld and Philippine and preventing a wedding that would have been bad business for Wilibald. She thereby also clears the stage for two potential weddings between couples that are clearly better suited for one another: Zierfeld and Philippine, both plagued with the vanity and arrogance of a thousand years of noble ancestry, and Wilibald and Amalia, the representatives of bourgeois Virtue and Reason. But the end of the play leaves the viewer to assume that neither of these weddings will ever come off. With regard to the eminently logical match between Zierfeld and Philippine — an ending the viewer is clearly led to expect — Herr von Ahnenstolz gives his reluctant consent, but still has to obtain his wife's permission, and "can't yet promise anything definite" when the play closes.[37] In the final scene of the play, the other potential wedding falls through: Amalia rejects Wilibald's marriage proposal and ridicules him as a bourgeois upstart who is unable to take a lesson from his failed negotiation with the Ahnenstolzes and still insists on buying his way into the aristocracy.

In *The Last Will*, marriage as financial transaction is thematized in similar ways: Amalie, bent on marrying at all costs, is presented as a negative character similar to that of Dorchen in *Pietism*. Her severe failings — she flatters and deceives her aunt at the outset and stoops to instigation of murder at the end — are attributed directly to her crazed wish to marry, which must therefore be considered her principal character flaw. Because Amalie is greedy enough to view a large inheritance as the sole means for marriage and deluded enough to consider marriage the sole means for happiness, her aunt's testament becomes an existential question for her. Her sister Caroline, on the other hand, is content with "bread, water, and the noble freedom to utter my opinion to everyone without hiding anything."[38] Throughout the play, she uses this freedom to good purpose by trying to convince her aunt of her health and by repeatedly warning her sister Amalie not to enter into marriage with a man who would marry her for her money. Indeed, both of Amalie's suitors, Herr von Kreuzweg and Captain von Wagehals, admit openly to everyone concerned that they are interested in Amalie's inheritance rather than her person. Both immediately drop her when she is disinherited, and Kreuzweg proposes to Caroline at the end of the play because she was named in her aunt's testament. Needless to say, Caroline rejects him — and vows to remain unmarried as long as her aunt is alive.

Her aunt, in the meantime, has no intention of dying. She is the only one in the drama who actually becomes engaged to marry, knowing full well that her wealth provides a motive for her fiancé. She comments sarcastically on his flattery that she looks twenty years younger than her actual age: "Well, I've always regarded him as a cavalier who has enough sense to perceive the change that great wealth can make in a person's intelligence, age, and privileges."[39] Frau von Tiefenborn here ironicizes an axiom that Amalie takes seriously — "Only the rich are clever"[40] — in a manner that indicates that she can afford this detached attitude towards both her wealth and her wedding. For she is not about to relinquish her financial independence: the Last Will around which the play revolves makes her fiancé her heir after her death. Until then, she will remain, in her own words, "mistress in my own home." Unlike Caroline or Amalie, whose property would have gone over to their husbands, and unlike the Luischens and Lottchens of other comedies who narrowly escape being married off for their wealth, Frau von Tiefenborn, the play's middle-aged but by no means infirm female authority figure, is finally in a position to afford marriage.

On Tradition and Influence:
Late Eighteenth-Century Drama

The recurring issue expressed in Gottsched's characterizations, her narrative structure, and her endings, is the question of women's self-determination, and the issue is treated in a manner perhaps disappointing to critics expecting a bolder statement from the century's most acknowledged woman writer. Gottsched's daughters are deprived of any authority to act on their own behalf by their parents and guardians, and those women in her plays who are in positions of authority, the mother figures, abdicate this authority by turning hypochondriac — a recurring motif that can easily be read as a symbol of psychological self-defeat. Her Reasonable Female Critics occupy positions on the margins of the play and comment on the action more than they participate in it. Solely Frau von Tiefenborn, *The Last Will*'s unlikely heroine, manages to engineer a Happy Ending to her liking and exercises her authority successfully to the end. The question of female self-determination in Gottsched's plays, then, is answered by a rift between intellectual/volitional and social empowerment: those who are intellectually capable and willing to make decisions are deprived of the authority to do so, while those in authority refuse to exercise it and mask this refusal by recourse to physical debility. To some extent, this can be regarded as narrative logic, since it mirrors women's powerlessness in the world outside the theater (cf. Johann Christoph Gottsched's demands for verisimilitude). On another level, it demonstrates a certain amount of pragmatism: portraying a woman of Caroline's intelligence and decisiveness in a position to *capitalize* on these talents, as, for example, head of her own household without male supervision, would surely have been considered nothing short of a provocation. Gottsched's characterization of women characters is indeed unusual in the sense that she accurately depicts the *condition des femmes* as dependent, accurately describes their own participation in the processes that keep them dependent, and does this by using little more than the stock female characters available to the contemporary comic repertoire — the hypochondriac and ridiculous woman, the cunning maidservant, the witty and ironic daughter, the Virtue in distress.

If the *condition des femmes* in Gottsched's plays is depicted true to life, her elimination of marriage as the Happy Ending of comedy makes narrative sense: women whose self-determination has been revoked can either be forced into marriages or they can — at best — narrowly escape that fate, as Gottsched's heroines do. In neither case can marriage be identified with the "happiness" that the comic ending is charged to provide. Gottsched does more here than adhere to her husband's demands for verisimilitude (although arranged marriages for purely financial reasons were far from unusual in her day, cf. Stone), rather, she provides an ending congruent with the narrative structure of her plays. On the narrative level, she refuses to be put in the dilemma that later playwrights have viewed as virtually inescapable: that of making the inevitable appear plausible and subordinating the narrative to the generic. On the ideological level, she could easily be interpreted as critiquing the notion of a permanent and conflict-free state of happiness that is evoked by the stereotypical marriage-at-the-end-of-comedy.

It is particularly these aspects of her comedies that should prompt us to rethink Gottsched's reception as a playwright. Reading her plays as forerunners to those of the male "greats" of the late Enlightenment and Classicism (particularly Lessing, Goethe and Schiller) places her in an automatically inferior position, a position frequently articulated in extremely prejudicial terms. Schlenther's revealing remarks about the "firm tread of a man" (read: any male author) following Gottsched's childish "four-legged crawling and groping" (208) are far from unusual here. Reading Luise Gottsched as a precursor to the male "greats" is problematic, not only because of the different genre choices and the conclusions commonly drawn from this (that is, presupposing the inferiority of both the comic genre and the woman author writing in it), but also because there is really no evidence, beyond the common commitment to dramatic reform, that Gottsched's plays had any influence on late eighteenth-century drama by men. Her genre, her themes, and her narrative technique were neither appropriated nor acknowledged in that tradition. The reverse is true of contemporary women's comedies: from the 1770s on (that is, simultaneously with Lessing's dramatic efforts and early plays by Goethe), there is an entire tradition of sentimental comedies authored by women that can be much more fruitfully interpreted as inspired by Luise Gottsched's comedies of the 1740s.

Comedies by authors such as Friederike Sophie Hensel-Seyler (1738–89), Victoria von Rupp (ca. 1755–ca. 1824), Sophie Mariane von Reitzenstein (1770–1823), or Marie Antonie Teutscher (1752–84)[41] reiterate some of Gottsched's character constellations (her incomplete families) and take up some of her themes (the Virtue-in-Distress motif) and techniques (self-referentiality). Most significantly, however, these dramas display a very similar uncertainty with regard to the traditional Marriage-as-the-Happy-Ending, an uncertainty that is played out in the rift between narrative and generic demands on the play, a technique analogous to Gottsched's. Unlike Gottsched's plays, however, these comedies usually end in marriage: they retain the Happy Ending as a generic function but relativize it on the narrative level. Like Gottsched's comedies, these comedies relativize the identification of marriage with "happiness" by eliminating happiness while retaining the marriage theme, by emphasizing the extreme unlikelihood of the portrayed ending, or by thematizing the unsavory ways in which the marriage is brought about (usually rape, coercion, or abduction).[42] Elsewhere, I have argued against reading these flawed "happy" endings as incompetence on the part of the playwrights and in favor of viewing them as a "tradition" in the sense that we perceive traditions when male writers create them, defined through commonality of occurrence to such a degree that the occurrence can be generalized, and a canon of stylistic, generic or narrative conventions used consciously and with sufficient conformity to established rules to guarantee their recognizability (cf. "All's Well," 193). Although in view of women's marginalization in canonical literature, "tradition" is an admittedly problematic term when applied to women's writing, a tradition of problematized "Happy" Endings can clearly be demonstrated to exist in their comedies — a tradition of which Luise Gottsched's comedies mark the beginning.

In the absence of biographical or poetological material by the authors of this alternative comedic tradition, we are reduced to speculation as to the *function* of women's compromised Happy Endings. The speculation I have to offer here is this: a seemingly flawed ending or, in many cases, complete nonclosure may indicate a doubt on the author's part that the end *should* justify the means, that an ending can be charged to confer meaning on a narrative or even serve as the "touchstone for aesthetic accomplishment" (Hinck 126), or that a piece of writing can and should be judged by its ending alone (cf. "All's Well," 193). In reading endings of comedies by eighteenth-century women, it is most fruitful to follow Schmidt's lead in considering alternative endings, that is, those alternatives that are suppressed in the play to make room for the Happy Ending, both the documented ones (the ones the playwrights themselves considered) and the hypothetical ones suggested by the plot (Schmidt 19, 26–8 and 34). Comedies by eighteenth-century women, beginning with Luise Gottsched's, imply the following hypothetical alternatives: a truly "happy" ending for a woman would entail some measure of self-determination, rather than pre-determination, for women. A Happy Ending on the narrative level would grant such self-determination to the countless women forced into arranged marriages and be "convincing" in the sense that this ending would match the viewers' experience of social possibilities (pre-supposing the possibility for female self-determination in real life as well). On the meta-narrative level, a Happy Ending might be one in which the play would be read for its narrative rather than its ending — marking the end of the era in which literature by women is read, based on their conformity to genre, as "inferior" to that of men, and the beginning of the era in which readers can see beyond the genre and rediscover the complexity of the narrative.

Notes

[1] Cf., among many others, Richel, *Luise Gottsched* 28. In the single instance of *Pietism*, in which the play was written before the marriage and the literary collaboration began in earnest, critics take care to detract from the play's "originality" by reducing it to a mere translation, by citing a biographical inspiration (the persecution of Luise Gottsched's father at the hands of the Pietists, Linke 27), by pointing out that the play coincided with the beginning of Johann Christoph Gottsched's campaign against the Pietists (Critchfield 114) or even by misrepresenting it as her husband's work, with the author herself reduced to the role of collaborator (Rieck et. al., 185). Cf., on the other hand, Zelle, who claims that Luise Gottsched had been working on the play since 1732 and intended it as a surprise for her fiancé, which would indicate that she wrote it independent of his direct supervision (165).

[2] See chapter I, note 26: both *The French Housekeeper* and *The Mésalliance* are supposedly illustrations of remarks made in her letters (Schlenther 39, 183, 222; Bryan/Richel 194); Schlenther speculates that the playwright's exaltation of marital fidelity in *Panthea* may have been inspired by her own husband's unfaithfulness (62–3); *The Witling* is reduced to a satire on her husband's opponents (Richel, *Luise Gottsched* 48; Schreiber 58; Bovenschen 136).

[3] Cf., for example, Buchwald's and Köster's comment in their re-edition of her comedies ("Schlußbericht", II 533–43; here 540).

[4] "How happy I am in fancying that the image of my beloved will one day eclipse the portrait of a Chatelet, Bassi, Frau Gottsched." (Quoted in Nenon 52)

[5] Cf. Johann Christoph Gottsched, "Von Comödien oder Lustspielen," *Versuch einer Critischen Dichtkunst* VI, 2, 337–60.

[6] I agree here with Gudrun Loster-Schneider, who has argued that interpreting Gottsched's comedic writing as part of her role as her husband's "helpmate" amounts to a "monologization" of Gottsched's comedies (the term is Bakhtin's), a move that simultaneously makes it impossible to view the author as anything beyond an incompetent mimic of his theories. (67–68)

[7] "The persons who belong in a comedy are average burghers, or at least people of moderate standing, among which also, if unavoidable, barons, marquis and counts can be included: it is not as if the notables of this world did not commit any ridiculous follies, no, but rather that it would offend the respect one owes them to portray them as deserving of ridicule." ("Die Personen, die zur Comödie gehören, sind ordentliche Bürger, oder doch Leute von mäßigem Stande, dergleichen wohl auch zur Noth Barons, Marquis und Grafen sind: nicht, als wenn die Großen dieser Welt keine Thorheiten zu begehen pflegten, die lächerlich wären; nein, sondern weil es wider die Ehrerbiethung läuft, die man ihnen schuldig ist, sie als auslachenswürdig darzustellen." Johann Christoph Gottsched, "Von Comödien" 351)

[8] "One cannot use a complete human character, which expresses itself in countless deeds, for a comic story line, as little as for a tragic one . . . . One has to choose one single highly important act of mischief, . . . that then makes up the plot [of the comedy]." ("Zu einer comischen Handlung nun kann man eben so wenig, als zu tragischen, einen ganzen Character eines Menschen nehmen, der sich in unzähligen Thaten äußert . . . . Es muß eine einzige recht wichtige Spitzbüberey genommen werden, . . . die . . . also eine Handlung ausmacht." Johann Christoph Gottsched, "Von Comödien" 349)

[9] Cf. Kord, *Ein Blick* 58–70.

[10] Cf. Hart's article for a more extensive discussion of the elimination of mothers from late-eighteenth-century drama by men, as well as Möhrmann and Kraft.

[11] *Pietism* 27–8. Unless otherwise stated, all translations from comedies are cited after Kerth/Russell's edition (*Pietism in Petticoats*); all original quotations in notes are taken from *Die Lustspiele der Gottschedin*, vol. I.
"HERR SCHEINFROMM. Ach Mademoiselle! seit dem Falle unserer ersten Eltern (mercken Sie sich das!) ist unsere Natur so verderbt, daß alles, wie sie liebt und thut, Sünde ist.
JUNGFER LUISGEN. Was muß man denn thun?
HERR SCHEINFROMM. Die Gnade muß durch ihre überwindende Krafft sich zur unumschränckten Beherrscherin unsers Willens machen, und demselben unvermerckt zum Guten lencken. Als denn (geben Sie wohl acht!) werden wir durch ein himmlisches Band geleitet, daß wir nicht widerstehen können. An statt, daß in Ermangelung dieser Gnade uns die himmlische Lust nothwendig zum Bösen antreibt.
JUNGFER LUISGEN. Gantz gut! Haben wir diese Gnade aber allezeit?

HERR SCHEINFROMM. Ach! was wollten wir doch? Die liebsten Kinder GOttes besitzen sie nicht immer.

JUNGFER LUISGEN. So sind sie alsdenn gezwungen, irrdisch gesinnt zu seyn?

HERR SCHEINFROMM. Freylich wohl!

JUNGFER LUISGEN. Nun, Herr Magister! das ist eben der Zustand, darinnen ich mich befinde.

HERR SCHEINFROMM. Wie so?

JUNGFER LUISGEN. Ich habe die Gnade noch nicht, meine Neigung zu überwinden: Ich werde noch durch die irrdische Lust fortgerissen.

HERR SCHEINFROMM. Wie wissen Sie, daß Sie die Gnade nicht haben?

JUNGFER LUISGEN. Weil sie mich nicht zwingt, darum habe ich sie nicht. Ich erwarte sie.

HERR SCHEINFROMM. Ja! man muß sich aber bestreben - - -

JUNGFER LUISGEN. Wie kan ich mich bestreben ohne Beystand der Gnade? Ich erwarte sie.

HERR SCHEINFROMM. Wie? so wollen Sie so geruhig seyn? und immerfort in einer Sache beharren, die der Mama zuwider ist?

JUNGFER LUISGEN. Ich erwarte die Gnade.

HERR SCHEINFROMM. Sie müssen den lieben GOtt drum bitten.

JUNGFER LUISGEN. Wie kan ich das thun, wann mich die Gnade nicht zum Gebeth zwinget?

HERR SCHEINFROMM. Wahrhafftig, Sie sündigen sehr, daß Sie in einer Leidenschafft beharren, welche nicht ein Werck der Göttlichen Barmhertzigkeit ist.

JUNGFER LUISGEN. Sagen Sie vielmehr, daß ich unglücklich bin. Dann wie kan ich mich versündigen, wenn ich keine Schuld habe? Ich erwarte die Gnade.

HERR SCHEINFROMM. Sie sind Ihrer Mama ungehorsam.

JUNGFER LUISGEN. Was kan ich davor? So bald ich die Gnade haben werde, will ich ihr gehorsam seyn: Doch, weil das Ihre Lehre ist, Herr Magister, so bringen Sie ihr wohl bey, damit sie mit meinem Ungehorsam ein Mitleiden habe.

HERR SCHEINFROMM. Wie? wollen Sie denn etwa, daß die Mama Sie mit Gewalt zum Gehorsam bringen soll?

JUNGFER LUISGEN. Ach! sie kan mich freylich wohl zwingen; Aber die Gnade allein ändert unser Hertz. Ich erwarte sie." (*Die Lustspiele* I, 490–2)

[12] Compare, for example, virtuous Luischen in *Pietism* who refuses to defend herself against being forced into marriage even by the most respectable means with Lottchen, the Reasonable Female Critic in *The Witling*, who essentially finds herself in the same situation but chooses to expose the treachery of her intended spouse instead of obeying her unreasonable parent. In *Pietism*, Luischen plays no part in the unmasking of her suitor's treachery.

[13] *Pietism* 18–9.

"FRAU GLAUBELEICHTIN, *(fällt in Ohmacht.)* Ach Cathrine! halt mich! Ach! - - - Ach! - - - ich sterbe! - - -

CATHRINE. Zum Hencker! wen haben Sie da genennt! Sie hätten lieber den Beelzebub und seine Engel ruffen mögen. Da bleibt mir die arme Frau unter den Händen todt.

HERR WACKERMANN. Wie denn? bey Fechtens und Wernsdorffs Nahmen fällt sie in Ohnmacht?

CATHRINE. Allerdings! Sie thut es allezeit. Diß ist schon das drittemal.

HERR WACKERMANN. Ja! das weiß ich nicht. Bestreichet sie geschwinde mit Ungarischem Wasser: Da habt Ihr welches.

CATHRINE. O! das hilfft gar nichts. Dieß ist ihre Artzeney! Schreyen Sie brav mit mir: *(Sie schreyt.)* Arnold! Petersen! Lange! Gichtel! Francke! Tauler! Gnade! Wiedergeburth! Der innere Funcke! Die geistliche Salbung! Zum Hencker! so schreyen Sie doch mit.

HERR WACKERMANN. Ich glaube, Ihr seyd rasend.

CATHRINE. Nein, nein, mein Herr Obrister; Sie werdens sehen, daß sie wieder zu sich kömmt. *(Sie schreyt.)* Die Gnade! der innere Mensch! der heilige Jacob Böhme! Sehen Sie! sehen Sie! sie erholt sich." (*Die Lustspiele* I, 474–5)

[14] On self-referentiality in other women's comedies, cf. my article "All's Well that Ends Well?"

[15] *Pietism* 18: "Ich wolte zwar in die Comödie gehen; allein ich werde nichts dabey verliehren." (*Die Lustspiele* I, 474)

[16] *Pietism* 24: "ists denn jetzo Zeit zu lachen?" (*Die Lustspiele* I, 484) In the translation, Herr Liebmann's outburst is erroneously attributed to Luischen.

[17] *The Mésalliance* 80.

"FRAU VON AHNENSTOLTZ. Ay! Ay! nennen Sie mir nur das Weib nicht! der Name fährt mir durch das Herz, wie ein Pfeil! Sie können mir meinen Polypus rege machen, und mich im Augenblick ersticken.

HERR VON WILDHOLZ. Behüte der Himmel! ich habe nicht gewußt, daß Eure Gnaden auch einen Polypus hätten. Bedencken Sie aber nur, gnädige Frau - - -

FRAU VON AHNENSTOLTZ. Bedencken? Meynen Sie denn, daß ich die Kraft habe, etwas zu bedencken? Das Denken erschöpft mir alle Lebensgeister: und seitdem ich das Malum hypochondriacum habe, so muß ich mich vor allem Denken, wie vor der Pest, hüten." (*Die Lustspiele* I, 16)

[18] *The Mésalliance* 81–2: "daß ich alle nur ersinnliche Krankheiten an mir habe, und daß ich ohne Lebensgefahr keine Bewegung des Leibes vornehmen kann." (*Die Lustspiele* I, 18)

[19] *The Mésalliance* 82: "ich sehe wohl, daß noch keine Frau in der Welt den Character eines schwachen Werkzeuges so sehr behauptet hat." (*Die Lustspiele* I, 19)

[20] The exemplariness of the "weaker sex" is, in my opinion, reinforced rather than negated by the plain-talking blustering criticism of the "reasonable" and

"robust" men, the Wackermanns and Wahrmunds. Their ridicule of the women's frailty is, of course, the surface notion communicated to the audience, but the commendation of the same condition lies embedded in the play's structure and in the men's own conception of themselves as contrast characters: only feminine frailty defines them as the "stronger sex," the sex that deserves the authority the women have usurped.

[21] *Die Lustspiele* I, 41: "die Ehre des Geschlechts"; translation by Kerth and Russell: "the honor of my family" (*The Mésalliance* 94). Semantically, "Geschlecht" could of course indicate either Philippine's gender or family; the fact that no male of the family suffers any ailments in the play seems to support the theory that Philippine refers to her sex rather than her lineage in this passage.

[22] *The Last Will* 219–20.

"HERR DOCTOR HIPPOKRAS. Unterthäniger Knecht, gnädige Frau, ich wünsche, daß Eu. Gnaden sich heute etwas leidlicher befinden mögen, als gestern.

FRAU VON TIEFENBORN. Ach! was wollte ich doch, Herr Doctor! ich habe eine recht elende Nacht gehabt. . . . Nicht wahr? mein Puls ist ganz matt und unruhig?

FRÄULEIN AMALIE. Ach ja, die Frau Muhme sehen auch heute recht elend aus!

FRAU VON TIEFENBORN. Nun, recht elend sehe ich wohl eben niemals aus . . . .

FRÄULEIN AMALIE. O! ich wollte auch nur sagen, blaß . . . kränklich . . . . *(schmäuchelnd.)* Wer in seiner Jugend so schön gewesen ist, als Eure Gnaden, der kann freilich niemals elend aussehen. *(Sie winkt seitwärts ihrer Schwester zu.)*

FRÄULEIN CAROLINE. Ohne der Frau Muhme eine Schmäucheley über ihre ehemalige Schönheit zu machen; so kann ich wohl sagen, daß sie mir gar nicht krank aussehen. Sie müssen recht gut geschlafen haben.

FRAU VON TIEFENBORN. . . . Nun was sagen Sie, Herr Doctor?

HERR DOCTOR HIPPOKRAS, *bedenklich.* Der Puls - - - der Puls ist - - - etwas bewegt.

FRAU VON TIEFENBORN, *kränklich.* Ich habe eine sehr elende Nacht gehabt!

HERR DOCTOR HIPPOKRAS. So? so haben Sie eine elende Nacht gehabt? *(Caroline schüttelt den Kopf.)*

HERR DOCTOR HIPPOKRAS. Haben Sie denn auch Beängstigungen gehabt?

FRAU VON TIEFENBORN. Ach! erschreckliche.

HERR DOCTOR HIPPOKRAS. So? So haben Eu. Gn Beängstigungen gehabt? Haben Sie denn gestern Abend etwas gespeiset?

FRAU VON TIEFENBORN. Etwas weniges, aber ohne Appetit.

FRÄULEIN CAROLINE. Nun da müssen Sie Ihrem Appetit große Gewalt anthun können. Ein ganzes Rebhuhn, ohne die Voressen zu verzehren? Und das wider den Appetit? *(Sie schüttelt den Kopf.)*

FRÄULEIN AMALIE. *winkt der Schwester.* Ich habe genau drauf Acht gegeben, daß die Frau Muhme fast alles auf dem Teller hat liegen lassen.

FRAU VON TIEFENBORN. Ach! mein Essen hieß gar nichts!" (*Die Lustspiele* I, 274–6)

[23] *The Last Will* 247: "Frau in meinem eigenen Hause." (*Die Lustspiele* I, 329)

[24] *The Last Will* 246: "Ach! was ist eine Wittwe nicht für eine geplagte Frau! In solchen Dingen, die eigentlich nur für Mannsleute gehören, muß man sich von allen Bedienten weiß machen lassen, was sie wollen. O wie ordentlich hielt mein seliger Gemahl nicht seinen Stall! Wenn er das sehen sollte! *(Sie weint.)*" (*Die Lustspiele* I, 327)

[25] *The Last Will* 247: "was gilt's! die Pferde werden den Augenblick alle gesund seyn." (*Die Lustspiele* I, 328)

[26] *The Last Will* 217: "Wenn ich an ihrer Stelle wäre, ich heirathete noch einmal, und genösse mein Vermögen recht." (*Die Lustspiele* I, 271)

[27] This section and the conclusions in the following section are indebted to my article "All's Well that Ends Well?," as well as passages in *Ein Blick* 44–8.

[28] In the words of Lord Byron: "All tragedies are finished by a death,/ All comedies are ended with a marriage . . . . The future state of both is left to faith" (quoted in Gardner, without source, 42). Byron expresses here precisely the uncertainty that the Happy Ending is charged to eliminate: we no more know what lies beyond marriage than what lies beyond death. The Happy Ending, in this sense, does not convey the message of The End, but rather a state of limbo that can be dispersed only by the viewer's "faith" in the permanence of the happiness that is presented at the comedy's conclusion (cf. Gardner 40). Schopenhauer may have felt the same uncertainty when he made his assertion that the author of comedy hurries to drop the curtain at a joyous moment so that the audience cannot see what comes after (cf. Hinck 129 and Schmidt 2). The list of post-eighteenth-century authors who objected to the "false definiteness" of the Happy Ending of comedy is virtually endless, from Eugene O'Neill, who condemned audience perception of the ending of his *Anna Christie* as "a happy ever-after which I did not intend" to Gerhart Hauptmann, who termed the ending of a play as "almost always a constraint imposed by the playwright upon himself or upon his plot. Yes, in most cases the last act represents a criminal assault upon the plot" (both quotations cited in Schmidt 9; the Hauptmann quotation in Schmidt's translation). What emerges from these comments is a near-universal sense that the ending is neither determined by the author (as creator of the piece, including its ending) nor by the play (its inner cohesiveness, narrative demands, plot developments or structural logic), but by the viewer: Happy Endings in particular are written exclusively for the audience, whereas tragedies are more likely to end in a manner consistent with the rest of the play.

[29] "Diese Materie aber ist schon so abgedroschen, daß ich nicht begreifen kann, wie man sie nicht längst überdrüssig geworden. Eben so kömmt es mir vor, wenn sich alle Stücke mit dem Heirathen endigen. Ist denn weiter nichts

in der Welt, als das Hochzeitmachen, was einen frölichen Ausgang geben kann?" ("Von Comödien oder Lustspielen" 351)

[30] *Pietism* 72. "Der Contract ist schon seit zwey Jahren fertig, wir dürffen ihn nur unterschreiben." (*Die Lustspiele* I, 572)

[31] *The Mésalliance* 92. "Ein jeder hat seine Ursachen warum er heirathet, und diese gründen sich immer auf den Eigennutz; er sey nun beschaffen wie er wolle." (*Die Lustspiele* I, 38)

[32] *The Mésalliance* 87: "daß er sich für sein Geld ein immerwährendes Unglück an den Hals kaufet." (*Die Lustspiele* I, 28)

[33] *The Mésalliance* 100: "oder sich die Braut gar zu theuer verkaufen läßt." (*Die Lustspiele* I, 54)

[34] *The Mésalliance* 99–100: "daß Sie für Ihr großes Vermögen, wofür Sie sich unter Ihres gleichen, die vortrefflichste Person in und außer Landes hätten wählen können, . . . nur die Vorwürfe . . . und die Beschimpfung . . . gekauft haben." (*Die Lustspiele* I, 52)

[35] *The Mésalliance* 103: "Wie zankt Ihr euch so? Es ist nicht anders, als wenn Ihr schon verheirathet wäret." (*Die Lustspiele* I, 60)

[36] *The Mésalliance* 105: "Ihr guten Kinder fangt zu frühe an! Nach der Hochzeit habt ihr noch Zeit genug zu Uneinigkeiten." (*Die Lustspiele* I, 62)

[37] *The Mésalliance* 137: "Ich kann davon noch nichts gewisses versprechen." (*Die Lustspiele* I, 122)

[38] *The Last Will* 229: "Ich wünsche mir in der Welt Wasser und Brod, und die edle Freyheit, daß ich einem jeden meine Meinung unverholen sagen darf." (*Die Lustspiele* I, 295)

[39] *The Last Will* 233: "Ja, ich habe ihn immer für einen Cavalier gehalten, der Verstand genug hat, die Aenderung einzusehen, die ein großes Vermögen in eines Menschen Verstand, Alter und Vorzügen machen kann." (*Die Lustspiele* I, 301)

[40] *The Last Will* 212: "Wer reich ist, der ist allein klug." (*Die Lustspiele* I, 262)

[41] Cf. Kord, *Ein Blick* 48–57 and "All's Well that Ends Well?"

[42] Plays to which this applies include Friederike Sophie Hensel's *Die Familie auf dem Lande*, 1770, later revised as *Die Entführung, oder die zärtliche Mutter* (1771); Marie Antonie Teutscher's *Fanny, oder die glückliche Wiedervereinigung* (1773); Victoria von Rupp's *Marianne, oder der Sieg der Tugend* and *Jenny, oder die Uneigennützigkeit*, both 1777, and Sophie Mariane von Reitzenstein's *Die seltene Beständigkeit* (1792), among many others. For an interpretation of these plays, cf. Kord, *Ein Blick* 48–52 and "All's Well that Ends Well?"; for an interpretation of Seyler's plays, cf. "Tugend im Rampenlicht."

Luise Gottsched as a young woman. From a miniature belonging to the Prussian Society in Königsberg. Painter unknown. Courtesy of the Staatsbibliothek zu Berlin, Preußischer Kulturbesitz.

JOHANNES GOTTSCHED.

Johann Christoph Gottsched as a young man. Painter unknown.
Courtesy of the Bibliotheca Albertina, Leipzig.

Profile of Leipzig, mid-eighteenth century. By M. Engelbrecht. Courtesy of the Bibliotheca Albertina, Leipzig.

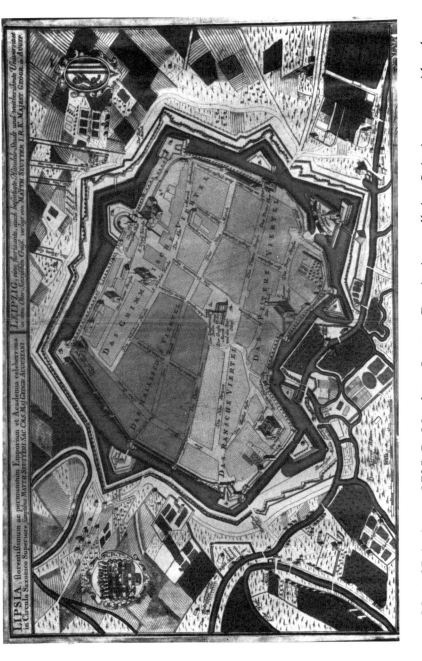

Map of Leipzig, ca. 1725. By Matthäus Seutter. Despite its small size, Leipzig was considered one of the predominant cultural centers of Germany in the mid-eighteenth century. Courtesy of the Stadtgeschichtliches Museum, Leipzig.

Der goldene Bär, Luise Gottsched's residence from the time of her marriage to her death. In: Reichel, Gottsched, I 752.

Luise Adelgunde Gottsched's status as an erudite woman was often visually reflected in her regal stance, with her hand on a book, and her portrayal in front of her library. Painting on left by E. G. Haussmann, undated, and engraving on right by J. M. Bernigeroth, 1757, after a painting by Haussmann. Courtesy of the Bibliotheca Albertina, Leipzig.

Johann Christoph Gottsched.
Engraving by J. M. Bernigeroth, 1757, after a painting by
Reiffstein, 1753. Like Luise Gottsched, Johann Christoph
Gottsched was frequently painted as a scholar, a status usually
emphasized by his portrayal in front of his library.
Courtesy of the Bibliotheca Albertina, Leipzig.

Excerpt from Luise Gottsched's letter to E. Chr. Count von Manteuffel, September 23, 1739. Women's letters of the period were judged for their natural style and the beauty and regularity of their handwriting. Courtesy of Bibliotheca Albertina, Leipzig.

la bonne grace dont il s'en sera acquité, a contribuée la moitié
à la reconvalescence de Vôtre Excellence, il sera amplement païé
de la peine qu'il s'est donné de contrefaire un sot homiletique.

Mon mari est vivement touché de la part que l'Ôtre Excellence
daigne prendre à sa fortune, et de toutes les peines qu'elle se donne
à cet egard, et Il ne manquera pas, Monseigneur, de Vous informer
au premier jour de la situation de ses affaires.

J'ai l'honneur d'assurer Vôtre Excellence que j'ai des rai-
sons bien anti-homiletiques, c'est à dire, très solides et très bien
fondées, pour être toute ma vie avec autant de zèle que de Respect

Monseigneur
de Vôtre Excellence

à Leipsic.
Le 8me du Mars. 1739.

la trésh. et trésob. Servante
L.A.V.Gottsched.

*Excerpt from Luise Gottsched's letter in French to E. Chr. Count
von Manteuffel, March 8, 1739. Luise Gottsched conducted her
own correspondence largely in French and German, and often
that of her husband as well in French, German, and Latin.
Courtesy of the Bibliotheca Albertina, Leipzig.*

Letter from Dorothea Henriette von Runckel to Johann Christoph Gottsched, January 31, 1753. Runckel's belligerent beginning is characteristic of the style of scholarly quérelles of the age and an indication that she saw her exchange with Johann Christoph Gottsched in that tradition. Courtesy of the Bibliotheca Albertina, Leipzig.

5: On Faith and Failure: Tragedy

LUISE GOTTSCHED'S *PANTHEA*, first published in the fifth volume of her husband's *Deutsche Schaubühne* in 1744 and revised in 1754,[1] marks the only time that she tried her hand at tragedy, thus claiming a place in the realm of serious "authorship." Not coincidentally, *Panthea* drew far harsher criticism, from both contemporary and posthumous critics, than any of her other works. Heitner regarded it as "Perhaps the weakest of the originals in the Schaubühne" (64); Kerth and Russell criticize the play as "incredibly cluttered" and marred by "relentless and essentially unvarying and uninspired Alexandrine couplets" (xxv); Bryan/Richel slam the play for its "faulty conception, wooden characters and excessive moralizing" (200), echoing word for word Richel's earlier criticism in *Luise Gottsched*, in which these points are supported with exaggeratedly lengthy quotations presumably intended to compound humiliating evidence of the author's incompetence (51). Almost universally, *Panthea*-criticism employs a derisive tone that is highly unusual in literary criticism of other works, including criticism of either Luise Gottsched's comedies or of any other author's tragedies published in *Die Deutsche Schaubühne*. The conclusions invariably drawn from these scornful analyses echo precisely the points made earlier about the connection between gender and genre. Luise Gottsched, so her reception has it, "failed" at tragedy (Hanstein I, 147), failed miserably, in fact: while her comedies may not amount to "art," either, "Frau Gottsched's one tragedy is little more than painful evidence that her talent lay with the comic genre" (Richel, *Luise Gottsched* 52) — a pronouncement that recurs verbatim in virtually all critiques of the play published to date.[2] "Frau Gottsched," one critic announces gleefully, "never again entered the realm of tragedy. Where truly high art was concerned, the means at her disposal for the everyday forms of naturalistic caricature failed" (Hanstein I, 147). To readers inclined to take this universal judgment on Gottsched's inability to produce a tragedy as unrelated to her gender, Heitner's commentary makes explicit what is implied in other accounts: "Madame Gottsched was the first authoress to publish a tragedy in German, but it can hardly be said that this work goes very far to prove that women have equal aptitude for the genre with men."[3]

Whereas posthumous criticism of the play is nearly universally vituperative, contemporary criticism tended to be partisan. The play was
indeed perceived as prototypical, as making an explicit statement about
modern tragedy in general as well as an implicit one about women's
potential authorship of such texts. What is highly remarkable is that the
initial reception of the play, while employing a vocabulary no less direct
than the above comments, also exercised an unusual degree of caution
by attributing commentary, both praise and invective, to anonymous third
parties. This is the method employed by both Bodmer, perhaps the first
reviewer to condemn the play in the cause of his long-standing exchange of polemics with Johann Christoph Gottsched, and Dorothea
Henriette von Runckel, whom Luise Gottsched asked for an assessment
of the revised version in February 1762, only a few months before the
author's death. Runckel's assessment of the play is attributed to an unnamed third correspondent, who praises *Panthea* as "a beautiful work"
with "strong, many strong parts" and found it particularly commendable for its clear attempt at the moral education of the aristocracy (*Briefe*
III, 158). Bodmer, too, put his critique into the mouth of an anonymous viewer who saw the play performed in Leipzig and undertakes to
debate it publicly as the audience is leaving the theater; in another letter, Bodmer admitted authorship of the review.[4] Bodmer, who of
course had an axe to grind with the author's husband, set the tone for
much later *Panthea*-criticism in dismissing the play as "a miserable
tragedy," and one, moreover, that propagated "a harmful moral." His
fictitious spectator claims to "have left the theater as poor in sentiment
as I entered it . . . . Cyrus, Panthea, Abradates, Gobrias, and all these
pretty names were just empty names to me, and left my heart as dry in
the fifth act as it had been in the first."[5] Bodmer also prefigured two
other important aspects of later *Panthea*-criticism. First, based on the
general perception of comedy as a lesser genre and tragedy as "truly
high art," is his insinuation that this tragedy is far too incompetently executed to be considered a worthy example of the genre. This is clearly
implied in his title, which refers to *Panthea* as "a so-called tragedy."
Second, he identifies the author with the title figure, a trope that first
appears in Bodmer's critique and has persisted in criticism to this day.
Bodmer's theory that "the Panthea of the tragedy possesses far more of
the character, lifestyle and opinions of his [Johann Christoph Gottsched's] wife than those of the queen of Susiana" (4) is reiterated more
than two centuries later in Heitner's clumsy allusion to Johann Christoph's infidelities: "Possibly for very good reasons of her own she decided to present the virtue of marital fidelity. Certainly, in her devotion

and obedience to her taskmaster spouse, she was herself a latter-day Panthea" (65). The conflation of author and title character serves, once again, to discredit the entire ("so-called") tragedy by locating its initial conception in the personal and the biographical, in the "everyday," to use Hanstein's expression — presumably an unlikely inspiration for "truly high art."

This ranking of genres, with comedy representing the "everyday" and mediocre and tragedy representing "high art," was already an issue in Johann Christoph Gottsched's *Critische Dichtkunst*, where he describes the switch from pre-Aeschylosian comedy to Sophoclean tragedy as follows: "From the most tasteless songs sung by drunk peasants sprung the most serious and moving piece in all of poesy .... The satirical jokes of earlier times metamorphosed into a quite splendid and edifying matter, in such a way that the most respected people no longer had reason to be ashamed to appear as viewers of such plays."[6] Tragedy gained in renown to such a degree that it was even considered "a kind of worship, which indeed was much more edifying for the people than all sacrifices and other heathen ceremonies."[7] Johann Christoph Gottsched's attempts to align comedy with the primitive and savage (drunk peasants, heathens and religious sacrifice) and tragedy with the educational, moral and intellectual (a genre befitting the "most respected" spectators) not only reflects the dichotomy between genres that is later universally echoed in criticism, it also makes important, and highly judgmental, assumptions about the *viewer* of each genre: elsewhere, he defines the early comedy crowd as viewers who, "in their backward coarseness, were unable to take pleasure in anything serious, but were instead merely bent on laughing all the time."[8] In an age concerned with dramatic reform, such commendation of one genre (and its viewers) and vilification of another (and its viewers), avowed by the age's principal reformer, could not have been entirely devoid of effect. Given the perception of women's authorship as secondary or diminished, the obvious message to women would have been one of discouragement from trying their hand at tragedies. And indeed, few ever have: women's tragedies are a comparatively rare occurrence in both the eighteenth and nineteenth centuries. I have been able to confirm the existence of only 86 tragedies published by women between 1700 and 1900 (compare this with the ca. 1000 comedies published by women authors during the same two centuries; cf. *Ein Blick* 93). By far the majority of these women's tragedies were written after 1770, long after Johann Christoph Gottsched's influence on the theater had been superseded by Lessing's theories and those of the Storm and Stress movement.[9]

Criticisms of *Panthea* as excessively moralizing and marred by stilted Alexandrine verse could be accused of a certain ahistoricity: a foundational moral and a strict verse form are common to all tragedies published in *The German Stage* and Johann Christoph Gottsched's *Critical Poetics* expressly calls for both as indispensable qualities of good "regular" tragedy. Aside from these points and from his advocacy of both elevated language and a strict dramatic form (five acts and observance of the Aristotelian three unities), Johann Christoph Gottsched's two most important points with regard to tragedy concern the creation of "mixed" characters and the establishment of poetic justice in the drama. Poetic justice in *Critical Poetics* is indispensable if any moral is to be successfully conveyed to the audience. In tragedy, it expresses itself not so much by rewarding the play's virtuous heroes, but predominantly in the punishment of the play's villainous characters and flawed protagonists. Indeed, one of the principal educational goals of tragedy is to instill admiration in the viewer for "divine vengeance which allows no vice to go unpunished."[10] The issue of mixed characters, already raised in Aristotle's *Poetics*, is related to this goal, since they are indispensable both for the audience's ability to identify with the characters and for the successful portrayal of the triumph of divine justice:

> The heroes of a tragedy must neither be too evil, nor too good: not too evil because one would otherwise not feel compassion for their misfortune but rejoice at it; but also not too good, because one could otherwise easily accuse Providence of having committed an injustice for punishing innocent people so harshly.[11]

It is on these two crucial points that Luise Gottsched's *Panthea* deviates from her husband's poetology: the characters of her tragedy can be neatly divided into "too evil" and "too good," with precisely the consequences for the establishment of poetic justice that her husband had envisioned. Since most scholarly critiques of the play adopt her husband's parameters, they have been unable to interpret these significant deviations as anything other than incompetence on the part of the author (cf., among many others, Bryan/Richel 199–200). But considering the author's subject position it seems more productive to attempt a reading that would interpret these deviations as *design*: it is inconceivable that any marginalized, secondary author, a "woman author" attempting for the first time to produce a work in a genre defined as "high art," could do so without implicitly or explicitly engaging the parameters that establish the genre as such. In the following, I would like to trace Gottsched's two most significant deviations from her husband's poetics — her characterization of hero(in)es and her establishment of the play's system of faith — in an attempt to determine what these moves might imply with regard to genre and gender. How does she define the central concepts of tragedy, such as "faith" and "justice"? To what extent are these definitions congruent with her husband's? To what extent can *Panthea* be read as an implicit commentary on the establishment of tragedy as "high art" within the parameters instituted by her husband? And is this commentary in any way reflective of her own daring undertaking as a first-time (not to mention *first*) female tragedian?

Temptations: The Implied Alternative

Gottsched's neat division of her characters into highly virtuous hero(in)es and despicable villains does indeed seem trite and undifferentiating, until it is contrasted both with her husband's call for characters that are neither "too good" nor "too evil" and with his move, elsewhere in *Critical Poetics*, to assign multidimensional characters to tragedy and one-dimensional types (like Molière's miser) to comedy ("Von Comödien" 351 and 354). It is her husband's relation of characterization to both *genre* and to an acceptable tragic *teleology* that makes Gottsched's unconventional characterization highly remarkable.[12] Her characterizations depend on a contrast so stark as to be obviously clichéd: her virtuous characters are reasonable, forgiving, brave, aware of temptation and trusting (in Divine Providence as well as the integrity of others), while her villains are cowardly, scheming, and uncontrollably passionate.[13] Cyrus and Panthea are centered as epitomizing masculine and feminine virtues respectively, with the other virtuous protagonists either at the margins (Abradates) or tableaued around these two central characters, ostensibly to learn from their example (Gobrias, Nikothris). By far the largest amount of text is given over to the praise of either Cyrus' or Panthea's virtues, which is, interestingly enough, sung by both virtuous protagonists and villains. Cyrus proves both his diplomatic skills and his virtue by returning Panthea to her husband Abradates, whom he has vanquished in battle. Panthea's return functions simultaneously as a political move to turn a conquered enemy into a new ally and as a means of maintaining his sexual virtue by evading temptation: having heard of Panthea's virtue and beauty, Cyrus chooses not to see her until the scene in which he returns her to her husband. This scene establishes two important points about his character: first, that Cyrus is not above temptation; second, that he is torn between the morality superimposed on the drama by the historical setting (in which the conqueror would have no qualms whatever about helping himself to female captives in the sexual sense) and the bourgeois eighteenth-century morality informing the play (wherein Cyrus is described as faithful husband to a woman who never enters the stage and marital fidelity is defined as sexual monogamy). His role in this scene as royal patron of matrimony is inverted in Panthea's criticism of other rulers for their sexual appetites, words that clearly prefigure the play's intended moral: "How few crowned heads are there on earth, who, like you/ Become matrimony's patrons instead of disturbers of marriages!" exclaims Panthea.[14]

This subtext of temptation accounts for one of the drama's more peculiar aspects: that no allowance is made for the characters' *positionality* when they generalize about virtue or vice on stage. The play seems to make no distinction between other characters extolling Cyrus' or Panthea's virtues and these characters *themselves* doing so, a breach of dramatic probability that can be explained only by the characters' awareness of the constant presence of temptation. Cyrus' references to "my honest heart" ("mein redlich Herz," 14), Panthea's mention of "my loyal breast" ("meiner treuen Brust," 16), Abradates' self-definition as "the best husband" ("den besten Mann," 46) are less indicative of the author's characterization of these figures than of her awareness of the play's inherent contradictions. Cyrus' frequent enumerations of his own virtue, for example, could be read as a constant grappling with the contrasts evoked by his position as conqueror and aristocrat in a world ruled by an antiquated ethics and the essentially enlightened bourgeois morality that he is charged to represent. Indeed, his rhetorical question "Is it only vice that makes us princes?"[15] would suggest just such an awareness of the apparent incompatibility of his rank with a virtuous lifestyle, one that he is committed to disprove. A similar preemptive function is perhaps served by the extensive self-acclamation with which he answers Hystaspes' suggestion of leading Abradates to his death in battle to gain possession of Panthea (7–10). Conversely, a similar situation seems to exist for Panthea: her many defensive assurances to her husband that she has remained faithful to him serve to extol her virtue, but also to indicate the presence of temptation.

> O, dearest husband! O that my mouth
> Could dispel all of your doubts, that I
> Am in constant care of our union! You have nothing to fear.
> All of the beautiful heroes that Cyrus' realm discloses
> from evening to morning, they all cannot move me:
> Even were it Cyrus himself; my duty,
> And you, my Abradates, would be inexpressibly dearer to me.

My life is fidelity, I cannot injure it.
O, do not, in the future, give room to doubt,
Because my breast has one heart, and it is yours alone.[16]

Panthea's remarks, while undoubtedly accurate on the surface (she does remain faithful to her husband to the end), hold an obvious subtext that bespeaks the existence of temptation, that defines this temptation as sexual ("from evening to morning"), and that views the presence of Cyrus as *the height* of temptation. Given that the viewer hardly needs to be convinced of Panthea's unimpeachable virtue, there can be no reason for the length of this passage (an entire scene is devoted to setting Abradates' mind at ease with regard to Panthea's fidelity) other than to emphasize the fact that like Cyrus' virtue, Panthea's virtue is not above temptation and in fact *depends*, to a very great extent, on verbal reiterations and reaffirmations.

The other instance in which the positionality of characters is disregarded in the play is the essential honesty of the villainous as well as the virtuous characters, honesty that diminishes only in scenes in which the villains move their devious schemes forward. Otherwise, the virtuous characters in the play essentially have no added credibility over the villainous seducers; all appear to sing the praise of virtue with the same gusto and credibility. It is Hystaspes, one of the characters responsible for the evil intrigue against the lovers, who initially establishes the motif of Cyrus as favored by the Gods (*Panthea* 6) and justifies Cyrus' invasion of Persia as a war of liberation: the Persians, he argues, would much prefer to live under such a virtuous king than continue to endure the vices of their current rulers (5). The following remarks certainly seem incongruous coming from the play's arch-villains and ardent opponents of the virtuous protagonists:

> ARASPES . . . . I do not doubt that the battle must be decided in our favor.
> The enemy, it is true, is strong, but many circumstances
> indicate
> That Cyrus is blessed by a Higher Power.

> HYSTASPES. And he indeed deserves it. A prince, who, even in his youth
> Was akin to wise men, is a son of virtue;
> And virtue is always protected by Heaven's high succor.[17]

Unlike other scenes, in which both Araspes and Hystaspes sing Cyrus' praise to his face, this scene, in which they are alone and plotting the downfall of Abradates, cannot be explained by the characters' desire to ingratiate themselves with Cyrus, although this is of course a motive attributed to them in other instances. Rather, this scene must be read as a parallel to the virtuous characters' extolling of their own moral qualities, since, like Cyrus' or Panthea's endless self-acclamations, it indicates an awareness of the other side. As Cyrus and Panthea recognize temptation and the role it plays in their lives, so Hystaspes and Araspes are conscious of the existence of virtue and occasionally speak of it with considerable longing. In their self-characterizations, both sides seem to imply the alternative, a reverse image of themselves. Just as Cyrus' valiant resistance to temptation must involve at least the ability to imagine himself *giving in* to it, so the villainous characters, in scenes like the one cited above, seem to allude to the possibility of returning to the path of virtue, thus placing themselves under Heaven's protection.

Of course, it could be argued that what I have referred to as the "implied alternative" amounts to a characterization of Gottsched's figures in the sense advocated by her husband: as neither "too good" nor "too evil." The problem with this is that these temptations, while constantly acknowledged, are not acted upon in a single instance; on the contrary, they merely serve to emphasize the characters' heroic ability to resist temptation. Johann Christoph Gottsched's mandate in *Critical Poetics* is clearly that the "mixed character" must *deserve* the misfortune he experiences "because one could otherwise easily accuse Providence of having committed an injustice." The play can only impart the desired moral to the viewer if it affirms the audience's faith in Providence and if the audience is able to identify with the tragic character. Using King Oedipus as an example, Johann Christoph Gottsched elaborates:

> Whoever claims that Oedipus is completely innocent or completely guilty would be wrong on both counts. He is as humans generally tend to be, that is, of the middling kind; he possesses certain virtues, but also certain vices: and it is only these latter that are the cause of his misfortune. For if he had only refrained from killing anyone, all the rest would not have happened. And it would indeed have been fitting for him to abstain from killing after the oracle had given him such a clear prophesy. For he should, by rights, have thought at all times: What if this was my father?[18]

Such a characterization would not hold for the virtuous hero(in)es in *Panthea*, who invariably resist the temptations to which they are exposed (in exactly the manner described by Johann Christoph Gottsched), who do indeed "refrain" from all acts that could call their indomitable virtue into question, and who cannot, by the wildest stretch of the imagination, be grouped with "humans generally." Nei-

ther they nor the villains can feasibly be considered "middling" characters; clearly, the downfall of the virtuous characters is not brought
about by any inherent flaws in their character. Gottsched's characterization of her virtuous hero(in)es as "too good" and her villains as "too
evil" has drawn intense criticism from contemporary and posthumous
critics alike, and it is clear why. It deprives the viewer of both the ability
to identify and the ability to admire the workings of Providence in the
characters' misfortunes, it fundamentally negates the *purpose* of tragedy,
and it represents such a radical departure from the model that the
viewer is led to expect that the play, read within Johann Christoph
Gottsched's framework, becomes virtually incomprehensible.

Ye Gods: Poetic Injustice

The direct relationship between human virtue and divine reward is established at the outset of the play as the philosophical basis of the tragedy and
evoked nearly constantly throughout it. Cyrus, the only character in
Panthea to harbor even the slightest doubt with regard to the battle's outcome, nonetheless postulates that victory depends entirely on his virtue
and that of his soldiers (41). As royal patron and protector of Panthea, he
advises her accordingly: "Continue, as you do, to adhere to purest Virtue;/ The highest favor of the gods will be your sure reward."[19] Panthea,
in turn, passes these convictions on to her protégée Nikothris: "Princess,
continue/ To cling to Virtue; it will reward you here as in Heaven."[20]
Panthea's faith in the gods and their protection of Virtue is so strong that
she unhesitatingly trusts the gods with her husband's life: "Because
Heaven's arm never abandons Virtue;/ It will most surely, in all circum-
stances,/ Watch over Abradates' well-being and ensure his victory./ All
my life I will trust in the gods' high protection."[21]

Ominously enough, the benevolence of Divine Providence is usually
evoked in the play immediately before human faith in it is disappointed.
To cite just one example: in the scene directly preceding the battle in
which he dies, Abradates orders Panthea not to doubt its successful
outcome, because "He who does not wish to perish must put his trust
in Heaven."[22] Just as judgments of Virtue and Vice sound practically
interchangeable whether from the mouths of virtuous characters or
heinous villains, both protagonists and antagonists are characterized by
an equally unshakeable confidence in Divine Providence. Similarly to
Abradates in the scene just cited, Araspes and Hystaspes voice their
certainty that virtuous Cyrus will surely emerge victoriously if Heaven

has anything to do with it (15). But this confidence is shaken in
Panthea's eloquent evocation of the gods while waiting for news of the
battle ("O Heaven! can you inflict such torture on me?"; / "Ye Gods!
do you delight in causing me such fear?")[23] and completely dissolves
into an otherwise speechless chant of "Ye Gods!" at the end of the scene,
when she is informed of the outcome of the battle and her husband's
death ("Ihr Götter!," 58–60). Her final outcry — "Wrathful Gods!
Oh!" ("Erzürnte Götter! Ach!," 62) — before she rushes off to commit suicide culminates less in a negation of her earlier faith, but —
worse — in a dismissal of the entire system of faith: "O Heaven! does
your wrath mete out reward and punishment so unfairly? . . ./ But why
should I, in my grief, accuse divine dispensation/ When I, with stead-
fastness, can help myself?"[24] In essence, what this final statement from
the play's virtuous heroine amounts to is a rejection of the will of the
Gods, and that rejection is carried beyond the limits of mere disobedi-
ence. It is a refusal even to *consider* the will of the Gods, a refutation of
any attempt to find meaning in it, and this very attempt to interpret
Divine Providence by matching it against human moral expectations
constructs the play's entire moral frame.

After Abradates' incomprehensible death in battle and Panthea's
suicide, the only paragon of virtue left in the play to rescue the moral
frame is Cyrus. But Cyrus finds himself plunged into fundamental
doubts by these events. Like Panthea, he is unable to interpret the will of
the Gods; unlike her, he does not withdraw his compliance from a faith
system he no longer understands. "[I]s it possible?," he wonders. "Oh!
does Heaven's/ Shielding Arm thus fail? and it does not protect them
[Panthea and Abradates, S. K.]?/ You, who never proclaim the reasons
for your actions,/ Ye Gods! do not be angry if my doubts are sinful./
This case is too difficult for me! - - - No, I do not understand."[25] Nor
does the audience: the Gods to whom Cyrus here still pledges his alle-
giance, albeit with a great deal more bewilderment than faith, have not
only failed in the protection of Virtue, but also allowed Vice to go unpunished. The fact that only one of the villains responsible for the tragedy is punished — Araspes, who dies in precisely the same manner as
Panthea — and the fact that Hystaspes escapes undiscovered, unpunished, and even retains his position as Cyrus' protegé and right-hand
man completely contradict the constantly reiterated human faith that
Heaven metes out reward and punishment justly (62). In the words of
one of Cyrus' allies: "The God we acknowledge/ . . . would have to
admit his own guilt/ If his arm further spares such a barbarous villain/
And does not punish his wickedness with destruction and distress."[26]

It is this failure to punish wickedness, even more so than the complete destruction of the virtuous heroine, that amounts to an absolute negation of faith in providence. Whereas one might still explain Virtue Unrewarded as divine wrath and incomprehensible to humans, as Cyrus attempts to do, Vice Unpunished is a heavenly crime, evidence of God's guilt and, perhaps not coincidentally, an unheard-of occurrence in tragedies authored by male writers. Conversely, Gottsched's tragedy ends with Cyrus' renewed expression of disbelief towards the Gods ("How to reconcile your kindness with so much dreadful anguish?"[27]) and with his relatively hapless attempts to atone to the dead bodies for Divine Ineptitude towards the living. The Gods being unavailable for comment, Cyrus takes over their part and metes out "justice" — reward and punishment — on the corpses of Panthea, Abradates and Araspes.

> Let us immediately erect a grave of honor
> In which Panthea and Abradates shall be laid to rest:
> So that this couple can enjoy their rest in the same grave.
> *(Pointing at Araspes):*
> But you, murderer, feel even after your spirit has fled
> That all vice and guilt are subject to royal punishment;
> And that the strict justice of Cyrus' royal house
> Will punish your life's wickedness even on your corpse.[28]

It is inconceivable that Gottsched could have written these final lines of the play with the intention of restoring the viewer's faith in Providence: the meaninglessness of this ersatz equity following upon the play's staggering injustices does little more than to reiterate both divine incompetence or disregard for the dramatic world order and human impotence to repair what the Gods have botched up.

The Teleology of Suicide

What, then, is the meaning of suicide within a philosophical framework like the one described here? Interpretations of death in tragedies are usually founded on three premises: that the tragic hero's demise is always brought about by his own fallacies, that the death is *not* to be equated with the inadequacy of virtue, and that his death, for that reason, cannot be valorized by a positive depiction on stage — for instance, to use Steinmetz's example, as a stoic suicide (*Das deutsche Drama* 44–5). Accordingly, scholars have unanimously and strenuously objected to the ending of Gottsched's tragedy, in particular to the fact that Panthea's suicide is not relativized by the other characters. "The

authoress evidently sees no fault in her heroine, makes no effort to set
Providence in a better light, and lets suicide stand as a virtuous act"
(Heitner 69). What is being criticized here, of course, is the implicit
statement about Divine Providence, which, even in the minds of twentieth-century critics, must be upheld as absolute by any means necessary. Hollmer interprets Panthea's suicide as a "failure" on the part of
the heroine to keep her feelings under control (199). Kerth and Russell, the most recent critics to engage Gottsched's writing, conclude
with some bewilderment that "this work is not really a tragedy in the
classical sense, where a tragic moral flaw or error in judgment causes a
character's downfall: Panthea's 'flaw' is that she loves her husband"
(xxv). Richel (*Luise Gottsched*) views Panthea's suicide as the denial of
enlightened Reason and optimism and as an abandonment of faith in
Providence (51) and points out, as Heitner had already done, that
Panthea's "suicide is viewed with approbation, thus negating the moral
purpose of tragedy" (50). This reiteration of Bodmer's criticism that
Panthea propagated a harmful moral is taken up once more in
Bryan/Richel's accusation that "Gottsched fails to make that behavior
[suicide, S. K.] reprehensible, consequently negating the moral purpose
of tragedy" (200). What is intriguing here is the honest sense of baffle-
ment permeating all of these assessments. All point out that Gottsched
denies the most essential facet of the genre (the "moral purpose of
tragedy," "poetic justice," "Providence"); all seem helpless to interpret
this as an act of anything but authorial incompetence. The alternative
would be to accuse the author of transgressing a dramatic world order
that seems almost as unshakable to twentieth-century critics as it did to
the author's husband. But there are good reasons for assuming a purpose
behind Gottsched's conclusion, "moral" or otherwise, the most glaring
being the character of Hystaspes. In Xenophon's *Cyropaedia*, on which
the plot of *Panthea* is based, Hystaspes is portrayed as "a brave and
virtuous man" (Richel, *Luise Gottsched* 50). In Gottsched's play, he becomes the play's driving evil force and escapes unpunished, to the
complete mystification of future critics. Hystaspes' escape, or rather the
reversal of his character, thus originated with Gottsched's version of the
story; it cannot be explained by the author's faithfulness to the source,
but must be read in the context of the drama's system of poetic justice.
The universal sense of puzzlement on the part of scholars who have written about the play is understandable because their criticism of the denial of poetic justice, evidenced in the positive portrayal of Panthea's
suicide and in Hystaspes' inexplicable escape, is based on the premise
that an intact and benevolent world order be portrayed and vindicated

within the play. Only by abandoning that premise, only by considering the possibility of a conscious subversion of the dramatic world order can the play's deaths (and survivals) be interpreted in a way that is supported by the teleology of the drama.

I would like to attempt such an interpretation by looking at three deaths — those of Abradates, Panthea and Araspes — and at Hystaspes' failure to die, since these are the instances in which the play's teleology is most obviously played out. The first commonality seems to be that the virtuous characters die off-stage, whereas the villains meet their end — death or survival — onstage, eye-to-eye with the audience. In the case of the virtuous characters, the audience is spared the actual death scenes but subjected to lengthy and tortuous presentiments that seem to serve the single purpose of calling the workings of Divine Providence into question. Abradates' last scene onstage, in which he takes his leave of Panthea, has been sensibly interpreted as a scene that establishes a change in Panthea's character (Hollmer 204). Less transparently, Panthea is blamed indirectly for her husband's death: "In the conflict between morality and sensuality, Panthea finally succumbs to emotion and thus contributes to her husband's death" (Hollmer 199). But Panthea's emotionality in this scene, for which she is frequently berated in scholarship, is fully explained by the fact that she is plagued by a vision of her husband's death. This instance of clairvoyance comes on the heels of her bravely supportive speech with which she intends to send her husband off to battle and to which he responds with all signs of approbation: "Your support makes me strong. Ye Gods! lend your aid/ To my endeavors to be worthy of such kindness, such a wife."[29] Until that point, Panthea behaves exactly as is expected of her — as the loving, supportive wife who has yet to exhibit even the slightest doubt in the benevolence of the Gods. Her directly subsequent vision is expressed in despairing statements that are nothing short of foreshadowing: she announces to her husband that she will lose her life to her grief for him (47), and after he has left the stage, marching bravely and trustingly off into battle, she states clearly where she sees him going: "He's going? O dire distress!/ And going to his demise; he's going to his death!/ Yes, yes! I can already see the enemy's murderous swords/ Deprive me of all my happiness, of Abradates./ O vision of such horror! Brazen villains, desist!/ And if you need a victim, let it be me!/ I will die if he dies."[30] Clearly, the contrast being played out here is that between Abradates' laudable faith in Providence — which, however, turns out to be ultimately unfounded — and Panthea's melancholy visions, which accurately predict the course of the play: Abradates' death (due to "murderous swords") as well as her own ("I will die if he dies"). It is in this scene, before any of the subsequent catastrophes have taken place, that the faith in Divine Providence so universally expressed by the play's virtuous characters is first doubted and then negated: what *should be*, what *must be*, according to the most basic principles of tragedy, according to the faith system that every tragedy is charged to vindicate and that enables the audience to interpret what they are seeing, is here invalidated by what *will be*. In every other tragedy, this is the scene in which the protagonist's faith in Providence is sorely tempted; invariably, the denial of Divine Providence turns out to be either merely a temptation to be valiantly resisted or the cause of the protagonist's eventual demise. Not here: Panthea's precise predictions leave the viewer little choice but to conclude that the outcome of the play is at this point already decided — not by anything the virtuous protagonists say or do, as Hollmer claims in a feeble attempt to rescue the concept of poetic justice, but due to the sheer non-applicability of the concept to the poetic world created here.

If the Gods are indeed still in charge of this world, they play a particularly cruel joke on Panthea. Her suicide is introduced by two consecutive scenes in which she receives messengers. The first is a false messenger in Araspes' employ who brings Panthea the news of Cyrus' complete devastation in battle and hints at the possibility of both Cyrus' and Abradates' deaths (57–8). His purpose is to force Panthea to flee under Araspes' protection. When the second messenger enters, Panthea receives him with the question: "What message do you bring? How is the battle going?/ Is Abradates still alive?"[31] A lengthy correction of the first messenger's report ensues, along with the discovery of Araspes' renewed villainy and elaborate reproaches of Araspes by Panthea (60–2). During the entire scene, the messenger studiously avoids answering Panthea's third question. Only after she has been reassured of Cyrus' victory and survival does Panthea have the opportunity to ask again after her husband, and even then the terrible news is further delayed by the messenger's hesitancy to tell her the whole truth: "O, Princess, do not ask!" ("Ach, Fürstinn, frage nicht!" 62) Aside from the repeated retardation technique employed at this most crucial juncture in the play, what seems particularly well designed to evoke doubts in the benevolence of Divine Providence is the paradox played out in the appearance of the messengers: the first messenger, whose whole purpose it is to scare Panthea into flight, actually evokes hopes that Abradates might have escaped, while the second messenger, ostensibly the bearer of good news, confirms his death in battle. To the audience, the news of Abradates' death must come as completely unexpected. The first messenger, who is charged with painting the blackest scenario possible, lies about the outcome of the battle and Cyrus' fate, but inexplicably does not invent a similar fate for Abradates; the second messenger is set up to be perceived by the audience — as well as Panthea — as the bearer of happier tidings, only to deliver to her, at the very end of the scene, the devastating blow. If Divine Providence is indeed at work here, it is in the form of a cruel bait-and-switch. It is at this point that Panthea abandons all of her earlier attempts to interpret, or even to contemplate, Divine will and leaves the stage, determined to "help myself" (63). Such a determination does not cohere in a universe guided by a benevolent deity, but it does make sense if seen as a response to what Panthea — and the audience — must perceive as an unpredictable and utterly capricious divine order.

The aspect of the play which has evoked the most criticism from later scholars is the fact that Panthea's suicide, which *cannot* make sense in a world under the guidance of Divine Providence, is treated by all surviving virtuous characters — who are, ostensibly, the ones to provide the audience with a discernible moral result of this tragedy — as if it *did* make sense to them. Nowhere is it explicitly stated that Panthea's choice should be regarded as a morally acceptable response because Heaven abandoned its virtuous heroes. But two facets of the ending would seem to support such a daring conclusion: first, the play's earlier evocations of Divine Justice are abandoned completely at this point, and second, the play makes allusions that this faith system is replaced by a theology of Love, with the lovers Panthea and Abradates elevated to divine status not only by their love, but by the very aspect of their lives that has wreaked such havoc on the play's faith system and caused critics such consternation: their untimely deaths by treason and suicide. *Panthea*'s conclusion can be read not merely as a negation, but as a complete reversal of the dramatic world order. Critics who have asserted that Gottsched fails to make Panthea's suicide reprehensible are guilty of a vast understatement: Panthea's suicide is not only condoned, it is *celebrated*. Nikothris serves as the messenger in this instance; brandishing the bloody dagger with which Panthea has killed herself, she introduces her tale as follows: "My King!/ See, what Love has now done for its own rescue,/ What Panthea has dared do for her Abradates!"[32] She answers the men's shocked outcries of "Ye Gods!" (69) with a depiction not of brutality but of peace and serenity, as if Panthea had died in her sleep: "O! her spirit has slipped away!/ It has found the most beautiful path back to her Abradates."[33] Nothing in her further elaboration — her repeated evocation of Panthea's deed as a "virtuous death" ("tugendvollen Tod," 69), her admiration of Panthea's "more than manly courage" ("mehr als Männermuth," 69), her exact rendition of Panthea's moving final remarks, her report of Panthea's own interpretation of her suicide as an act of love and loyalty — contradicts this peaceful scene. Unthinkably, Panthea is not, as tragic teleology would otherwise seem to demand, pitied and forgiven *despite* her suicide, but rather, and ostentatiously, reaffirmed as the play's epitome of virtue *because* of her suicide: Nikothris ends her tearful tale with the summary judgment, "O, that I knew of a similar paragon of virtue!" ("O wär zur Tugend mir ein ähnlich Bild bewußt!," 70)

Even more unlikely, in light of the viewer's expectations, is the play's final scene, which features Araspes' death and Hystaspes' escape. Unlike Panthea, Araspes, who kills himself in precisely the same manner she did and with the same dagger, dies on stage. In other words, he confronts the audience directly with both the act and his own rationale for it; like Panthea, he defines his death as an act of loyalty and love. His final words, which include a confession of the murder of Abradates, could otherwise easily be transferred to any of the play's virtuous characters:

> Yes, my liege, only now have I found Love,
> Who rules over us with a force never vanquished.
> It was Love who led me to Abradates' murder
> In order to be happy with Panthea after him.
> Now that all my hopes are dashed at her grave,
> *he tears the dagger out of Cyrus' hand and stabs himself.*
> May my spirit, like that of others, flee my body.
> May an early grave enshroud my unhappy loyalty;
> So that I will not be a disgrace to thy court;
> And if my failing surpasses my youthful loyalty,
> Take your revenge for Panthea and her expired virtue.[34]

Araspes' final statement is unusual in several ways. On the one hand, he acknowledges Panthea's virtue and even suggests that his death could be viewed as some sort of atonement for her fate; on the other, he attributes the exact same reasoning to his suicide as Panthea did to hers. The fact that he not only imitates the manner of her death in his own and echoes her motivations, but also uses the weapon she used to kill herself, lends his interpretation of his own death as a death for love a certain amount of dramatic support: like Julia drinking from Romeo's poisoned cup, Araspes manages to follow his beloved in death.[35] The parallel between both the manner and motivations of both suicides is clear; the assessments of each death are diametrically opposed. Panthea's suicide reaffirms her as the paragon of virtue; Araspes' body is subjected to indignities after his death, in a feeble attempt to "take revenge for Panthea." In the final lines of the play, Hystaspes, co-conspirator of Araspes, reports that Araspes had admitted his evil intentions towards Abradates before the battle (which is true), but claims that he had thought to have succeeded in persuading him to drop this plan. This is a fairly transparent lie for the audience, who have watched Hystaspes agree eagerly to Araspes' plan in the final scene of Act II, admit to having harbored very similar plans on his own (37) and heard him suggest this very plan to Cyrus at the outset of the drama (7–10). Since neither Panthea nor Nikothris was aware of Hystaspes' participation in the plot to kill Abradates, there is nobody to contradict him; thus there is nothing to impair Hystaspes' continued position as Cyrus' right-hand-man and confidant.

Araspes' suicide is the only instance in the drama that could be interpreted as evidence of poetic justice, were it not for the fact that he is presented in this scene neither as the remorseful misguided scoundrel (who could be pitied and forgiven) nor as the hardened sinner (whose death could serve as an indication that justice is being served). Araspes does not repent or recant, and although he uses the words "murder," "failing" and "disgrace," no awareness that he has committed a crime seems to inform his final statement. Incredibly, he is permitted to die, emphasizing — and in words intended to be moving — merely his motivations (love and loyalty) for the crime as well as its self-inflicted punishment and leaving judgment of his deeds to others. Although Araspes has throughout the drama served the *function* of the arch-villain whose evil deeds move the plot steadily on toward catastrophe, his *character*, in this scene, seems closer to that of the traditional "middling hero" envisioned by Johann Christoph Gottsched in his treatise on tragedy. But this tragic hero, if indeed he can be considered as such, is not only responsible for his own downfall, but also for the destruction of Virtue and the faith in benevolent Providence, that faith on which tragic teleology ultimately depends, in every virtuous character in the play as well as the audience. The fact that Hystaspes ends the play in Cyrus' good graces, with the audience watching helplessly, merely reaffirms the fact that what it has witnessed is not an affirmation of a benevolent world order, but the dismantling of order per se. Virtue is not triumphant, and Vice is either left unpunished or accorded the dignity of the tragic in death-scenes which are every bit as moving and sentimental as that of the virtuous heroine who has fallen victim to that same villain's machinations. Viewer identification, if possible at all, is confused; viewer edification is compromised; indeed, one could argue forcefully that the play purposely withholds the "moral" from the audience, depriving the spectator of what he or she came to the theater to experience: *catharsis*, that tearful edification from which all moral improvement flows.

A So-Called Tragedy

It is undoubtedly this experience that Bodmer's fictitious viewer gave voice to when he claimed to "have left the theater as poor in sentiment as I entered it," with his "heart as dry in the fifth act as it had been in the first." It is also more than likely this experience that caused future critics such consternation. Their critique that Gottsched's tragedy fails to uphold Providence, that it negates the "moral purpose" of tragedy, is entirely justified in its assessment, if utterly mistaken in its rationalization. Their helplessness in interpreting the phenomena exhibited in Gottsched's play are an indication of the apparent inability even of twentieth-century critics to read Gottsched's literature outside of the parameters established by the cultural context now called "Enlightenment" in general and by her husband in particular. But there are at least three other (related) ways of reading this "first" tragedy in German ever to be authored by a woman: by adopting a different focus in reading the biographical, the aesthetic, and the generic. The biographical must be considered because Gottsched's was a harnessed creativity: as an author who wrote mostly dramatic (and other) works commissioned by her husband, as a *woman* author whose creativity was expected to extend no further than the trite and the trivial, her one foray into tragedy constituted a major exception in her entire oeuvre. Perhaps the author saw what critics today read as merely a failure to adhere to established norms as an opportunity for experimentation with those norms, which were, after all, still fairly recent and not, as today's critics might read them, produced in the nebulous regions of the dawn of a "great" literary past. Perhaps her creativity, for the very reason that it was harnessed, was more likely to turn to experimentation than to attempt to reproduce the work of male tragedians; perhaps her status as a lowly "woman" author, the knowledge that whatever she produced would invariably be viewed as inferior, freed her from the necessity of having to adhere to tragedic conventions at all.[36] The aesthetic must be considered because there are good reasons to suspect that reading the play as it always has been read, in the context of Enlightenment morality, ignores crucial aspects of the play. Perhaps *Panthea*'s purpose is *not* to enlighten the viewer; perhaps it is, rather, an exploration of an antique world and faith system — complete with unenlightened, amoral, cruelly capricious Gods by whom the play's protagonists and antagonists are alternately tempted, plagued and disregarded. Perhaps Panthea's virtue-by-suicide lies in the very fact that she emancipates herself from their domination. Finally, the generic must be considered because ultimately, *Panthea* is not a tragedy in the traditional sense in that the play points at the most basic tenets and assumptions of the genre as well as to the author's own daring enterprise. In its denial of tragedy's most basic principles, in its experimentation with alternatives, it is less a tragedy than an aesthetic commentary on Tragedy. *Panthea* is a play that raises questions not only about Enlightened morality and not only about the bases on which the tragic ultimately rests — an inviolate faith in poetic justice not being the least of them — but also, no less perceptibly, about the universal applicability of the worldview presented in and by tragedy. Ultimately, Bodmer was right when he referred to *Panthea* as a "so-called tragedy," and he was also right when he rooted this critique, subtly, to be sure, in the dubious legitimacy of female authorship within the genre. What he and future critics missed entirely is the author's awareness of this most principal of all authorial dilemmas and her remarkable ability, demonstrated aptly in *Panthea*, to manipulate not only the play's "inside" story, but also dramatic convention and with it, viewer response.

Notes

¹ The play was performed by Schönemann's troupe in Breslau in 1744, 1745 in Königsberg (Devrient, *Schönemannsche Truppe* 28 and 40); further performances are documented in Devrient, *Johann Friedrich Schönemann* 90.

² Cf., among others, Robinson 121: "particularly a tragedy, *Panthea*, she reworked for the rest of her life, but this last work shows clearly that this 'Sappho,' the name by which her friends liked to call her, was entirely devoid of any poetic talent"; Bryan/Richel 200: "*Panthea*, then, is little more than painful evidence that Gottsched's talent and potentiality lay with the comic genre"; most recently Kerth/Russell xxv: "*Panthea* makes it clear why the prose comedy was Frau Gottsched's theatrical métier."

³ Heitner 65. The only earlier tragedy by a woman that I have been able to find, other than the numerous Latin tragedies by the tenth-century nun Hrotsvitha von Gandersheim, is Catharina Salome Link's (1695–after 1743) *Poleyctes ein Märtyrer*, a translation of Corneille's tragedy, which appeared in 1727 in Strasbourg. To my knowledge, the only direct contemporary of Luise Gott-

sched's who worked in the genre was the actress Christiane Friederike Huber (?-1799); her tragedy *Cleveland* appeared in 1756, twelve years after *Panthea*. Until this research is superseded, we can assume that Luise Gottsched was indeed the first woman author to publish original tragedies in the German language. Having said that, I would like to caution feminist scholars with regard to any such summary statement: I myself would question it both with regard to canonical literary history (because the elevation of authors as "firsts" is a well-worn trope in the establishment of canonical hierarchies that *must* be demolished if women's literature is to be considered anything but secondary) and to *women's* literary history. Many women's plays were never published or performed, and many women's publications have yet to be discovered, so that Gottsched's status as the "first" female author of tragedies is likely to be temporary. Nonetheless, it seems clear that Gottsched, as a woman author of tragedies in the 1740s, was in very limited company, and that she must certainly be acknowledged as a pioneer woman tragedian in Germany.

[4] On the question of authorship. cf. Hollmer 194, note 370.

[5] Bodmer, *Beurtheilung der Panthea eines sogenannten Trauerspiels der Frau L. A. V. G.*, 14. All quotations from this text are cited in my translation.

[6] "Von Tragödien" 311–2: "Aus den abgeschmacktesten Liedern besoffener Bauern, ist das ernsthafteste und beweglichste Stücke entstanden, welches die ganze Poesie aufzuweisen hat. . . . Das vorige satirische Scherzen hat sich in ein recht prächtiges und lehrreiches Wesen verwandelt; so, daß sich die ansehnlichsten Leute nicht mehr schämen durften, Zuschauer solcher Schauspiele abzugeben."

[7] "Von Tragödien" 312: "eine Art des Gottesdienstes; die auch in der That für das Volk viel erbaulicher war, als alle die Opfer und die übrigen Ceremonien des Heidenthums."

[8] "Von Tragödien" 311: "Zuschauern . . ., die in ihrer ersten Grobheit an etwas ernsthaftem noch keinen Geschmack finden konnten; sondern nur allezeit lachen wollten."

[9] This is not to imply that later literary movements devalued tragedies enough to conceive of women as authors of the genre. On the contrary, tragedy remained the pinnacle of literary art in the minds of most authors and theorists through the late Enlightenment, Storm and Stress, and Classicism. The higher number of tragedies authored by women after 1770 must be seen in the context of the explosion of independent authorship in general that came with the development of a literary marketplace, independent publishing houses and public libraries. In other words, writing became an enterprise bound by the rules of supply and demand rather than one supported almost entirely by aristocratic patronage. The result was a much larger number of publishing authors in general and of women authors in particular. Complaints from male authors about the ubiquitousness of works by women begin in the

1780s and remain a constant theme in the epistolary exchanges and diary entries of male authors through the nineteenth century. Obviously, such complaints not only document the increased number of writing women, but also their male colleagues' fear of competition. Moreover, many of them, in an effort to demonstrate the seriousness of the situation, wildly exaggerate the actual number of publishing women authors. One of the most famous examples is Goethe's sardonic remark to Schiller that their co-edited journal *Die Horen* was so flooded with contributions by women that the journal was clearly entering its "feminine age" — made at a time (1795) when only seven of the journal's thirty regularly contributing authors were women (cf. Goodman/Waldstein, "Introduction" 1–27, this citation 16).

[10] "Von Tragödien" 314: "anderntheils aber bewundert man die göttliche Rache, die gar kein Laster ungestraft läßt."

[11] "Von Tragödien" 312–3: "die Helden einer Tragödie müßten weder recht schlimm, noch recht gut seyn: nicht recht schlimm, weil man sonst mit ihrem Unglücke kein Mitleiden haben, sondern sich darüber freuen würde; aber auch nicht recht gut, weil man sonst die Vorsehung leicht einer Ungerechtigkeit beschuldigen könnte, wenn sie unschuldige Leute so hart gestrafet hätte."

[12] Quotations of *Panthea* are taken from the second edition, published in Vienna in 1751; Gottsched reworked this version a few months before her death but made only minor changes. All citations are by page number; all translations from the text are mine. I have not tried to reproduce the original's Alexandrine metre in my translations, but I have otherwise attempted to remain faithful to the original in both content and style.

[13] This characterization remains essentially unvaried, with one interesting exception, Araspes' death scene, which I will discuss further below.

[14] "Wie wenig Fürsten sind, die, so wie du auf Erden,/ Der Ehen Schutzherrn sind, nicht ihre Störer werden!" (*Panthea* 16)

[15] "Ists denn das Laster nur, was uns zu Fürsten macht?" (*Panthea* 9)

[16] "Ach theurester Gemahl! O höbe doch mein Mund/ Dir allen Zweifel auf, das ich für unsern Bund/ In steter Sorgfalt steh. Du hast nichts zu besorgen./ Was Cyrus ganzes Reich von Abend bis zum Morgen/ An schönen Helden zeigt, das alles rührt mich nicht:/ Und wär es Cyrus selbst; so ist mir meine Pflicht,/ Und du mein Abradat, unendlich mehr zu schätzen./ Mein Leben ist die Treu, ich kann sie nicht verletzen./ O gieb doch fernerhin nur keinem Zweifel statt;/ Weil meine Brust ein Herz, für dich allein, nur hat." (*Panthea* 21–2)

[17] "*Araspes.* O ia, ich zweifle nicht, die Schlacht muß uns gelingen./ Die Feinde sind zwar stark, doch mancher Umstand zeigt,/ Es sey dem Cyrus noch ein höher Glück geneigt./ *Hystaspes.* Und dieß verdient er auch. Ein Fürst, der in der Jugend/ Schon Weisen ähnlich war, der ist ein Sohn der Tugend;/ Und diese schützet stets des Himmels hoher Arm." (*Panthea* 23)

[18] "Wer hier sagen wollte, daß Oedipus ganz unschuldig oder ganz schuldig wäre, der würde in beydem irren. Er ist so, wie die Menschen insgemein zu seyn pflegen, das ist, von mittlerer Gattung; er hat gewisse Tugenden, auch gewisse Laster an sich: und doch stürzen ihn bloß die letzten ins Unglück. Denn hätte er nur niemanden erschlagen, so wäre alles übrige nicht erfolget. Er hätte sich aber billig vor allen Todtschlägen hüten sollen: nachdem ihm das Orakel eine so deutliche Weissagung gegeben hatte. Denn er sollte billig allezeit gedacht haben: Wie? wenn dieß etwa mein Vater wäre!" ("Von Tragödien" 313–4)

[19] "Sey ferner, wie du thust, der reinsten Tugend hold;/ Der Götter hohe Gunst ist ihr gewisser Sold." (*Panthea* 17)

[20] "Prinzeßinn, fahre fort/ Der Tugend treu zu seyn; sie lohnt hier und dort." (*Panthea* 52)

[21] "Und da des Himmels Arm die Tugend nie verläßt;/ So wird er auch gewiß in allen andern Sachen,/ Für Abradatens Wohl und für sein Siegen wachen./ Der Götter hohen Schutz trau ich mein Lebenlang." (*Panthea* 20)

[22] "Wer nicht verderben will, der muß den Himmel trauen." (*Panthea* 45)

[23] "O Himmel! kannst du mich durch so viel Marter kränken?" (*Panthea* 56); "Ihr Götter! tragt ihr Lust mich so in Angst zu setzen?" (57)

[24] "O Himmel! theilt dein Grimm den Lohn so ungleich ein? / . . . Jedoch, was klagt mein Schmerz der Götter Fügung an./ Da, wenn ich standhaft bin, ich selbst mir helfen kann?" (*Panthea* 62–3)

[25] "Ists möglich? ach! gebricht/ Des Himmels Retterarm? und er beschützt es nicht?/ Ihr, die ihr nie den Grund von euren Thun verkündigt,/ Ihr Götter! zürnet nicht wofern mein Zweifel sündigt./ Der Fall ist mir zu schwehr! - - - Nein ich begreife kaum - - -" (*Panthea* 67–8)

[26] "Die Gottheit, die wir kennen,/ Der grosse Mithra muß sich selber strafbar nennen,/ Wofern sein Arm hinfort solch eines Wüthrichs schont/ Und nicht der Frevelthat mit Fall und Unglück lohnt." (*Panthea* 30)

[27] "Wie reimt sich deine Huld mit so viel herbem Wehe?" (*Panthea* 67)

[28] "Es werd indeß sogleich ein Ehrenmahl bestellt,/ Das Pantheen und auch den Abradat umschliesse;/ Damit dieß Paar die Ruh in einer Gruft geniesse./ *Auf den Araspes zeigend.* Du Mörder aber, spür auch nach entwichnem Geist,/ Daß jedes Lasters Schuld die Fürsten strafen heißt;/ Und daß das strenge Recht von Cyrus Königskrone/ Auch an der Leiche nicht des Lebens Boßheit schone." (*Panthea* 72)

[29] "Dein Zuspruch stärket mich. Ihr Götter! steht mir bey!/ Damit ich dieser Gunst und Gattin würdig sey." (*Panthea* 46)

[30] "Er eilt? o herbe Noth!/ Und eilt zum Untergang; er geht in seinen Tod!/ Ja, ja! ich sehe schon des Feindes Mörderklingen,/ Mich um mein ganzes

Glück, um Abradaten, bringen./ O Anblick voller Graus! Verwegne, haltet ein!/ Und fehlt ein Opfer euch, so laßt mein Haupt es seyn./ Ich sterbe, wo er stirbt." (*Panthea* 48)

[31] "Was bringst du für Bericht? Wie geht es in der Schlacht?/ Lebt Abradates noch?" (*Panthea* 60)

[32] "Mein König!/ Schau, was die Lieb anietzt zu ihrer Rettung that,/ Was Panthea gewagt, für ihren Abradat!" (*Panthea* 69)

[33] "Ach! ihr Geist ist schon verschwunden!/ Er hat den schönsten Weg zum Abradat gefunden." (*Panthea* 69)

[34] "Ja, mein Fürst, nun kenn ich erst die Liebe,/ Sie herrschet über uns mit nie bezwungnem Triebe./ Sie gab mir diesen Mord des Abradates ein,/ Um bey der Panthea nach ihm beglückt zu seyn./ Jetzt, da bey ihrer Gruft mein kühnes Hoffen fehlet,/ *Er reißt dem Cyrus den Dolch aus der Hand und ersticht sich.* So werd auch diese Brust den andern gleich entseelet./ Es deck ein frühes Grab die unglücksvolle Treu,/ Damit ich nur kein Schimpf von deinem Hofe sey:/ Und übertrifft mein Fehl die Treue meiner Jugend;/ So räche Pantheen und die erblichne Tugend." (*Panthea* 71)

[35] Subsequent fictionalizations of Xenophon's story reflect these complex relationships between Panthea and her real and potential suitors: in their titles, Panthea is rarely paired with her husband (as in Edwards' 1803 tragedy *Abradatas and Panthea*) and more frequently with either Araspes (Wieland's "moral tale" *Araspes und Panthea*, 1760) or torn between Cyrus and Araspes (Wieland's *Cyrus, Araspes und Panthea*, 1804).

[36] These suppositions are phrased as such because they cannot be substantiated outside of a reading of the play; certainly, there is little "biographical" evidence that this was the author's "intention." In letters, Gottsched never commented on her authorial "intentions," or on the play as a whole, other than to state near the end of her life that the play assumed, for her, a special place in her entire work. This is another fact that has been marvelled at by critics: "For inexplicable reasons, *Panthea* remained the personal favorite of its author" (Richel, *Luise Gottsched* 52). It is indeed difficult to read the author's attachment to this play within a biographical context that assumes that she merely intended to produce an exemplification of existing tragedic theories, most prominently her husband's: in that case, *Panthea* would in nothing have distinguished itself from any of her comedies. My explanation would be that *Panthea*'s status as Gottsched's personal favorite was rooted in the apparent immutability of the genre, its aesthetic and ethical tenets, and in the challenge in adapting these tenets for her own purposes. That *Panthea* did assume a special place in the author's assessment of her own work is evidenced by the fact that she reworked the play almost to the end of her life (cf. the letter to Runckel cited above); that she did *not* view it merely as an exemplification of her husband's dramatic theories is perhaps indicated by the fact

that she did not show her husband the final revision of the play — of which he apparently remained unaware to the end of his life.

6: On Guilt and Innocence: Authorship

IN A SHORT LIST of eighteenth- and nineteenth-century authors that includes Karoline Neuber, Charlotte von Stein, Karoline von Günderrode, Bettina von Arnim, Annette von Droste-Hülshoff, and Marie von Ebner-Eschenbach, Luise Gottsched is one of a handful of women writing in either century who are still known today. This relative fame (compared with the absolute obscurity of thousands of her colleagues) has, in her readers' perception, very little to do with the quality of her literature, as the open contempt accorded her work in most scholarship to date attests. Neither can her relative fame be explained entirely with the fact that she was married to and supported in her literary endeavors by a famous man, one of the literary "greats" of his time, although her husband was of course a pivotal influence on her literary career. This influence was both negative and positive: she was forced to spend virtually all of her creative energy on commissioned works for him, thereby almost certainly preventing increased engagement with literary forms and subjects she may have been more interested in, but his influence also afforded her easily accessible venues for publication. The association with a "great man" has, of course, stimulated scholarship on some women who would otherwise have remained obscure (such as Charlotte von Stein), but historically that has occurred only when his and her audiences — that is, the consumers of literature on the "great man" and the readers of works on the woman attached to him — have intersected. Such is the case in early research on Charlotte von Stein, which was written by and for Goethe scholars and viewed more or less as an interesting footnote to *his* life. Goethe biographies, for example, usually acknowledge Charlotte von Stein as a pivotal influence in his life and writing, and Charlotte von Stein scholars have traditionally made it explicit that her connection with Goethe was, in their consideration, the only reason to research her at all: there is hardly a work on Charlotte von Stein in which she is not paired with Goethe in the title.[1] A parallel case cannot be made for Luise Gottsched: readers (and writers) of works on Luise Gottsched appear to form a group entirely distinct from readers (and writers) of works on her husband. If scholarship on Luise Gottsched acknowledges her husband's influence in passing, it is usually made clear that his influence is not the purpose of investigation, and scholarship on Johann Christoph Gottsched has entirely ignored his wife — a tendency exactly parallel to her complete effacement in general works on the literature of the Enlightenment.[2] Clearly, there is very little overlap in scholarship on Johann Christoph and Luise Gottsched, despite their life-long collaboration; given her absence from many works on the period, Luise Gottsched is equally clearly hardly considered a standard Enlightenment author, despite her fame.

Luise Gottsched's reception, then, marks her as anomalous in several ways. While she remains one of the most famous eighteenth-century women writers, this fact, in the minds of most critics, is unrelated to the quality of her work (unlike, for example, Marie von Ebner-Eschenbach). Unlike Charlotte von Stein's, her fame is not viewed as occasioned by her association with a more famous male author. What makes her central, in the minds of most critics, is neither her work nor her connectedness to other authors, but on the contrary her *dis*connectedness from any context, biographical, socio-historical or aesthetic. This position is frequently expressed in emphases of her position as abnormal: she is viewed as the "most famous" Enlightenment woman author, the "first" female tragedian in Germany, and so on. Such designations, while providing a surface justification for establishing Gottsched as the object of scholarly inquiry, also serve to deprive her of the context in which she is best examined: women's literary history and their historical reception as authors. Traditional modes of inquiry, which tend to view women in exclusively biographical contexts or to examine their writing in aesthetic contexts which a priori devalue women's authorship, have proven inadequate to an examination of Gottsched's writing. The following is an attempt to revitalize the discussion of Gottsched's authorship — both as a historical occurrence and as an issue conceptualized by the author herself — by placing it in the broader context of the conceptualization and reception of contemporary women's authorship.

The Innocent Ruse: Making a Name for Herself

Any discussion of women's authorship in the eighteenth (or nineteenth) century is intimately connected with the issue of women's anonymity and pseudonymity. Anonymity and pseudonymity, as I have stated elsewhere (*Sich einen Namen machen*), were the single most consequential modes of publication for female writers in both centuries. For various reasons, not the least of which may be the numerical increase of writing women during the nineteenth century and concomitant issues of competition with their male colleagues, nineteenth-century women writers were accorded a very different status from their eighteenth-century colleagues, who were still, by and large, considered "exceptions." This difference in status is reflected in the discussion of female "erudition" in both centuries: in the eighteenth century, the term *Gelehrte* ("erudite woman") was largely used in non-vituperative, sometimes even complimentary, terms, for example in works by early bibliographers and literary historians like Johann Caspar Eberti (1677–1760), Georg Christian Lehms (1684–1717) and Christian Franz Paullini (1711–78).[3] Conversely, "erudite" became a taboo designation for women in the nineteenth-century, a century during which many of the most renowned philosophers, educators, and authors of literary and aesthetic works spent a substantial portion of their life's work prescribing for women an exclusive existence as housewives and caregivers for husbands and children.[4] Women's activity as writers was very often seen in the context of these treatises, that is, negatively: at best as distractions from housework, at worst as proof positive that they had failed in their "calling" as "true women" (*weibliche Bestimmung*). One could speculate that this situation was both caused and exacerbated by the fact that there were many more women writing during the nineteenth century than there had been during the eighteenth. An eighteenth-century woman writer could still be regarded as "exceptional," a fact that may explain the more lenient treatment she was generally accorded by her male colleagues and critics. Nineteenth-century women writers, on the other hand, were legion and regarded as serious competition on the literary marketplace. In my investigation of this problem, I have been able to find 323 women writing between 1700 and 1820; between 1820 and 1900, that number jumps to 2617 (*Namen* 52). The reasons for this are too varied to be discussed here at length, but among them are the general broadening of opportunities and venues for authors that accompanied the gradual switch from the authors' utter dependence on courtly patronage to a "free" literary marketplace (complete with independent publishers, incorporated publishing houses, much wider journal distribution, and lending libraries) and the increased activity of women writers in specifically "feminine" genres like children's literature, which had, in the eighteenth century, still been largely furnished by male writers. In addition, it can be assumed that more eighteenth- than nineteenth-century women writers have never been recovered from obscurity because of their usage of anonymity or pseudonyms, which tended to be more generic in the eighteenth century than in the nineteenth. This applies to at least five writers who published before 1830 and are now known only by their (non-descript) pseudonyms: Kreopola (ca. 1816), Richa (ca. 1820), Mara L. (ca. 1830), Frau von Mauritius (ca. 1820) and the author of the drama *Ortinde* (1792), of whom we know neither a first nor a last name. Pseudonyms in the nineteenth century were composed, as a rule, of a first-name/last-name combination; they are therefore more easily attributable than eighteenth-century pseudonyms that consisted, more often than not, of common feminine first names or mere initials. In the eighteenth century, I have been able to determine the pseudonyms of 60 authors (approximately 19% of publishing female authors throughout that century), in the nineteenth of 38% of all publishing women (1394 writers). Their usage of pseudonyms at a glance:[5]

Years	Publishing Authors	Initials	Abbreviation of First Names	Abbreviation of Last Names	Male Pseudonym	Female Pseudonym
1700 –1820	60 100%	17 28%	5 8%	2 3%	7 12%	91 152%
1820 –1900	1394 100%	45 3%	498 36%	14 1%	476 34%	702 50%

The most obvious discrepancy appearing from this overview is the historically varied usage of initials and male and female pseudonyms. The popularity of initials that serve to mask both the author's identity and her gender diminishes in the nineteenth century (from 28% in the eighteenth century to only 3% after 1820). Surnames appear to be initialized with equal frequency in both centuries, but there is an astonishing divergence with regard to initializing first names: before 1820, only 5 authors chose this route (8%) vis-à-vis nearly 500 (36%) after 1820. Even more astounding is the contrast in the usage of male versus female pseudonyms: in the eighteenth century, only seven authors (12%) used a male pseudonym, in contrast with 91 female pseudonyms employed during the same era: that means that every female author of that century that we know of used at least one, many times two different female pseudonyms. In the nineteenth century, only half of all writing women employed this method; simultaneously, the number of male pseudonyms jumped to 476 (34%). From a purely mathematical viewpoint, female pseudonyms in the nineteenth century occurred only one third as frequently as they had in the eighteenth, while the percentage of male pseudonyms used during the same timeframe *tripled*.

The usage of initials marks the same trend towards pretended masculine authorship in the nineteenth century. The fact that the popularity of initial pseudonyms that abbreviate both first and last name diminishes so sharply in the nineteenth century can perhaps be explained by the fact that such cryptonyms were among the most common pseudonyms for female authors of the eighteenth century: with 28% of authors using it, this method is the second most common mode of pseudonymous publication for women. Because of famous trendsetters like Luise Gottsched (L. A. V. G.) and Catherine the Great of Russia (I. K. M. d. K. a. R.[6]), such initials became practically identified with female authorship. In the eighteenth century, women's pseudonyms often consisted entirely of such initials or, at times, of abbreviated last names (Susanne von B., Eleonore F.); whereas in the nineteenth, the tendency is towards abbreviation of the first name (P. v. Husch, F. S. Koch, C. Wedi, H. Sakkorausch, A. Weimar). Authors who used such pseudonyms in the nineteenth century almost certainly played on the readers' likely assumption of a male author behind the abbreviated personal name.

Elsewhere I have contended that such pseudonyms were used deliberately and consciously, that is, that users of initials or abbreviated first names steered their readers towards the assumption of either a male or a female author. By virtue of the fact that neither initials nor abbreviated first names comment on the author's gender, authors who use these methods speculate on the readers' prejudices and assumptions. If one, based on this assumption, experimentally counted all full initials as "female" pseudonyms and all abbreviated first names as "male" pseudonyms, the result would be the following comparison: in the eighteenth century, the time during which each woman author used one to two female pseudonyms, 80% of all authors insisted on being recognized as female — hiding their identity, but not their gender behind names like Jerta, Jenny, Glycere, Minna, Nina or Therese. In the nineteenth century, these female pseudonyms diminish by two-thirds; 70% of all authors now hide behind abbreviated first names (assuming that readers would automatically presume male authorship) or behind a male pseudonym. Abbreviated first names and male pseudonyms now begin to outnumber female ones substantially. Perhaps another indication of the urgency of the situation for nineteenth-century women writers is the proliferation of *emphatically* masculine names: women now call themselves Wild, Ernst Ritter, R. Edmund Hahn, Max Stein, Lork Alban, Julius Willborn, Franz Fels, Max Hero, Alexander Römer, Sigismund Mannsperg, Schwucht von Zinken, Eichen-Löw, Werner Kraft, Josef Trieb. The trend is very clearly one from personal to gender anonymity: throughout the eighteenth century, women attempt to mask their *identity*, whereas throughout the nineteenth, they attempt, to a much greater degree, to hide their *gender* (Kord, *Namen* 51–5).

Obviously, there were many other variants in the use of anonymity and pseudonyms of female writers throughout both centuries, among them age, popularity, class membership, text type and genre (cf. *Namen*, particularly chapters 3 and 4). In this context, however, I would like to concentrate on four conclusions which I view as a central background for my investigation of Luise Gottsched's anonymity and authorship: that the anonymous and pseudonymous publication of women authors is a steady occurrence throughout both centuries and must indeed be considered the primary mode of publication for women during that era; that this mode of publication is intimately connected with the author's gender; that this fact was universally known to both male and female writers; and that anonymity in fact can be seen as much more than merely a mode of publication for most writing women of the age, but as a problematization of their *authorship* and a veiled discussion of the permissibility of authorship for women, a connection that might then, obliquely or obviously, also express itself in their texts. One telling example for the connectedness of pseudonymity and gendered authorship is Johann Christoph Gottsched's remark in the preface to the 1738 reprint of his journal *Die vernünftigen Tadlerinnen* (The Reasonable Female Critics), originally published in 1725 and 1726, in which he defends the authorial choice of pseudonym with the pedagogical goals and potential success of the journal:

> The intention of its first authors was as innovative as it was laudable. They sought to bring to the German woman a piece that would serve her to pass the time pleasantly, but also have a more useful and instructive content than the usual novels. In order to preserve this intent, they employed an innocent ruse in pretending that they themselves were women, since they foresaw clearly that this pretense, even if it was not universally believed, would greatly contribute to the positive reception of the journal.[7]

This "ruse," which I would argue was, in view of the author's clear awareness of the gender specificity of authorship and its consequences for the reception of the text, far from "innocent," constitutes a comparative rarity, a fact that is indeed instructive. Whereas we know of nearly one thousand women writers who sought to secure the greater acceptance accorded writings by male authors for their works by using a male pseudonym or abbreviated personal name, Johann Christoph Gottsched is one of only twelve male authors (in both centuries) who ever published under the pretense of female authorship (*Namen* 127–8). The large majority of texts published by men under this pretense were "instructive" manuals for women in the sense described in Johann Christoph Gottsched's preface. They ranged from moral pamphlets for women and tracts outlining the severely restrictive views of *The Whole Duty of Woman*, published for obviously pragmatic reasons by "A Lady" (=William Kenrick, 1725?–79), to outright mockery of female authorship à la Benjamin Franklin, who expressed the intended moral directly in the pseudonyms he chose ("Alice Addertongue," "Celia Single," or "Busybody"; cf. *Namen* 127–8). Like most of his eleven male colleagues who used the same "ruse," Johann Christoph Gottsched surmised that a text prescribing and restricting female behavior would be more easily accepted by a female readership if it were read as coming from a woman author. By virtue of this admission, his preface demonstrates clearly both the connection between pseudonymity and authorial gender and the fact that the author's gendered pseudonym was consciously employed to steer the reader's reception of the text (particularly in cases where, as was the case here, the reader was also presumed to have a specific gender).

In the following, I would like to investigate to what extent Luise Gottsched's comments on female authorship can be read within the same context, a context that represents female authorship as both impeded and defined by the author's anonymity and pseudonymity. Luise Gottsched, both as the paradigmatic "first"/"only" woman author of her time and as an author who published everything she wrote either anonymously or under (clearly recognizable) pseudonyms, seems to me a particularly apt case for this investigation. Together with famous women colleagues like Christiane Mariane von Ziegler and Sidonia Hedwig Zäunemann, she became not only a trendsetter for female use of pseudonyms and anonymity, but also an exemplification of how far female authorship as a phenomenon could go. Gottsched is also one of the first women who saw, and expressed in writing, a variety of complex aspects circumscribing and defining the comparatively rare phenomenon of female authorship — among them the woman writer's ambiguous relationship with her own anonymity and authorship, male tutelage and directed writing, and the seemingly foregone reception of the woman writer's text.

The Innocent Translator:
On the Guilt of Female Authorship

Interestingly enough, and this fact alone merits investigation, Luise Gottsched's commentary on female authorship in general and her own in particular does not appear in those texts in which readers would expect to find it, her letters and her paradigmatic essays on women and erudition in *The Reasonable Female Critics*, but in her fiction. Her views are thus far removed from the obvious pedagogical and social "instruction" of women that her husband pursued in his early writing. Luise Gottsched engages the issue of female authorship in an indirect, opaque, and strangely contradictory way. Her letters and articles in the moral weeklies, the only venues in which unequivocal comments on women's authorship could have been made publicly, are both strangely silent on the issue. Indeed, the only aspect that does testify to the centrality of the issue for Luise Gottsched is its recurrence in dramatic texts and the telling difference with which the issue is treated in these texts, compared with the entirely non-committal, almost disinterested, treatment the theme is afforded in her articles in the *Reasonable Female Critics*. In these pieces, Gottsched rather generically treats related themes like women's work ethic and industry ("Lob der Arbeit"), clearly distinguished from masculine "erudition, which is, of course, far beyond our sex" ("Wissenschaften, die freylich für unser Geschlechte zu hoch sind," 62). She pleads for education for women, again strictly differentiating between such education and true "erudition" ("Gelehrsamkeit"): the goal of women's education, she claims, would be "to instill reason, but certainly not scholarly erudition, in the woman" ("daß sie [the woman, S. K.] dadurch zwar vernünftig, aber noch lange nicht gelehrt werden wird"; "Die Rolle der Frau" 249). In keeping with the traditional debate on women and erudition in the moral weeklies, women in Gottsched's journal entries appear predominantly, if not exclusively, as housewives and mothers, rarely or never as authors. Where women's authorship is thematized at all, it is discussed indirectly, defensively, and with an acute display of embarrassment and shame. One example is a passage in the 29th piece of the re-edition of *Die Vernünftigen Tadlerinnen* (1738) in which Gottsched declares that true *Gelehrsamkeit* is beyond women's capabilities, but she then exempts a number of activities from the definition of *Gelehrsamkeit*, redefining them as mere "skills." Among these "skills" she lists "music, painting, dancing, writing, fencing, basic mathematical skills, and languages (excepting the scholarly languages)."[8] But even in such passages, in which Gottsched *appears* to lay the argumentative foundation for a justification of women's right to write, the reader has to infer her point. Nowhere does she state explicitly that this redefinition of activities as "skills" rather than the tabooed *Gelehrsamkeit* permits women, through the back door as it were, to engage in these activities. Readers who did infer this meaning and expected this to be followed by a spirited defense of women painters, musicians and authors were disappointed. On the contrary:

> I suppose they [women, S. K.] are able to cite their basic multiplication tables, at times, they can even add. They can write one neat and orthographically correct page in three or four hours using a lined piece of paper: this last I say in defense of my sex, but I wouldn't guarantee it. But now for the best part: they write verse! But what verse? Are they pure? Are they regular? Are they full of noble, elevated, virtuous and reasonable expression? What genres are used? Are they heroic epics? Is it dogmatic poetry? Are they noble, new and innovative inventions? I would not like to answer these questions. Readers can find the answer in the printed works of my sisters. But I wish that nobody would ever notice the great formal flaws as well as the mean, pompous, empty, saucy, vulgar, coarse, and lewd passages showing the inner nature of their poetry, which I have often lamented in my heart.[9]

Granted, despite her snide remarks on women's deplorable mathematical skills and orthography, Gottsched blames this situation on their general lack of education, a condition which she would like to see improved. Nonetheless, her unilateral condemnation of contemporary German women writers is remarkable in its vehemence, in its unfavorable comparison to France (she concludes that "we cannot point to a single Deshoulières in poetry, a single de Sevigné in letters, a single Gomez in rhetoric, and a single Barbier in tragedy"[10]) and in the fact that her essay makes *no* suggestions to remedy this deplorable situation. Instead, she ends by recommending a basic education for women to aid them in the fulfilment of their primary duties: "obedience toward men, the management of the household, and the education of children."[11] Women's authorship is thus presented as a dubious phenomenon to the female readership of the journal: in *principle*, it may be permissible for women to engage in such activity, but Gottsched paints a picture of actual contemporary women authors so sinister that it serves as a practical discouragement for women. This stance is further emphasized by the fact that Gottsched epitomizes "authorship" in three authorial modes or genres that most contemporary readers would indeed have deemed "beyond" women's capabilities or inappropriate for women: heroic epics, "dogmatic" poetry, and "new and innovative inventions." Most discouraging for female readers of Gottsched's piece who considered themselves aspiring authors, perhaps even as following in her footsteps, is Gottsched's self-stylization as the shamefully embarrassed *reader* of women's writings. Her ostensible refusal to engage in open critique of their works effectively pronounces them as beneath criticism and simultaneously conveys a good sense of the shame, guilt and embarrassment involved in even exposing oneself to such filth by assuming the reader's role. How much worse would it be, as is clearly implied, to have *written* this filth, to sign it as author? Were it not for the entirely different treatment of the theme in her dramatic works, Gottsched's views on women's authorship as expressed in her journal essays could well be viewed as prefiguring the nineteenth-century discussion on the theme, a discussion dominated by a sense of restrictiveness that was still, in her own age, comparatively rare.

Gottsched takes up the theme again in the foreword to her first play, *Die Pietisterey im Fischbein-Rocke*, her adaptation of Bougeant's *La Femme Docteur* (1730), in which she adapted not only Bougeant's text, but also his mode of publication for her purposes. Both plays appeared anonymously and with a false place of publication and publisher on the frontispiece: Gottsched's play was not published, as the frontispiece claims, in Rostock and "auf Kosten guter Freunde" (published by friends of the author), but in Leipzig with the renowned publisher Breitkopf (who lived in the same house as the Gottscheds). Both plays are preceded by an exchange of letters between the "author" and the "editor," which is presumably fictitious in Bougeant's case and certainly so in Gottsched's. There was good reason for all this subterfuge: both plays attacked contemporary religious groups (Bougeant's the Jansenists, Gottsched's the Pietists) and proved exceedingly controversial in their day; Gottsched's play was outlawed in most German cities and even inspired some new censorship laws in Prussia (cf. Consentius). But despite all similarities, there are some telling differences between Gottsched's manner of proceeding and Bougeant's, and it is these differences that most clearly illuminate the gendered nature of Gottsched's anonymity.

Gottsched's exchange between "author" and "editor" that precedes her play reads essentially similar to Bougeant's. Her editor, who addresses the author as "Most worthy, highly learned Sir!" (*Pietism* 1: "Hoch-Ehrwürdiger, Hochgelahrter Herr!," *Die Lustspiele* I, 442), apologizes profusely for the printing of the comedy without the author's knowledge or consent. The story that now unfolds in both Gottsched's and Bougeant's case borders on the absurd: the editor took the liberty of reading the manuscript, with which he had been entrusted by the author (and ostensibly not for purposes of publication), to a gathering of friends. The piece proved an immense success, and the listeners were immediately determined to publish the play at their own expense, ignoring the editor's desperate objections. "They simply took possession of your manuscript, and it was not possible for me to get it back into my hands."[12] The printing was concluded so quickly that the editor was presented with the galley proofs before he even had a chance to notify the author. Thus he is reduced to sending the galley proofs to the author, along with his feeble assurances that "I have done everything within my power to prevent the publication of this text."[13] The author figure, in his answer letter to the editor, reacts to these revelations with a great deal of "dismay" and assures the editor that he never intended to have the drama printed — on the contrary, he claims to have written it "simply for my own amusement and at most for the entertainment of a few intimate friends during idle hours."[14] He attempts to pre-empt his own fear of public censure ("What will the world think of me . . .?"[15]) and of potential "aggravation and quarrels" (*Pietism* 3; *Lustspiele* I, 447: "Verdruß und Streitigkeiten") with the best defense imaginable:

> Did you not consider where I live and how easily people will develop the suspicion that I am the author of this manuscript? Even though, to tell the truth, I should not be regarded as such. A certain anonymous Frenchman had more to do with it than did I, and I should be regarded more as an innocent translator than as the author of this comedy. I see myself compelled to acknowledge this to you because I noticed that you ascribe it to me and me alone, which honor is not due me at all.[16]

Gottsched's foreword is highly descriptive of, indeed paradigmatic for, the problematic phenomenon of female authorship in general, in that it raises four issues that later become a tradition in women's forewords to their works: the strangely unresolved contradiction between the "honor" and "guilt" of authorship, which is mirrored in Gottsched's revealing designation of the "innocent translator"; the fear of public judgment which has to be pre-empted with exaggerated statements of modesty; the transfer of all pride in authorial achievement to masculine go-betweens (in this case the editor and the enthusiastic gathering of friends); and the privatization of authorship, in which literature is produced not for publication, but for the private edification of the author and her ("his") intimate circle of friends. In subsequent forewords by women, such manoeuvers are employed particularly in cases in which the author's identity or at least her gender was known. Gottsched, conversely, uses these pseudonymous tactics *in addition to* her complete separation of author and text, which she achieves by means of five diversionary tactics: her insistence on her own personal anonymity as the actual author, her insistence on her *gender* anonymity, her redefinition of her authorship as a translatorship, her fictionalization of place of publication and publisher, and her insistence — in the fact that within the text, all these poses are struck by a fictitious *male* author — that even a male author would not approve of the publication of this text.

In this respect, Gottsched's exchange of letters between author and editor differs markedly from Bougeant's, even and especially where she merely translates his original. The simplest and most obvious example is the appellation: like Bougeant's, her author figure ("Most worthy, highly learned Sir!") is clearly a man. What was a non-committal form of address in Bougeant's original becomes an effective tool to conceal gender identity in the translation. And it is gender anonymity that is intended here, as becomes abundantly clear in Gottsched's changes to Bougeant's original. Gottsched's author figure insists that "his" name never be revealed in public, that the edition of the play be kept as small as possible, and that no copies be sold in "his" place of residence. He even goes so far as to announce his wish to buy all copies already printed and destroy them. At the very least, he exhorts a promise from the editor "to suppress my name and in your introduction to convince the world that I had no part in the printing of this text."[17] None of these fears and exhortations appear in Bougeant's epistolarly exchange: Bougeant's author figure does not insist on the preservation of his anonymity, nor does he worry about the potential consequences of his play's publication for him personally. His main fears, and these I would identify as a component of a male authorial voice, concern the reception of the play: he worries about negative reviews, boring the public, and the possibility that the play might be misunderstood as an attack on the Jesuits instead of the Jansenists.[18] Where Bougeant's introduction remains clearly text-centered, Gottsched subtly shifts the emphasis to the author. The features dominating Gottsched's foreword include an insistence on the author's personal and gender anonymity, the use of pseudonymous tactics, and a simultaneous denial of the main objective of the subterfuges (to obscure the author's gender) via the fiction of the male author figure. All of these are conspicuously absent from Bougeant's, and these same features later become standard manoeuvers in forewords by women writers. Gottsched's foreword can thus be regarded as one of the earliest and one of the most representative texts by women writers on the issue of their own anonymity and authorship.

What makes Gottsched's text representative of women's discussions of their own authorship is the fact that Gottsched is establishing a discourse here that becomes the starting point for later discussions of the issue. Whether or not Gottsched's play actually *is* a translation,[19] her emphasis on her "innocent" translatorship is the principal point that marks the difference between male and female authorship. In addition to her own anonymity, her insistence on her mere translatorship exempts her from the suspicion of authorship. Her exact translation of Bougeant's original, with all masculine appellations and pronouns in place, exempts her from the suspicion of *female* authorship, and her rhetoric of the "innocent" translator clearly implies a commentary on the "guilt" of female authorship. This commentary is entirely absent from Bougeant's original but endlessly repeated in forewords by women writers throughout the eighteenth century and, with increased frequency and fervor, in the nineteenth. Gottsched's rhetoric reveals what may have been at the bottom of many fake translations issued from eighteenth-century women's pens[20]: like anonymity and pseudonymity, pretending to be the "mere" editor or translator served as a demonstration of "feminine" modesty while enabling women to proceed with their "masculine" literary activities. In a literary climate that was already beginning to pronounce female authors guilty, the "innocent" translator became a way of resolving an unsolvable conflict: a woman could thus write and publish but still adhere to already emerging restrictive notions of femininity, she could become known but remain unknown at the same time.

Guilt by Dissociation:
Women Writers and the Editorial Voice[21]

The problematic theme of feminine authorship and publication, which Gottsched introduced in the foreword to *Pietism*, is taken up again in the first scene of the fourth act, incidentally one of the longest scenes of the drama. The satirical barb of the play in general and of this scene in particular is directed at the ridiculous arrogance of women who mingle in religious affairs, in marked contrast to the female models of virtue portrayed in the play who pass their time with "sewing, knitting, embroidery" and "make it a point of honor to have nothing to do with religious quarrels."[22] Frau Glaubeleicht, Frau Seufftzer and Frau Zanckenheim, by contrast, not only presume to know something about "religious quarrels," but also — worse — aspire to the creation of "a useful document" ("ein nützliches Werck"); they wish to have it "appear under our names" ("unsere Nahmen darunter setzen") and even — this is presented as the height of female haughtiness — to "make our names immortal" ("uns einen unsterblichen Namen machen").[23] The desired comic effect of the scene relies entirely on the contrast between these lofty ideas and the reduction of the three would-be authors to epitomes of female ignorance and quarrelsomeness. Their plan to jointly produce and publish a document outlining a new article of faith concerning spiritual rebirth disintegrates quickly when each of the three authors offers a definition that is rejected by the other two. Each co-author, in other words, attempts to establish herself as primary author of the document, and thus comes into conflict with the authorial ambitions of the other two. Each attacks the writing of her co-authors for its obtuseness and lack of clarity. When Magister Scheinfromm enters the scene, he is called upon immediately to serve as judge (and editor) of the work in progress. Herr Scheinfromm has to exercise his masculine authority repeatedly in order to keep the three from interrupting each other, but when he finally hears the various definitions, he approves of all three: he calls Frau Glaubeleicht's definition "very beautiful and clearly explained," Frau Seufftzer's "elevated" and Frau Zanckenheim's "very beautifully put."[24] Nor does he demur when each author cites the greatest male authorities in the field, Francke, Spener and Böhme, as precursors for her writing. He withdraws his support only when he realizes that this is not a personal conversation, but "an article of faith,"[25] that is: a document intended for publication. At the end of the scene, the women are left with nothing but the title, which is quite representative of contemporary religious tracts in terms of both its baroque length, its assumed self-importance, and its evocation of a very specific audience: *Collection of Selected Arguments Concerning the Most Difficult Articles of Faith, Published for the Use and Edification of the Doctors of Holy Scripture and the Theological Faculties, by Frau Glaubeleicht, Frau Seufftzer and Frau Zanckenheim.*[26] In the hands of female authors, the message to the reader appears to be, the erudite theological "arguments" alluded to in the title disintegrate into the usual quarrels among women.

It is precisely the provocative tone employed in the title and throughout the discussion that marks the women's blatant authorial ambition as a transgression: above all, their intention is to "show these gentlemen that we are cleverer than they are" and to "silence all the theologians."[27] Obviously, then, this authorial ambition that manifests itself in the insistence on publication under the author's name and in the resistance to masculine authority over the text is charged with the "guilt" alluded to in the foreword. This guilt is punishment neither for the women's act of writing nor for their presumption of viewing their own literary production equal to that of the most central and respected male authors in the field, but for the act of orthonymous publication unmediated by male editorship. Scheinfromm limits his contributions to vague compliments until the point in the discussion at which it becomes clear to him that the document is intended for publication, when he forcefully dissociates himself from the entire project: "What? . . . Your servant, ladies, but I'll have nothing to do with that."[28]

If read against Luise Gottsched's biographical background, this scene presents an insoluble paradox, as many critics have pointed out: "The Learned Lady" ridiculed in the subtitle and in this scene is, of course, an all-too-obvious likeness of the author, a woman who by no means limited herself to "sewing, knitting, embroidery," but on the contrary — just like the three women of this scene — voiced her opinion on religious matters *through authorship*. But read in conjunction with Gottsched's analysis of female authorship in the foreword, the scene makes sense: female authorship is presented as admissible to the extent that it does not represent a usurpation of male privilege. Female authorship is acceptable insofar as it revokes itself, redefines itself as a mere translation, and humbly places itself under male protection. Its self-presentation must be appropriately demure rather than provocative, and orthonymous publication by a woman is clearly viewed as a provocation. When female authorship opposes or defies male protection, when it understands itself as independent from such patronage, and when it is demonstratively *female* (with publication under the author's own name planned), it loses its "innocence" and is given over to castigation and ridicule.

Mitigating Circumstances:
Women Writers and Male Mentorship

Nearly ten years later, in the penultimate scene of *The Last Will*, Gottsched comments on the problems of the shackled female authorship that she presented as permissible in her first play and that she herself had exercised paradigmatically during the preceding decade.[29] If one reads this scene, with Arnd Bohm, as a "fictional analogue" to Gottsched's own authorial situation, (137–8), the scene becomes a commentary on the rules governing female authorship, a commentary that establishes, once again, that legitimate female authorship (that is, authorship under male mentorship) is characterized above all by female submission to male authority. In Bohm's interpretation, the last will appears as the central text of the drama, Frau von Tiefenborn as its author and her wards as the readership breathlessly awaiting the appearance of this text. Thus, the entire drama centers on Frau von Tiefenborn's potential authorship: "Will she write? When will she write? What will she write?" (Bohm 134) Caroline, the Reasonable Female Critic of the play, accepts her role as a mere reader and critic of the text in question, whereas Amalie confuses her own desire as reader with the author's intention and attempts to influence the content of the text: "Amalie represents an extreme position of those who would deny the writer's autonomy and would make it serve absolutely the requirements of the reading audience." (Bohm 135) When Frau von Tiefenborn finally writes and publishes this long-awaited text at the end of the drama, she nonetheless has to submit to the rules outlined by the (male) notary, whom Arnd Bohm reads as a "fictional analogue" to the author's husband, Johann Christoph Gottsched. The notary insists, with the utmost exactitude, on the adherence to the rules he has laid down. In this manner, he dictates perhaps not the content, but certainly the form of her document:

> NOTARY [*makes an entry and reads on*]. ". . . Frau Veronika Eustasia Tiefenborn, Hereditary and Liege Lady and Chief Adjudicator of Goldenloh, Rententhal, Reichenhof, Schatzleben and Frohenloh, a servant by the name of Matthew Nicholas Pulverhorn, by profession a huntsman, with a dark, scowling face, stubby red nose, large lips, bristly black hair, thirty-seven years of age, wearing green hunting garb with old gold braid, yellow buttons, rather worn leather leggings. . ." [*They all begin to laugh.*]

> FRAU VON TIEFENBORN. Must all that be in my will?

> NOTARY. Yes. Your Ladyship.

> FRAU VON TIEFENBORN. How in the world can it be of any concern whether my huntsman's leggings are old or new?

> NOTARY. Yes, Your Ladyship. Otherwise the whole will is invalid. I shall have to request patience from all of you, for there are several more such passages to come.

FRAU VON TIEFENBORN. All right, whatever must be, must be. Read on!

NOTARY [*resumes reading*]. ". . . worn leather leggings, stuttering of speech, stinking of breath [*They all hold their handkerchiefs before their faces.*] appeared before me and gave me a report, according to which the above-named Frau Veronika Eustasia von Tiefenborn is resolved to prepare her legal last will and testament, the which is to take place outside the court at her own residence, to which place I was to proceed today, the fifteenth of June, in the year seventeen hundred and forty-five, with an already completed instrument. Since such a request conforms to my professional and notarial authority, I, Remigius Leodegarius Gänsekeil, Notary Public, have on this evening of the fifteenth of June, in the year seventeen hundred and forty-five, towards six-thirty in the evening betaken myself to the above named Honorable and Highborn Frau Veronika Eustasia von Tiefenborn, to her proper residence at the manor of Rententhal, a lordly residence situated with one side toward the East, with the second toward the West, with the third toward the South and with the fourth toward the North, which is painted in white and blue and has a large stone stairway on which there was lying a black, fat, shaggy, large, and barking poodle, then up a twenty-seven step entry into a room decorated with bright wallpaper and provided with . . . [*He looks around and makes an entry.*] . . . with eight windows [*He jumps up.*] . . ."

FRAU VON TIEFENBORN. Where are you taking us, Notary?

NOTARY [*returns and makes an entry.*] I was just counting the panes.

FRAU VON TIEFENBORN. Must you do that?

NOTARY. Yes, Your Ladyship. Just trust my manuscript. I'm a seasoned practitioner: There's not a single syllable too many here.[30]

What has changed in the nine years of regulated authorship between *Pietism in Petticoats* and *The Last Will* is the author's perspective. In *Pietism*, the object of satire is the rebellious female authorship that refuses male patronage; in *The Last Will*, it is the male desire to manipulate female authorship. Nonetheless, the fact remains that only male authority, represented here by the characters of Herr Scheinfromm and Notary Gänsekiel, can legitimate female texts, even over the author's objections. This process of legitimation, it is made clear, can far transcend its own editorial authority and mentorship role; it can even, as it does in *The Last Will*, supplant, subsume or obscure female authorship altogether. Either the credit for the work is given to the male editor by the female author, in the context of the now-infamous "discourse of modesty," or female authorship is simply subsumed under that of the man,[31] as apparently also happens in this text: "Just trust my manuscript," the notary advises Frau von Tiefenborn, who is, at this point, merely the nominal author of the text. Frau von Tiefenborn cannot even begin to speak (write) until the notary finally shuts up, and both are perfectly aware that her text is "invalid," null and void, without his signature and approval:

> FRAU VON TIEFENBORN. Stop! That's truly enough! Is there no end to
>   this business?

> NOTARY. Madam, he must go in here; otherwise your will is null and void![32]

The authors' protests are registered in both *The Last Will* and in *Pietism* (cf., for example, Frau Glaubeleicht's defiant repudiation of university study, from which women were excluded, as the sole legitimation for all engagement with theological concepts[33]), and in both plays, their objections remain unheeded. Both texts, in advocating and circumscribing such authorship, indirectly expose the conditions and inefficacy of a female authorship that exists exclusively in direct dependence on male editorship and mentorship. In this context, any aspiration to creativity, originality and self-sufficiency on the part of women authors is kept tightly in check. This is enforced on the inside by the discourse of the "guilt" of female authorship, first analyzed by Luise Gottsched and a nearly ubiquitous presence in the forewords of nineteenth-century women authors. From the outside it is enforced by the threat of non-publication — a destiny that could well be seen, for any author, male or female, of any age, as the most effective means of "voiding" and "invalidating" a text.

Notes

[1] The fact that most books that term themselves von Stein biographies are actually limited to accounts of her relationship with Goethe goes a long way toward explaining that phenomenon. Once defined as "Goethe's Friend" (Düntzer), von Stein herself appears in second place — "Goethe and Charlotte

von Stein" (Höfer; Hof; Martin; Petersen; Susmann) — or in parentheses, as an afterthought: "Goethe's Immortal Friend (Charlotte von Stein)" (Voß). Clearly, von Stein's biographers were less concerned with von Stein herself than with her diverse roles as Goethe's friend, Goethe's muse, one influenced by Goethe (Seillière), and competitor for Goethe's affections with Christiane Vulpius (Kahn-Wallerstein). The rare biographies that grant her the first and only place in the title — Bode's extensive *Charlotte von Stein* and Maurer's *Charlotte von Stein* (in which ubiquitous Goethe appears as a limiting factor in the subtitle *Ein Frauenleben der Goethezeit*) show the same emphasis on her relationship with Goethe. Cf. Kord, "Not in Goethe's Image," 54–5 and p. 69 n. 3.

[2] Reichel's two-volume biography of Johann Christoph Gottsched, spanning over 1700 pages, mentions Luise Gottsched on only a few pages and entirely ignores her literary oeuvre; in the 770–page GDR work on *Aufklärung*, Luise Gottsched is treated in one single paragraph and a few honorable mentions; in the monumental *Geschichte der deutschen Literatur*, edited by Rieck, Krohn, Reuter, and Otto, she is accorded less than a paragraph on 955 pages; Waniek records biographical detail on only a few pages of his monumental work on her husband.

[3] Cf. the discussion in Kord, *Namen* 36–51; on the status of erudite women during the early Enlightenment, cf. also Gössmann, *Eva, Gottes Meisterwerk* and *Das wohlgelahrte Frauenzimmer*.

[4] Cf. writings by Humboldt, Hegel, Kant, Fichte, Pockels, Campe and Knigge, among many others, and the discussion of some of these texts in Kord, *Namen* 36–44 and Cocalis. On women's self-perception as "erudite" or "scholarly women" in both centuries, cf. Kord, "Die Gelehrte." In a broader context, cf. also the seminal works by Hausen, Duden, Dotzler, and Frevert.

[5] The table and following interpretation are taken over from *Sich einen Namen machen* 53–4. I am, of course, aware that the statistical value of this table is limited due to the enormous discrepancy of the sample between centuries, but I would contend that the comparison at least serves to describe general tendencies in pseudonym use.

[6] = Ihre Kaiserliche Majestät, die Kaiserin aller Reussen (Her Imperial Majesty, Empress of all Russians).

[7] "Die Absicht, so die ersten Verfasser derselben hatten, war auch so neu, als unsträflich. Sie suchten dem deutschen Frauenzimmer ein Blatt in die Hände zu bringen, welches ihm zu einer angenehmen Zeitkürzung dienen, und doch von nützlicherm und lehrreicherm Inhalte seyn sollte, als die gewöhnlichen Romane. Diese Absicht zu erhalten, bedienten sie sich des unschuldigen Kunstgriffes, sich selbst für Frauenzimmer auszugeben; weil sie wohl vorhersahen, daß dieses Vorgeben, wenn es gleich nicht überall Glauben finden sollte, dennoch viel zu guter Aufnahme derselben beytragen würde." (Johann

Christoph Gottsched, "Vorrede," *Die Vernünftigen Tadlerinnen. Der erste Theil*, no pagination)

Johann Christoph Gottsched's remarks in this context are somewhat disingenuous, to the extent that he admits neither to his principal editorship of the journal nor to the fact that the decision to publish the journal under the pseudonyms Phyllis, Calliste and Iris was his, rather than the authors' of whom he commissioned separate pieces of the journal (a list that included his wife). As we shall see, this implicit disavowal of authorship is a trope that later occurs in the writings of Luise Gottsched as well.

[8] "Es kann also derselbe [the term "Gelehrsamkeit," S. K.] in der Tonkunst, Malerey, Tanzkunst, Dichtkunst, Fechtkunst, in den Anfangsgründen der Rechenkunst, in den Sprachen (die gelehrten ausgenommen,) nicht gebraucht werden." ("Die Rolle der Frau" 249) By "scholarly languages," which she here implicitly defines as inappropriate for women, Gottsched indicates ancient languages, i.e., Latin, Greek, and Hebrew. Latin and Greek continued to be used for scholarly works and correspondence throughout the eighteenth century; Gottsched herself had learned both — an "exception" she justified with her role as a scholar's wife who frequently answered correspondence with other scholars in her husband's name to free him for other projects.

[9] "Das Einmaleins können sie auch noch wohl; zuweilen gar addiren. Sie schreiben nach einem Linienblatte in vier oder drey Stunden, eine ordentliche und orthographische Seite: Das letztere sag ich meinem Geschlechte zu Liebe nach; ich mag aber durchaus nicht dafür gut seyn. Nun kömmt das beste: Sie machen Verse! Aber was für welche? Sind sie rein? Sind sie regelmäßig? Sind sie voller edlen, erhabenen, tugendhaften, und vernünftigen Ausdrückungen? Was sind es für Gattungen? Sind es Heldengedichte? Sind es dogmatische Gedichte? Sind es edle, neue und sinnreiche Erfindungen? Ich mag diese Fragen nicht beantworten. Man frage die im Drucke vorhandenen Werke meiner Mitschwestern selbst darum. Ich wünsche aber, daß niemand die grossen Mängel im äusserlichen, und die gemeinen, schwülstigen, nichtssagenden, frechen, pöbelhaften, groben und unzüchtigen Stellen, des innerlichen Wesens ihrer Gedichte, gewahr werden möge, worüber ich schon oftmals in meinem Herzen geseufzet." ("Die Rolle der Frau" 250–1)

[10] "Wie viel fehlt nicht noch daran, ehe wir eine einzige Deshoulieres in der Poesie, eine einzige de Sevigné in Briefen, eine einzige Gomez in der Beredsamkeit, und eine einzige Barbier in Trauerspielen aufzuweisen haben." ("Die Rolle der Frau" 251) Poet Antoinette du Ligier de la Garde Deshoulières (1637–94), epistolary author Marie de Rabutin-Chantal, Marquise de Sévigné (1626–96), playwright and prose author Madeleine-Angélique Poisson, Dame Gabriel de Gomez (1684–1770) and playwright Marie-Anne Barbier (1670–1745) were all women that Gottsched had read and admired from very early on. She translated Gomez' *Triomphe de l'Éloquence* as "Triumph der

Beredsamkeit" (1735) and Barbier's tragedy *Cornélie, mère des Gracques* (1703) as *Cornelia, Mutter der Gracchen* (1741).

[11] "Daß diese meine Anforderung billig sey, wird man leicht erachten können, wenn man auf die Pflichten sieht, welche uns sowohl in geistlichen als weltlichen Gesetzen auferlegt sind. Diese sind aber der Gehorsam gegen die Männer, die Besorgung des Hauswesens, und die Erziehung der Kinder." ("Die Rolle der Frau" 252)

[12] *Pietism* 1: "Man hatte sich einmal Dero Manuscript bemächtiget, und es war mir nicht möglich, dasselbe wiederum in meine Hand zu bekommen." (*Die Lustspiele* I, 444)

[13] *Pietism* 2: "daß ich alles gethan habe, was nur in meinen Kräften gestanden, den Abdruck dieser Schrifft zu verhindern." (*Die Lustspiele* I, 444)

[14] *Pietism* 3: "eine Schrifft, die bloß zu meiner eigenen Vergnügung, und höchstens zur Lust einiger vertrauten Freunde bey müßigen Stunden aufgesetzet worden . . . ." (*Die Lustspiele* I, 446)

[15] *Pietism* 3: "was wird die Welt von mir gedencken?" (*Die Lustspiele* I, 447)

[16] *Pietism* 3: "haben Sie nicht bedacht, an was vor einem Ort ich lebe? und wie leicht man auf die Muthmassung fallen wird, daß ich der Urheber dieser Schrifft nothwendig seyn müsse? Gleichwohl, wenn ich die Wahrheit gestehen soll; so bin ich nicht einmal dafür anzusehen. Ein gewisser ungenannter Frantzose hat mehr Theil daran, als ich. Und ich bin eher vor einen unschuldigen Uebersetzer, als für den Urheber dieses Lust-Spiels anzusehen. Ich sehe mich genöthiget Ihnen dieses zu bekennen: weil ich gemercket, daß Sie mir dieselbe einzig und allein zuschreiben, welche Ehre mir doch gar nicht gebühret." (*Die Lustspiele* I, 447)

[17] *Pietism* 4: "Uebrigens werden Sie meinen Namen auf das sorgfältigste zu verschweigen, und in der Vorrede die Welt zu überzeugen wissen, daß ich an dem Drucke dieser Schrifft keinen Theil gehabt, auch meinen Beyfall darzu nicht gegeben habe." (*Die Lustspiele* I, 449)

[18] Cf. Bougeant's foreword; also Vulliod's line-by-line comparison between Bougeant's original and Gottsched's adaptation and the discussion in Kord, "Innocent Translator" and *Namen* 105–8.

[19] *Die Pietisterey* has in various contexts been read as a "translation," as an "adaptation," or even, based on her "original" fourth act, as an "original"; cf. Waters, Kaiser, Martens, "Nachwort," and Vulliod. In my opinion, Gottsched's self-presentation, or rather, her presentation of her fictitious male author as the mere translator of the play is disingenuous: she made substantial changes to the play, cut some characters and scenes and invented others, and rewrote the entire fourth act. In the modern sense, then, I would prefer to designate Gottsched's play as an "adaptation" rather than a "translation." The question is, of course, further complicated by the very different attitudes

toward translation and what modern readers would consider "originality" throughout the eighteenth century (cf. chapter 2).

[20] One example is Victoria von Rupp's *Jenny, oder die Uneigennützigkeit*, published anonymously, but as an original drama, in 1777 and later degraded to the status of translation: Rupp's subsequent play *Marianne, oder der Sieg der Tugend* appeared later the same year "by the Translator of Miss Jenny." Rupp does follow tradition in mentioning her first play in her pseudonym: "by the author of [a previously successful publication]" is possibly one of the most popular pseudonyms of women writers throughout the eighteenth century. More interesting here is Rupp's transformation of her first play *Jenny* into a translation: its frontispiece gives no indication that it is not an original, and a search reveals no original on which it could be based. The same is true for a host of other women's plays, published with vague references such as "adapted from the English" or "after Destouches," for which searches have usually revealed no originals to match these "translations." Cf. Kord, "The Innocent Translator" and *Ein Blick* 17–8.

[21] The following two sections are expanded from an earlier outline of the same argument, which appeared in German in my essay "Frühe dramatische Entwürfe."

[22] *Pietism* 17 and 16 respectively. The quotations are taken from Herr Wackermann's admonition to the three Pietistic women to stick with "Nehen, strikken, sticken": . . . "Sie täten viel besser, wenn Sies wie andere Frauens machten, die Sie kennen; welche, ohngeachtet sie sehr klug sind, sich dennoch eine Ehre daraus machen, von den Religions-Streitigkeiten nichts zu wissen." (*Die Lustspiele* I, 471–2) Kerth's and Russell's translation de-emphasizes the aspect of *knowledge*, which is in the original portrayed as forbidden fruit for women — a modification of the text in translation that I think is highly problematic, but occurs frequently throughout their translation.

[23] All quotations in *Pietism* 42; originals in *Die Lustspiele* I, 517–8.

[24] *Pietism* 47; original in *Die Lustspiele* I, 527–8: "sehr schön und deutlich erklärt"; "hoch"; and "sehr schön gesagt."

[25] *Pietism* 48; *Die Lustspiele* I, 529: "Glaubens-Artickel."

[26] *Pietism* 42; "Sammlung auserlesener Streitigkeiten über die schwersten Religions-Artickel, den Doctoren der heiligen Schrifft, und den Theologischen Facultäten zum Nutzen und Unterricht heraus gegeben, von denen Frauen: Glaubeleichtin, Seufftzerin und Zanckenheimin." (*Die Lustspiele* I, 518) The untranslated adage "von denen Frauen," of course, serves to underscore the female authorship of the document — and I think, deliberately so.

[27] *Pietism* 42 and 44 respectively. "Wir wollen uns also drüber machen, und diesen Herren zeigen, daß wir klüger sind, als sie." (*Die Lustspiele* I, 518) Frau Seufftzerin's gleeful "damit wird man allen Theologis das Maul stopffen können" (522) is intended to be indicative of her vulgarity and also, in direct con-

trast to her theological ambitions, as a sign of her lack of piety, an aspect that is entirely lost in the translation.

[28] *Pietism* 48: "Wie? . . . Ich bin Ihr Diener: Damit habe ich nichts zu thun." (*Die Lustspiele* I, 529)

[29] This scene has been brilliantly analyzed by Arnd Bohm in "Authority and Authorship"; my argument in this chapter owes much to his analysis.

[30] *The Last Will*, in *Pietism* 274–5.

"NOTARIUS, *schreibt ein, und liest weiter.* Frau Oberstinn Veronica Eustasia, von Tiefenborn, Erb- Lehn- u. Gerichtsfrau auf Goldenfluß, Rententhal, Reichenhof, Schatzleben und Frohenlohe, ein Bedienter, mit Namen Matthäus Nicolaus Pulverhorn, seiner Profession ein Jäger, schwärzlichen finstern Angesichts, stumpfer rother Nase, von großen Lippen, borstigen schwarzen Haaren, seines Alters im 37. Jahr, in grüner Jägertracht, mit alten goldnen Tressen, gelben Knöpfen, ziemlich abgetragenen ledernen Beinkleidern - - - (*Sie fangen alle an zu lachen.*)

FRAU VON TIEFENBORN. Muß denn alle der Plunder in meinem Testamente stehen?

NOTARIUS. Ja gnädige Frau.

FRAU VON TIEFENBORN. Was ist der Welt daran gelegen, ob meines Jägers Beinkleider alt oder neu sind?

NOTARIUS. Ja gnädige Frau; sonst ist das ganze Testament unrichtig. Geduld werde ich mir von Ihnen allerseits ausbitten: denn es kommen noch viel mehrere solche Sachen vor.

FRAU VON TIEFENBORN. Nun, was seyn muß, das sey! Lese er weiter!

NOTARIUS, *liest weiter.* Abgetragenen ledernen Beinkleidern, stotternder Sprache, stinkenden Athems, - - - (*Sie halten sich alle die Tücher vor.*) bey mir gewesen, und mir berichtet; demnach hochbemeldete Frau Oberstinn Veronica Eustasia von Tiefenborn entschlossen sey, ihr Testament und letzten Willen gerichtlich aufzurichten, und solches in Dero eigener Behausung außergerichtlich geschehen solle, ich mich heute, den 15. Junii des 1750. Jahres, mit einem bereits fertigen Instrumente zu denenselben verfügen möchte. Alldieweilen nun solches Begehren meiner Profession und Notariatsautorität gemäß ist, habe ich Remigius Leodegarius Gänsekiel, Notarius Publicus, mich den heutigen 15. Junii 1750 gegen Abend um halb sieben Uhr, zu hochgemeldeter Hoch- und Wohlgebohrnen Frauen, Veronica Eustasia von Tiefenborn, nach Dero ordentlicher Behausung auf dem Rittergute Rententhal, in das daselbst mit einer Seite nach Osten, mit der andern nach Westen, mit der dritten nach Süden, und mit der vierten nach Norden gelegene Herrschaftliche Haus, so von außen weiß und blau abgeputzt ist, und eine große steinerne Vortreppe hat, worauf ein schwarzer, dicker, zottiger, großer, mich anbellender Pudel gelegen, eine 27. Stuffen hohe Stiege hinan, in ein mit bunten Tapeten ausgeziertes, und mit - - - (*er sieht sich rund um und schreibt ein*) 8 Fenstern versehenes - - - *er springt auf* - - -

FRAU VON TIEFENBORN. Wo will er hin, Herr Notarius?
NOTARIUS, *kömmt wieder und schreibt ein.* Ich habe nur die Glastafeln gezählet.
FRAU VON TIEFENBORN. Muß das auch seyn?
NOTARIUS. Ja gnädige Frau. Trauen Sie meinem Aufsatze nur. Ich bin ein alter
    Practicus, hier ist keine Sylbe zuviel." (*Die Lustspiele* I, 382–4)

Why the translators changed the year named in the text from 1750 in the
original to 1745 in the translation is unclear to me.

[31] Both were historically frequently the case — the most famous cases being
Wieland's editorship of Sophie von La Roche's *Die Geschichte des Fräuleins
von Sternheim*, of which he was held to be the author, Dorothea Schlegel's
novel *Florentin*, which was likewise edited by and attributed to her husband,
and Marianne von Willemer's poems in Goethe's *West-östlicher Diwan*, which
appeared without attribution to her and hence under Goethe's name.

[32] *Pietism* 277.

"FRAU VON TIEFENBORN. Ach! es ist schon genug! das Ding hat ja kein Ende!
NOTARIUS. Gnädige Frau, er muß herein; sonst ist Ihr Testament null und
    nichtig!" (*Die Lustspiele* I, 386)

[33] "HERR WACKERMANN. . . . But you know nothing of theology.
FRAU GLAUBELEICHT. And why not? Perhaps because I didn't study in Rostock?
    Does the pastor's black vest and coat grant this learning? Must one be so very
    learned to know the mysteries and basic precepts of Religion?" (*Pietism* 17)

"HERR WACKERMANN. . . . Aber von der Theologie wissen Sie nichts.
FRAU GLAUBELEICHTIN. Und warum nicht? Vielleicht weil ich nicht in Rostock
    studiret habe? Giebt dann der schwarze Priester-Rock und Mantel diese
    Gelehrsamkeit? Muß man denn so gar gelehrt seyn, um die Geheimnisse
    und Grund-Sätze der Religion zu wissen?" (*Die Lustspiele* I, 471)

In this scene, Gottsched takes up one of the most controversial issues of her
day with regard to women's involvement in theology, namely that Pietism
was indeed one of the rare religious movements that granted women a voice
as mystics and visionaries, without insisting on traditional theological study as
a justification for their involvement (cf. Critchfield).

7: Between Friendship and Love: Letters to Dorothea Henriette von Runckel

"My heart is disposed toward friendship more than toward any other emotion."

— Luise Gottsched, *Briefe*

LUISE GOTTSCHED'S LETTERS to Dorothea Henriette von Runckel, written during the last ten years of Gottsched's life, constitute perhaps the most remarkable corpus of texts credited to her authorship, for two reasons. First, as I hope to have shown earlier, they can, strictly speaking, be considered neither texts authored by Luise Gottsched nor an "accurate" depiction of the author's life in the historical sense. They can, however, be read as attempts to depict Luise Gottsched's emotional state towards the end of her life and certainly as inspired by events in her life. In the creation of that document, Dorothea Henriette von Runckel played a tripartite role, as addressee of the emotional expressions, as the object of the affection expressed and described in the letters, and ultimately as the person who prepared the letters for publication. As I have already stated, we cannot, in this case, infer an unproblematic "editorship" in the usual sense of the word (which would imply an objectivity towards the text that Runckel could not possibly have mustered, and that she demonstrably did not practice). For that reason, it is worth reminding ourselves that these are not "letters" describing a "life"; they were not "authored" by Luise Gottsched and then "edited" — in the modern sense — by Runckel. But neither do I choose to read them as a contaminated edition, a move that would still presuppose a modern editorship role. My reading of these letters assumes that they attempt to depict an emotional condition and that this depiction is co-habited by both the original and the secondary author, that it was to some degree "co-authored" by both people involved in the creation and perpetuation of that condition. "Co-authorship" is here understood in the eighteenth-century sense, by which the "author" furnished nothing but a rough template and all further authority over the text was assumed by its "editor."

The second reason why these letters are highly remarkable is that they attempt to define two terms central to late-eighteenth-century discourse, namely friendship and love. As such, I would argue, following Magdalene Heuser's lead,[1] that they participate in the creation of a new literary culture, a culture exemplified by names such as Klopstock, LaRoche, Richardson and Young, a culture valuing the expression and analysis of feelings and experimentation with literary forms over the adherence to poetic rules and precursors that Johann Christoph Gottsched advocated. Like Heuser, I see this participation as a crucial step in Gottsched's writing, one that can be interpreted both as a rebellion against her husband's regulation of her own authorship and as an implicit protest against his dominance of the literary scene.[2] During the time in which these letters were written, that predominance increasingly came under attack, and while Gottsched privately lamented the vituperative criticism to which her husband was exposed, she remarked on the emergence of the new literary culture and assessed her own writing — and with it she may well have implied her husband's — as "outmoded" and unable to follow where the new authors were leading.[3] But through the same letters in which she bemoaned her inability to participate in the new literary movement, she did just that: both the new direction in literature and the reconceptualization of friendship, a development that culminated in the mid- to late eighteenth-century "Cult of Friendship," were intimately connected with the epistolary genre. As Steinhausen has expressed it, the eighteenth century was the Golden Age of Friendship *because* it was the Golden Age of letter-writing.[4] The new aesthetic demanded a "natural" style of personal letters while the public devoured epistolary novels. When viewed as documents of a significance beyond the personal, Gottsched's late letters, unlike her early letters and dramatic works, cannot be read as literature of the early Enlightenment: her letters to Runckel are situated in a different context. The initial composition of Gottsched's letters to Runckel followed on the heels of Gellert's 1751 treatise *Praktische Abhandlung von dem guten Geschmacke in Briefen.* Equally significantly, the appearance of Runckel's edition of Gottsched's letters in 1771/72 coincides with several other seminal publications: the first German translation of Samuel Richardson's wildly successful epistolary novel *Pamela* (orig. 1740, first appeared in Germany in F. Schmit's translation *Pamela oder die belohnte Tugend eines Frauenzimmers,* 1771), the first publication of Sophie von LaRoche's epistolary novel *Die Geschichte des Fräuleins von Sternheim* (The History of Lady Sophia Sternheim, 1771), and, on the heels of this bestseller, Goethe's *Die Leiden des jungen Werthers* (The Sorrows of Young Werther, 1774).

Along with numerous stylistic facets in the letters themselves, it is these concomitant developments that should lead us to suspect that Gottsched, and certainly Runckel, were well aware that they were participating in a literary tradition, and it is one of the most consistent paradoxes of female authorship that this participation hinged upon the very fact that these were, at least nominally, *personal* letters, that is, documents not intended for publication. Toward the end of her life, Gottsched increasingly took her own advice as expressed in the foreword to her first play: she privatized her authorship. The claim that Gottsched had made of her first drama, namely that it was written "simply for my own amusement" and for the edification of a friend, that nothing could have been further from her mind than actual publication (*Pietism* 3) certainly seems more credible when applied to her letters. One could well speculate that Gottsched gained a space for literary experimentation because she did *not*, or not initially, write for publication, because she moved into the "private" realm — the only realm in which literary experimentation on the part of women was condoned.[5]

Chercher la Femme: Lesbianism, Friendship, and the Sentimental Discourse

Most of the final two volumes of Luise Gottsched's letters, edited by Dorothea Henriette von Runckel, is devoted to a portrait of their friendship and love for one another. As such, they document a phenomenon that, according to contemporary discourse on friendship and love, could not exist: much of that discourse affirms that women are incapable of either friendship (with either men or women) or love (for another woman).[6] Particularly the latter fact has led to a noticeable difference in the acknowledgment and punishment of male and female homosexual activity throughout the century: because "lesbianism," in the minds of contemporaries, existed neither legally nor conceptually, lesbianism was largely ignored at a time when male homosexual activity was harshly punished. While later scholarship has made much of the sensationalistic case of Catharina Linck, whose execution in 1721 makes her the sole eighteenth-century lesbian we know of who was punished by death,[7] there is good reason to assume that Linck, like many other women before her, was executed not so much for her lesbianism as for male impersonation. Linck used several different male names, dressed as a man, served in the military, married another woman, and had sex with her using an artificial penis. All other executed lesbians that we know of

were also accused of male impersonation or of using an artificial phallus
during intercourse; in each case, the court ruling placed special emphasis on this fact as a rationale for the death sentence.[8] There is no single
death penalty case in which it is clear that the woman in question was
executed purely and exclusively for her lesbianism, and good evidence
to suggest that mere lesbianism was considered a lesser offense: Linck's
wife, Catharina Mühlhahn, who had by her own admission voluntarily
engaged in sex with Linck after she discovered the true gender of her
spouse, got away with three years in jail.[9] The nonexistence of lesbianism as a crime in legislation (and the complete absence of same-sex love
among women in literary and philosophical discourse) is not an over-
sight but a *conceptualization,* or rather, an inability to conceptualize:
women, lacking a penis, were simply deemed incapable of "love"
among each other.

"Friendship," the other term that could possibly be used to describe
emotional attachments among women, was generally viewed as an emotion confined exclusively to men. Carl Friedrich Pockels, author of the
monumental *Versuch einer Charakteristik des weiblichen Geschlechts*
(Attempt at Characterizing the Female Sex, 5 vols., 1797–1802), claims
authoritatively that women, constantly vying and competing for the love
of men, are thereby prevented from forming lasting friendships with either
men or women (I, 349–51; II, 176–88). Adolph Freiherr von Knigge,
whose work *Über den Umgang mit Menschen* (Human Interaction, 1796)
became a standard for well over a century, characterizes love by its ex-
ceeding irrationality and the inequality of partners (always a male-
female couple) and friendship by the equality and emotional distance
between partners (always male).[10] Knigge's work stands at the beginning of a long tradition that differentiates strictly between friendship
and love by virtue of a mandatory gender distribution (friendship as
existing solely between men, love solely between a male-female couple)
and by virtue of the kind and intensity of emotion attributed to each
attachment. "Friendship" in this discourse was desexualized and juxtaposed to its "irrational" cousin love, a move that freed later scholars to
interpret the late-eighteenth-century "cult of friendship" among men
as simultaneously inspired by the Socratic tradition *and* freed from any
aspersion of homosexuality (and thus within the bounds of nineteenth-
and twentieth-century propriety). What made it possible to publish the
most ardent love letters of the age under innocuous titles like *Letters
Between Friends* (Schenck) is what is now commonly termed the "sentimental discourse": the assumption is that even where men and women
openly declare their love, they do not mean it unless they are writing to

a member of the opposite sex. It is, of course, impossible to "prove" sexual activity between these authors, and that is not the purpose here. The purpose is to point to a discrepancy in scholarly thinking on the issue. Where women (or men) declare their love to members of the same sex, all suspicion of possible sexual activity or desire is immediately brushed aside with reference to the sentimental discourse of the age, while similar avowals in letters among heterosexuals have led to centuries of "scholarly" speculation as to whether or not the two were actual lovers (witness the case of Goethe and Charlotte von Stein).[11]

The eighteenth-century conceptualization of friendship and love is of obvious relevance here, particularly since I see the letters co-authored by Gottsched and Runckel as documents spanning an era during which this conceptualization changed considerably. In the course of the Enlightenment, with its emphasis on virtue and reason, "love" was disavowed because of its connotations with "irrational" passion, while "friendship" was raised to the status of an ideal mode of human interaction and advocated as the best reason for marriage in the moral weeklies (Martens, *Botschaft*). For women, the new valorization of friendship as superior to love permitted emotional, even passionate interaction with other women under the rubric of "friendship." Relationships that frequently fluctuated between *agape* and *eros* appear to have been tolerated as an emotional outlet in an age when marriage had nothing to do with love and divorce was impossible. Toward the end of the century, however, the love match began to supplant the enlightened "reasonable" marriage (Friedli 235–6), which ultimately came to mean that all female emotion was now supposed to be centered around men. With the return of love to the marriage, same-sex attachments among women were increasingly denounced, a tendency that culminated in the criminalization and medicalization of lesbianism as a "disease" in the nineteenth century (Tubach 4, Hacker 33–92). Concomitant with these developments was the increasing emphasis on women's domestic role and their "natural vocation" as housewives and mothers at the turn of the nineteenth century.[12]

Given my own reservations about the authenticity of Gottsched's letters and their ability to "describe a life," the purpose of my discussion here is not to take these letters as evidence that she and Runckel were "lovers" in the twentieth-century sense of the word, although I think this question is far from beside the point. I do wish to emphasize here that scholarship that insists on the *impossibility* of any passionate attachment among women and that reads all utterances that seem to transcend the bounds of "friendship" as mere "sentimental discourse" is engaging in a serious underreading of these letters. Gottsched's and Runckel's letters attempt to define both "friendship" and "love" at a time when women were deemed incapable of either and at the same time that the male "Cult of Friendship" was coming into vogue.[13] As such, they must be read not only as documentation of a personal attachment, but also as both contribution and antithesis to one of the most pivotal discussions of their age.

"Inseparable and Eternal": Friends and Lovers

Gottsched first met Runckel in the summer of 1752, on one of the many journeys that Gottsched undertook to repair her failing health. Her ensuing correspondence with Runckel differs from her earlier letters to her husband in two respects: they display an openness uncharacteristic of Gottsched and an emotionality unprecedented in her earlier letters. Her very first letter to Runckel, written the day after they separated, reads like a Lover's Lament written during the Age of Sentimentality, complete with an inserted poem:

> Why did I have to meet you for such a short time? Why did I have to discover in you everything I have sought so ardently, but never found united in one person? Why did you have to grant me your friendship immediately? A fortune that I wished for the moment I met you, but did not dare to hope for.
>
> > My tranquil happiness, the bliss of a few hours,
> > Has vanished, tracelessly, has vanished like a dream,
> > Vanished like the rapture felt on a summer night.
>
> . . . You are right, nothing is more enchanting than the friendship of two upright souls. Let ours be inseparable and eternal. Permit me to write to you often and often to share with you my sorrows, of which you are the innocent cause. I will look forward to all your letters with joyous impatience, and will receive them with pleasure as a small atonement for your absence . . . . I am yours with tenderness and reverence . . . .[14]

This first letter to Runckel is characteristic of the entire correspondence: while Gottsched defines their attachment as a "friendship," she uses the vocabulary of love. In the ensuing correspondence, Gottsched sent Runckel love poems (*Briefe* II, 45, 238; III, 53–4), her picture (an emotionally "loaded" gift that she had earlier refused Johann Christoph Gottsched; I, 15 vs. II, 236–7), her "tender embrace" (II, 58), and "one thousand kisses" (II, 108 and 173); she spoke of "unspeakable tenderness" (II, 91), "love eternal" (II, 94; III, 133) and "tenderness that cannot be matched" (II, 131); she at times employed a playful and teasing tone also unknown from her earlier letters (II, 109 and 121–2). She exhibited clear signs of jealousy with regard to other women and, conversely, assured Runckel that their relationship had nothing to fear from Gottsched's contact with other women (II, 252; men were not considered adequate competition). She railed at the fate and the husbands that kept them separated (II, 63 and 117) and fantasized about a life without them that would free Gottsched and Runckel to live together (II, 63); she counted the miles that separated them (II, 123, 135–6, 236–7, 302); she swore she only lived for Runckel (II, 157; III, 37 and 145) and fantasized about dying with her (II, 276–7; III, 138). Gottsched, who in her earlier letters took great care to present herself, and who was in fact seen by many of her contemporaries as the model of wifely virtue, went so far as to call housework a miserable occupation for a thinking being (II, 151), to wish podagra on her husband (II, 152–3), to refer to him as a perjurer for falsely promising to let her visit Runckel (II, 305), and to claim that she would rather travel the thirteen miles that separated her from Runckel than go on a nine-mile trip with her husband (III, 18). What makes this sudden emotionality on Gottsched's part even more remarkable is that Johann Christoph Gottsched, despite the Enlightenment rhetoric of "reason," had clearly expected such passion from his fiancée and been refused. During the years of their courtship, Gottsched frequently had to defend herself against Johann Christoph's accusations of "coldness" (cf. chapter 3).

"Friendship" and "love" become constant themes in Gottsched's correspondence with Runckel. Her attempts to arrive at a clearer understanding of each attachment are born partly out of the dichotomy between the intensity of her feelings and her awareness of these same attachments as subjects of contemporary philosophical and literary discourse. In one letter to Runckel, she attempts an analysis of friendship, emulating the style of contemporary sentimental epistolary writing:

> . . . I cannot believe that any tender pain could transcend mine over your loss. In this way, my sorrow is based on your merit, whereas your friendship for me is nothing but generosity. You assure me that you were not indifferent to me before you even knew me. You have, in other words, blessed me with your friendship even before you knew of the loyal admiration which awoke in me the first hour that I had the happiness of knowing you. Hence my conclusion:

A friendship which is based on knowledge of true merit takes deeper root than one that is based on purely undeserved generosity. Whereas my friendship for Frau von R[unckel] is based on her merit.

Atqui, ergo, say the logicians . . . . Oh! why did not a single one of all my attempts to meet you succeed? Why did the entire French nation have to be in danger of becoming foolish with joy before I found out that the person that I had sought in Saxony for 15 years and that I was despairing to find was living a few streets away from me? My heart is disposed toward friendship more than toward any other emotion.[15]

Gottsched's "analysis" of friendship incorporates the style of philosophical argument and certainly alludes in more than one way to the contemporary masculine "Cult of Friendship," but she also recognizably alludes to the context beyond friendship: unless one reads this letter as part of a "sentimental discourse," the lover's quarrel she engages in with Runckel as to who loves the other person more seems inappropriate to the sober context of "friendship" to which she returns at the end of her letter. To read her final outburst as a heartfelt, if slightly more stylish "Where have you been all my life?" would not be an exaggeration: it is precisely this kind of emotional, almost juvenile, intensity that collapses the sober analysis of the thirty-nine-year-old woman philosopher.

Throughout her correspondence with Runckel, Gottsched repeatedly invokes love and draws comparisons between a love relationship and their own (II, 217; III, 45 and 116). At least once, she seems to have transcended the discourse of "friendship," no matter how "sentimental," and crossed over into forbidden territory. In the following letter, she apologizes for this transgression:

Never have I waited as long for news from you as this time. I imagined one hundred reasons for your silence, I built the most beautiful castles in the air, I hoped you would unexpectedly appear at our fair, but nothing of all this happened. Finally, I remembered that I had declared myself to be your lover, and your silence indicated to me that this role did not meet with your approval. To me, this conclusion seemed demonstrably certain, and since I was utterly unable to bear this condition, I sat down and wrote the following letter [the inserted letter is originally in French, S. K.]:

Madame,
Your friend, who lives only for your letters, is slowly killed by your silence, to which you subject her as if she were your lover. If it is thus that you treat those who adore you, I had rather not adore you and take up my former character again. Return to me your tenderness, Madame, return to your fervor in sharing with me news of you and be

assured that I will never aspire to another title but that of your friend. It is with the most pure and faithful sentiments of friendship that I will remain, all my life long, your devoted G.

Perhaps your husband's curse is on my audacious proposal. If this is the case, he shall in the future be content with me. I do not desire to charge myself with his sighs. I will, in the future, seek all my happiness in preserving, until death, all emotions of a pure and constant friendship towards his and my friend.[16]

This letter is highly revealing in several ways: whereas most of Gottsched's letters fuse both emotions by collapsing the nominal invocation of friendship with the vocabulary of love, this letter makes a clear distinction between the two and expresses a desire that could be neither explained nor fulfilled in the context of mere friendship. It also expresses an awareness that this desire would amount to a transgression of the most severe kind, in that Gottsched as "lover" would trespass on the rights of Runckel's husband. Gottsched thus retracts her "adoration" in favor of a "pure" friendship (an adjective that is certainly laden with meaning in this context), underscoring the formality of this arrangement by virtue of the fact that she uses French, still the language of official rather than personal letter-writing, to initiate the truce. Conversely and importantly, she does nothing to camouflage or deny her actual feelings, despite the fact that she felt punished and rejected because they were perceived as inappropriate. On the contrary, she felt justified in asking her friend for the same "tenderness" and "fervor" that had previously characterized their exchange. In the final analysis, Gottsched places herself beside Runckel's husband in the designation of Runckel as "his and my friend," adeptly using the contemporary discourse of "friendship in marriage," thus turning her rejection into a valorization and putting her relationship with Runckel on an equal footing with Runckel's marriage.

This letter did not mark the only time that Gottsched attempted to transcend the bounds of friendship with Runckel: the letter in which she proposed this illicit affair to Runckel, in which she styled herself her "lover" and for which she apologizes here, is not surprisingly omitted from the collection. We know that the letters were censored by Runckel, clearly for reasons of propriety: Runckel's goal in publishing the letters was to establish Gottsched, post-mortem, as the Enlightenment paragon of feminine virtue. In light of this knowledge, we must suspect editorial intervention from Runckel at other junctures at which Gottsched transgressed in terms of propriety, specifically, that Runckel may have deleted other letters that were obvious love letters and difficult to reconcile with the image Runckel wished to convey of their author. That Gottsched's letter of apology was not censored or at least edited to omit her impropriety is somewhat surprising if read as a personal document. If, on the other hand, one reads this letter as an example of Gottsched's and Runckel's attempt at participation in a new discourse, a discourse that was largely literary although it took its cue from private life, its inclusion makes sense because it establishes why, even in future letters written under the heading of "pure friendship," the vocabulary of love could continue unabated:

> Yes, dearest friend, I have found in you . . . bliss . . . . In short, I only live for you, to love you and to give over my future life to every joy and every pain, every contentment and every murderous uneasiness, in short, to all emotions that accompany this divine passion.
>
> Farewell, my only friend; write me more frequently than I do, and longer letters than mine, because you have more leisure than I. Every word that comes from your pen is dear to me. I am so impatient at the beginning of all your letters that I hurry towards the end; and I again begin to read them because I am finished too soon. Laugh at me, but only love me. I live and die wholly your friend.[17]

Whether read biographically, as an expression of love for Runckel, or aesthetically, as "a literary embellishment of her own feelings" (Heuser, "Angedencken" 158), the most remarkable contrast in Gottsched's letters is that between her expressed desire for emotional intensity toward the end of her life and the "philosophical equanimity" dominating her early letters addressed to her then-fiancé Johann Christoph Gottsched. And whether read as "friendship" or "love," one of the most obvious contradictions that emerges from Gottsched's/Runckel's attempts to define the nature of their emotional attachment is the fact that while the feelings explored here were undoubtedly inspired by real-life experience in some fashion, there was no aesthetic, literary or philosophical context for them beyond the masculine Cult of Friendship. When Gottsched speaks of precursors or fictional analogues, she invokes Plato and Socrates[18] — not, for example, Sappho and Anactoria. In part, this paradox can be seen as a contributing factor to their perception of their attachment as unique and matchless that is so frequently expressed in the letters.

The Third Wheel: Rivals

The implicit jealousy Gottsched exhibited in her letter of apology to Runckel is not an isolated incident, but a recurring theme in the letters. It appears occasionally with regard to third persons who enter the correspondence as possible competitors for one friend's affection, but more generally with regard to the husbands, in particular Gottsched's. In some cases, the rivalry theme is discernible as a literary embellishment, but the fact that it is so prominent in the letters points, once again, to the fact that their "friendship," as described in their letters, was quite unlike the detached emotion that characterizes Pockels' term in that it demanded exclusivity. The rivalry depicted in these letters does not clear up the question of how much Gottsched's and Runckel's stylized epistolary love was rooted in biographical fact, but it does give us an indication as to what extent it can be regarded as literary embellishment (two possibilities that do not necessarily rule each other out).

One episode that demonstrates this aspect of the rivalry theme particularly clearly is the arrival of the Countess Charlotte Sophie von Bentinck in Leipzig, who immediately sought Gottsched's acquaintance and who is occasionally discussed in the correspondence during her stay in Leipzig from November 1753 until January 1756. Because Runckel perceived her presence in Leipzig as a threat to her own relationship with Gottsched, the episode becomes an indicator that both correspondents desired exclusivity, or at least predominance of affection, from the other. In its obvious reverberation of the principle of monogamy among lovers, this claim transcends those that could normally be made on a friendship. Gottsched attempted to reassure her friend as to her fidelity on November 22, 1754:

> You fear that the Countess B. will supplant you in my heart? No, my best friend, fear nothing. She has, up to this point, shared her heart only with princesses, and her rank places her in such a distance from me that nothing detrimental to our union could enter into this acquaintance.[19]

It appears that Runckel did indeed voice such fears consistently throughout the Countess's two-year-stay in Leipzig, and one of the most interesting letters documenting her jealousy is one written to Johann Christoph Gottsched on September 9, 1755. This letter is highly revealing, both in terms of the light it throws on the question of the extent to which Gottsched's and Runckel's union was open or secret and in terms of the roles Runckel assigns both to the Countess Bentinck and Johann Christoph Gottsched:

I discover, despite the pleasure I promised myself upon opening your most esteemed letter, that forthrightness does not always have the most beneficial effect. I had hoped to read assurances that I still possess, in the tender heart of your and my friend, that same place that this exceptional woman was pleased to grant me on the happiest day of my life, and if you had only seen fit to flatter me with this news, nothing would have been more pleasing to me than to be betrayed in such a desirable manner; but how disquieted I am now by truths that I wish I had never found out!

I see now that my fear of such a dangerous rival, which consumed my entire heart upon the arrival of the Countess in Leipzig, was not entirely unfounded. If she was cunning enough to flatter Apollo in order to win his dearest muse, and if she succeeded in this assault, how easy will it be to supplant a far-away friend from a heart which this dangerous countess wishes to possess entire . . . .

The one-act play which your erudite friend has authored to please the Countess, a play which, as you said, you and I would not have asked of her, is not yet proof that we have lost that place of which we are rightly proud . . . . You, Highly esteemed Sir, you my familiar rival, you and I would have been more modest in our wishes and not asked anything of our tender friend that could have caused her even the slightest effort . . . .

You see, my most highly esteemed Herr Professor, how I carefully seek out anything to suppress the painful thought that we should have to take second place to our enemy in the exceptional heart that we know. I beseech you by everything that is holy not to change your good resolution and to come to Dresden next winter with your exceptional wife.[20]

If one reads between the lines of this letter — which has come down to us unmediated and unedited in manuscript form — one gets a much clearer picture of what the real issues were in the correspondence between Runckel and the Gottscheds. Runckel uses essentially the same discourse as Gottsched. She views her role as Gottsched's friend to some extent as infringing on the rights of the husband, whom she regards as her "familiar rival"; like Gottsched, she equalizes and identifies her friendship with their marriage by referring to Gottsched as "your and my friend." The Countess Bentinck poses the same threat to both "friends" of Luise Gottsched. But the fact alone that Runckel could write such a letter to Gottsched's husband indicates clearly that the third wheel and the jealousy theme function as a literary embellishment; and while this fact does nothing to prove that these feelings were not rooted in real-life experience, it does indicate clearly that Runckel intended Johann

Christoph Gottsched to read these remarks aesthetically rather than biographically. It defines the union between Runckel and Gottsched as a publicly known affair, as a "literary" friendship. Gottsched corroborated this idea in her plans to publicize their friendship when, for example, she asked Runckel to write her a letter that she could copy for the benefit of the Countess von Zerbst in order to show her "that two friends, in their mutual affection, can enjoy everything that often, all too often, is lacking among the exalted of the earth."[21] I do not view this, in and of itself, as evidence that love and jealousy were not aspects of the friendship between Gottsched and Runckel as they experienced it in real life, but it also reveals the jealousy theme as a literary device, as a red herring in a letter essentially concerned with different issues.

In this letter, Runckel attempts, in the only indirect fashion available to her, to prevent Johann Christoph Gottsched from overworking his wife, whose complaints about overwork on her husband's "learned galleys" had become a steady theme in her letters to Runckel,[22] and to persuade Johann Christoph to take Gottsched to Dresden to visit Runckel. As a woman and as an outsider, it was clearly impossible for her to plead with him openly not to kill his wife with work or to hold him to his frequent promises to permit Gottsched a journey to Dresden. Her jealousy of the Countess essentially functions as a foil which permits her to lend urgency to her request for a visit; simultaneously, the Countess's demanding behavior towards Gottsched and the flattering contrast with her husband's supposed moderation in this regard function as diplomatic reminders of the excessive demands Johann Christoph himself made on his wife's time.

The third wheel in the relationship, as becomes apparent in this episode, was Johann Christoph Gottsched. Consistently referred to as Gottsched's "friend," in keeping with contemporary discourse, he plays an important role in the letters particularly with regard to the implicit philosophical discussion of friendship. Like the dominant discourse of her time, Gottsched viewed friendship as the highest form of human interaction; unlike that discourse, however, which limited friendship to men, Gottsched considered women more capable of lasting friendships than men, as she wrote to Johann Christoph as early as 1734 (I, 157). In her letters to Runckel, she goes on to claim that "men rarely know the exquisiteness of friendship"[23] and that "it would be bad if two souls who love each other as we do should learn the rules of friendship from that deceitful sex [men]."[24] The Enlightenment discourse, in which friendship was valued more highly than love, enabled Gottsched both to define her relationship with Runckel in terms that did not conflict with her role as Johann Christoph's wife and to give it a special validation that distinguished this relationship qualitatively from the one she shared with her husband.

In Gottsched's letters, Johann Christoph did not appear, as he did in Runckel's letter to him, as a "rival" for Runckel's affection, but as the factor that stood in their way, the man who heaped upon her an excessive workload that became the source of constant complaints and severe health problems ("My friend has found it good not to leave me idle for a single hour"[25]), and the man who repeatedly refused to permit Gottsched to see Runckel again. There are so many letters in which Gottsched complains about overwork in the service of her husband that this must be regarded *the* dominant theme of the entire correspondence (examples in *Briefe* II, 104–6, 111, 118, 211, 260, 301; III, 39, 123, 150). It is important to note that Gottsched does not record any satisfaction or joy in this work:[26] on the contrary, she interprets her work in her husband's service as forced labor, as work done in captivity. She frequently speaks of working on the "learned galleys" ("gelehrte Galeere," *Briefe* II, 104–6, 211), in her "Carthusian cell" ("Karthäuserzelle," II, 275; III, 38, 47, 57), or even "in chains" ("Kettentracht," II, 211), all images that eloquently circumscribe both the context of imprisonment and her immense loneliness. Very frequently, these depictions of her forced labor are accompanied by a fresh report on her failing health (II, 105, 118, III, 39, 55, 123, 150) or with statements that she longed for an early death (II, 112, 118, 237, 239, III, 11–12, 150). The journey to Dresden in the summer of 1752, during which Luise Gottsched first met Runckel, was occasioned by her first severe illness, and this was the first time that her husband — by his own admission ("Leben") — permitted her a brief respite. After 1760, Gottsched was constantly ill, but her workload did not lessen. Her bitter speculation that she would be "buried, pen in hand"[27] turned out to be prophetic: she continued to work, interspersed with time off for bloodlettings and fainting spells, until shortly before her death. Her final translation commissioned by her husband, produced at a time when she could no longer write herself, had to be dictated. In one of her final letters to Runckel, she attributes her illness and death in part to the immense workload to which she was subjected. "You ask for the cause of my illness? Here it is. Twenty-eight years of uninterrupted work, hidden grief and six years of countless tears . . . ."[28]

The other role Johann Christoph assumes in Gottsched's letters, and explicitly rather than implicitly, is that of the man between the two women: his frequently retracted promise to allow them to visit each other is a subject in both Runckel's letters to Johann Christoph and Luise Gottsched's letters to Runckel. Whereas Runckel's letters are filled with pleas and reminders (in fourteen letters, she reminds him of his promise eight times, cf. Heuser, "Sprache" 65, 66, 68, 69, 70, 73), Gottsched's letters to Runckel are filled with witty sarcasms, even remonstrances.

> You invited me to visit you in G.[29] on occasion of my journey to Dresden in such a friendly manner that I feel everything that a friendship drawn towards fulfillment of all of her friend's wishes can experience. In spirit, I have already felt your most fiery embrace, I have slept in your room, eaten at your table, forgotten myself and the food on my plate in one hundred joyous conversations with my most gracious host; in short, since receiving your last letter, I have already completely been with you. But it will remain a metaphysical delight, as a punishment for the fact that my friend is a professor of metaphysics. However, he is also professor of logic, and here are the reasons with which he answers my pleas:
> 1) Twenty-six miles is exactly twice as far away as thirteen.
> 2) My business does not permit me to be absent from Leipzig for longer than eight days, and since a journey to G. would necessitate fourteen days, ergo — — —
> All of this is true, dearest friend, and I have yet to cite you the main stipulation that silences all of my protests: *Thy will shall be subject to* — — —[30]

Where Gottsched's bitterness over this repeated disappointment voices itself in harsh criticism of her husband, her husband is referred to under a code-name:

> I will say it again, our Asmodi is a bad boy. Do not pay attention to anything he says; he still bears the old grudge over the superior friendship of women . . . . He has already retracted his promise to accompany me to Dresden this year under many pretexts. Observe, now, whether the Asmodis of the world keep their word.[31]

Whether Johann Christoph's circumscription as "Asmodi," a devil or evil demon,[32] originated with Gottsched or Runckel, it is yet another indication how strictly these letters adhered, at least in their published incarnation, to the image of feminine propriety that furnished the impetus for Runckel's publication of the letters: inconceivable that a model of wifely virtue could directly and openly criticize her husband. Similar circumscriptions and circumventions are employed in passages in which Gottsched indirectly mocks her husband for the discrepancy between his moral philosophy and his failure to practice what he preached (e. g., II, 166–7) or in her veiled allusions to his possible infidelity (e. g., II, 6).

It is worth reminding ourselves that it is quite apparent from the manner in which the early letters were edited by Runckel that her desire and intention was to present Johann Christoph Gottsched and his relationship with the author in the best light possible. No other motivation can be attributed to her modification of his improprieties and excesses in the early letters, or to the fact that Runckel occasionally inserts terms of endearment for her husband into Gottsched's letters where no such expressions of affection can be found in the originals still extant (cf. chapter 2). Around 1755–6, at the same time that these letters were originally written, Runckel entered into obligations to Johann Christoph Gottsched, who acted as mentor and mediator for her own first literary attempts (Heuser, "Sprache" 53). While these obligations ceased with his death in 1766, five years before the appearance of her edition of his wife's letters, it is still likely that she would have taken steps, in her edition of Gottsched's letters, to modify the author's increasingly obvious expressions of disappointment and bitterness towards her husband, if only in the interest of presenting Gottsched, as her foreword states, as model wife through her letters. Conversely, Runckel may have tolerated the occasionally critical image of the author's husband in her published version of the letters because her emphasis was on a portrayal of Gottsched's emotional state toward the end of her life, which was inseparable from her relationship with Johann Christoph, her constant state of illness and overwork, and her frequently expressed death wish. It is, of course, equally possible that Runckel made only a token attempt to disguise Gottsched's critical attitude towards her husband because she was, as the letters implicitly state, involved in a real rivalry with him, one that expressed itself not so much in the writing of these letters, but in their publication. Gottsched, who had repeatedly refused Johann Christoph permission to publish her letters (in 1734; cf. I, 101 and 127), granted this permission to Runckel, rejoicing that "the magic of friendship can thus transform miserable remains into relics."[33] Runckel not only edited and published Gottsched's letters, but also reprinted, in the same collection, Gottsched's favorite drama *Panthea*.[34] After twenty-eight years of producing literary works for her husband's projects, many of which were never credited to her, it was Runckel who was finally responsible for publishing the works that Gottsched *wanted* to write — her tragedy and her letters. In view of Gottsched's publication history, the fact that Runckel published these works under the author's name becomes highly significant — indeed, Runckel's edition of Gottsched's letters, published eleven years after the author's death, is Gottsched's *first* orthonymous publication. And it was this last act of friendship for Gottsched that inspired Runckel's own ensuing literary and editorial activity.[35] As Heuser has pointed out, Gottsched's letters to Runckel represent an emancipatory act directed at both her husband Johann Christoph and at Johann Christoph Gottsched, the literary "Pope" of her time: her refusal to let him publish her letters permitted her to develop her passionate epistolary style and thus to participate in the development of the new emotional and linguistic culture of the eighteenth century ("Das beständige Angedencken" 160–1). Simultaneously, she managed to preserve the integrity of her relationship with Runckel by conferring the editorship of her letters on her and thus permitting her letters to become "relics" of their friendship.

Questionable Methods: The Sentimental Discourse versus Biographical Speculation

Until 1998, that is, until Magdalene Heuser's assertion that Gottsched's letters as edited by Runckel constitute a severely contaminated edition, they should have been a highly sensationalistic, popular and also productive subject of scholarly research — for Enlightenment scholars, for Gottsched scholars, for researchers on early women writers, the Cult of Friendship, or homosexuality in the eighteenth century. Not only was this collection authored by the most famous and best-researched woman writer of the period, it also provides broad documentary evidence of a same-sex attachment that clearly formed the emotional center of the last ten years of her life: it includes ninety-five letters to Dorothea von Runckel, which makes their ten-year friendship the best-documented friendship among German women of the age. The passionate tone of the letters, the open declarations of love, the analyses of friendship versus love, the many snide remarks about Johann Christoph Gottsched and men in general make this correspondence fairly scandalous by both nineteenth- and early twentieth-century standards. Eighteenth-century scholars, as extensive research on the exact nature of the relationship between Charlotte von Stein and Goethe has shown, are usually hesitant neither to engage sensationalistic materials nor to voice speculations with regard to personal relationships based on fairly flimsy documentary evidence. Nonetheless, this extraordinary correspondence has attracted virtually *no* scholarly attention, with the exception of Heuser's articles on the subject.[36] Even scholarly scandal-mongers, instead of picking up on the obvious, have mined the letters exclusively for evidence to what extent Gottsched was aware of her husband's amorous escapades (Schlenther 29 and 62–3; Waniek 674; Reichel I, 725–6, Buchwald 436), and the first major scholar to produce a book-length study on the author, Paul Schlenther, stated listlessly that a reprint of her letters would not be worth the trouble because of their insignificance in literary terms (227).

In light of the sheer rarity of women's letters of the age, of the sensationalistic potential of these particular letters, and of the fact that they were authored by the most prominent woman writer of the century, this scholarly disinterest would be baffling, were it not for two blind spots. One concerns genre and amounts to the automatic classification of the letters as "personal" documents and hence ineligible for literary interpretation; the other, the common inability to imagine women as lovers. The automatic classification of women correspondents as mere "friends" results in the scholar's inability to interpret the distinctly passionate tone of the letters in terms other than those dictated by the sentimental discourse. The question as to whether Gottsched and Runckel were lesbian lovers in the modern sense is, to my mind, less to the point than an examination of Gottsched's and Runckel's attempt at participating in a new literary culture. Moreover, biographical questions are difficult to ask of letters which have been edited for content to this extent, and one could rightly argue that even to entertain such questions would be to engage in questionable scholarly practice. They are biographically unanswerable and, given their interest in pure biography and "old historicism," would clearly be considered methodologically primitive. In another sense, however, I think it is worth asking the biographical question, even the one that suspects a love relationship between the correspondents based on nothing but repeated allusions in their letters that this was the case, for two reasons. First and foremost, methodological sophistication aside, it must remain defensible to ask biographical questions when researching early women authors, about whose lives precious little is known. Suspicion towards "old historicism" as a method of literary investigation may be fully justified when the method is applied to famous male writers of the age, authors who have been the subject of sustained and extensive study for centuries; in the case of women, even famous women, *no* data is reliable unless it is based on a laborious and painstaking evaluation of archival sources. Luise Gottsched, an author whose life appeared to be comparatively well researched until Magdalene Heuser's reassessment in 1998, is only one example. Second, when discussing passionate letters between female correspondents, the "biographical" question is the only one that can cast some doubt on the assumptions of the ubiquitous sentimental discourse, help us question *previous* (no less biographical, no more sophisticated) research methodologies that have, as I have maintained throughout this volume, determined how we read this author's life as well as her works to this day.

For these reasons, I think it is worth putting aside, for the moment, one's fear of questionable methodology (and rotten reviews) and engaging the dreaded "biographical question," based on the documentary evidence available and with all caution mandated by the volatile and compromised materials. A biographical interpretation of the materials at hand would have to recognize that Gottsched's and Runckel's demonstrable awareness of the contemporary cultural context surrounding their personal correspondence undoubtedly played a part in depersonalizing and literalizing the letters. Nonetheless, there can be little question that the emotions expressed in them, embellished or not, were rooted in real life. The highly erotic tone of the letters, of course, does not indicate actual sexual activity between the correspondents, which is unlikely simply because we know that the two women met only twice in person. (Although, as every reader of Gottsched's letters is well aware, they lived only thirteen miles apart for seven of the ten years of their correspondence, to Gottsched, without her husband's consent and accompaniment, this represented an insurmountable distance.) However, as long as we assume that Runckel's edition was in any way based on Gottsched's originals, in other words, as long as we assume co-authorship rather than sole authorship (Runckel's), it is evident from the letters that Gottsched's relationship with Runckel constituted the most intense love relationship of her life, as well as the emotional counterpart to what became an increasingly unhappy marriage. Tubach has defined "homosexual[ity] in the broad sense of the word" for the love story between Bettina von Arnim and Karoline von Günderrode thus: "[homosexuality] in the sense that Bettina was lovingly, if possessively, devoted to Karoline, that she desired the greatest possible degree of personal intimacy from her including some physical familiarity, that she adopted the language of love to speak to her." (261) This would certainly seem to apply to the letters discussed here. It is not unlikely that this volatile biographical context is to a very great degree responsible for the fact that these letters have been largely ignored in scholarship — both as documents furnishing biographical information and as evidence of Luise Gottsched's attempt toward the end of her life to participate in a newly emerging literary culture. Yet it is imperative that we recognize these letters as such because this new literary culture clearly harmonized both with her biographical circumstance and her literary interests, and it furnished her her only opportunity, in twenty-eight years of ceaseless writing, to engage in a literary activity that was *not* mandated and controlled by her husband.

Notes

This chapter relies on the research presented in an earlier article, "Eternal Love or Sentimental Discourse?" which also features a short section on the correspondence between Gottsched and Runckel.

[1] Cf. Heuser, "Das beständige Angedencken" 152–4. While Heuser is the first to state that Gottsched participated in the literary culture of "the next generation," Gottsched's interest in it, in marked dissociation from her husband's poetology, has often been remarked on by earlier scholars, for example Haberland/Pehnt 37, Brüggemann (*Gottscheds Lebens- und Kunstreform* 15) and Buchwald (437–8). Robinson's denial (133) of this late interest is untenable in view of the frequent mention made of some of the new authors, notably Young, in the correspondence (e.g., *Briefe* II, 57 and 267).

[2] If one takes the co-authorship of these letters seriously, then the same would apply to Runckel, who professed herself a disciple and admirer of Johann Christoph Gottsched in her letters. Cf. Runckel's letters to Johann Christoph Gottsched transcribed and published by Heuser in "Sprache," 70–1, 74, 76–8.

[3] *Briefe* II, 311 and III, 165.

[4] Steinhausen II, 307. On the intimate connections between the cult of friendship and epistolary writing, cf. Mauser/Becker-Cantarino; for a concentration on women, cf. Becker-Cantarino, "Leben als Text."

[5] Writing "for the drawer," mostly epistolary writing, was a mode employed by many eighteenth- and early-nineteenth-century women, the most notable being Rahel Levin Varnhagen, who published nothing during her lifetime and is now considered one of the most significant epistolary authors of her time. For a brief discussion of unpublished authorship, cf. Kord, *Namen* 174–80.

[6] For a general discussion of friendships among women, cf. O'Connor; for a more concrete analysis of homoeroticism among early German women writers as expressed in letters, cf. Kord, "Eternal Love" and Joeres. Joanna Russ has eloquently analyzed the prevalent inability to conceptualize lesbianism in both literary reception and social life in her article "She Wasn't, She Isn't, She Didn't, She Doesn't, and Why Do You Keep On Bringing It Up?"

[7] Crompton cites the case, among others, as evidence that lesbianism was persecuted along with male homosexuality (11); cf. discussion in Kord, "Eternal Love" 228–30.

[8] Cf. the cases cited in Crompton 17 and discussion in Kord, "Eternal Love" 230.

[9] Eriksson 39; cf. discussion in Kord, "Eternal Love" 230.

[10] "Über den Umgang unter Freunden," II, 130–61; "Über den Umgang mit und unter Verliebten," II, 81–94; "Von dem Umgange unter Eheleuten," II, 32–80; cf. Kord, "Eternal Love" 231.

[11] Cf. Maurer, Düntzer, Höfer, Petersen, Martin, Susmann, Hof, Voß, Kahn-Wallerstein, Boy-Ed, and Bode; discussion in Kord, "Eternal Love" 231 and "Not in Goethe's Image."

[12] Cf. the works by Hausen, Duden, Walter, and discussion in Kord, "Eternal Love" 232–3.

[13] Brüggemann, *Bürgerliche Gemeinschaftskultur* I, 14, sets the beginning of that tradition around 1750, simultaneous with the original composition of the letters.

[14] June 19, 1752: "Warum muste ich E. H. auf so eine kurze Zeit kennen lernen? Warum muste ich in Ihnen alles entdecken, was ich bisher so eifrig gesucht, und noch nie vereinigt gefunden hatte? Warum musten Sie mir sogleich Ihre Freundschaft schenken? ein Glück, daß ich in dem Augenblicke Ihrer Bekanntschaft wünschte, aber nicht so gleich hoffte.
    Mein stilles Glück, die Lust von wenig Stunden
    Ist wie das Glück von einer Sommernacht,
    Ist ohne Spur, ist wie ein Traum verschwunden.
. . . Sie haben Recht, es ist nichts reitzender als die Freundschaft zweyer redlichen Seelen. Lassen Sie die unsrige ungetrennt und ewig seyn. Erlauben Sie mir Ihnen oft zu schreiben, und oft meinen Kummer, davon Sie die unschuldige Ursache sind, zu klagen. Ich werde allen Ihren Briefen mit freudiger Ungedult entgegen sehen, und sie als eine kleine Genugthuung für Ihre Abwesenheit empfangen. . . . Ich bin mit Zärtlichkeit und Hochachtung . . . Ihnen ganz ergeben." (*Briefe* II, 44–5)

[15] ". . . weil ich nicht glauben kann, daß irgend ein zärtlicher Schmerz weiter gehen sollte, als der meinige über Ihren Verlust? Ueber dieses so gründet sich mein Gram auf Ihre Verdienste, da hingegen Ihre Freundschaft gegen mich nur Grosmuth ist. Sie versichern mich, daß ich Ihnen nicht gleichgültig gewesen, auch ehe Sie mich noch gekannt haben. Sie haben mir also Ihre Freundschaft geschenket, ehe Ihnen noch die treue Verehrung bekannt war, so die erste Stunde in mir erwachte, da ich das Glück hatte, sie kennen zu lernen. Nun schließe ich so:
    Eine Freundschaft, die sich auf die Kenntnis wahrer Verdienste gründet, schlägt tiefere Wurzel, als eine die auf lauter unverdienter

Großmuth beruhet. Nun gründet sich aber meine Freundschaft gegen die Frau von R. auf ihre Verdienste.

Atqui, ergo, sagen die Logici . . . . Ach! warum ist mir denn von so vielen Versuchen, die ich gethan, Sie kennen zu lernen, kein einziger gelungen? Warum mußte erst die ganze französische Nation in Gefahr gerathen, für Freuden närrisch zu werden, ehe ich erfahren konnte, daß die Person, die ich 15 Jahr in Sachsen gesucht hatte, und zu finden verzweifelte, wenige Straßen von mir anzutreffen wäre? Mein Herz ist zur Freundschaft mehr, als zu irgend einer anderen Leidenschaft geschaffen." (*Briefe* II, 64–6)

Runckel explains the allusion to the happy French nation rather cryptically in a footnote in which she states that the two had originally met due to an ode by Arnaud on the birth of the Duc de Bourgogne (II, 66).

[16] May 24, 1754: "Niemals ist mir die Zeit nach einer Nachricht von Ihnen so lang geworden, als diesesmal. Ich suchte hundert Ursachen Ihres Stillschweigens, ich baute die schönsten Luftschlösser, und hoffte irgends eine unvermuthete Erscheinung auf unserer Messe, aber nichts von alle dem ist geschehen. Endlich fiel mir ein, daß ich mich für Ihren Liebhaber erkläret hatte, und ich fand in Ihrem Stillschweigen, daß diese Rolle Ihren Beyfall nicht hätte. Mir war dieser Einfall demonstrativisch gewiß, und da ich mich in diesen Zustand gar nicht schicken konnte, so setzte ich mich nieder und schrieb folgendes Billet:

Madame,

Votre amie, qui ne vivoit que par Vos lettres, se voit tuer par Votre Silence dont Vous la régalés comme Votre amant. Si c'est ainsi que Vous Vous prenés à ceux qui Vous adorent, j'aime mieux ne pas Vous adorer & reprendre mon ancien caractere. Rendés moi Votre tendresse Madame, reprennés Votre empressement à me donner de Vos nouvelles & soyés persuadée, que je n'ambitionnerai d'autre titre que celui de Votre amie. C'est dans les sentimens d'une amitié pure & constante que je serai toute ma vie Votre trés devouée G.

Vielleicht ruhet Ihres Gemahls Fluch auf meinem verwegenen Antrage. Ist dieses? so soll derselbe künftig mit mir zufrieden seyn. Ich begehre seine Seufzer nicht auf mich zu laden. Mein ganzes Glück will ich in Zukunft darinne suchen, gegen seine und meine Freundin alle Empfindungen einer reinen und beständigen Freundschaft bis ins Grab zu erhalten." (*Briefe* II, 217)

I thank Professor Milena Santoro of the French Department at Georgetown University for checking my translation of the French portion of the letter.

[17] January 29, 1755: "Ja, liebste Freundin, ich habe in Ihnen die Glückseligkeit gefunden . . . . Kurz, ich lebe nur für Sie, um Sie zu lieben, und mein ganzes künftiges Leben aller Freude und allem Schmerze, aller Zufriedenheit und aller tödlichen Unruhe, kurz allen Empfindungen zu überlassen, die die Begleiterinnen dieser göttlichen Leidenschaft sind.

Leben Sie wohl, einzige Freundin; Schreiben Sie mir öfter als ich, und längere Briefe als ich, weil Sie mehr Muße haben als ich. Jedes Wort ist mir theuer, was mir Ihre Feder sagt. Ungedultig bey jedem Anfang Ihrer Briefe, eile ich das Ende zu wissen; und fange sie wieder an zu lesen, weil ich zu bald damit fertig werde. Lachen Sie, aber lieben Sie mich nur. Ich lebe und sterbe Ihre ganz eigene Freundin." (*Briefe* II, 269–70)

[18] For example in *Briefe* II, 177 and 215.

[19] "Sie vermuthen, daß die Gräfin B. Sie aus meinem Herzen verdrängen wird? Nein, beste Freundin, fürchten Sie nichts. Sie hat bisher ihr Herz nur mit Fürstinnen getheilt, und ihr Stand setzet sie in eine solche Entfernung mit mir, daß nichts, was unserm Bunde nachtheilig wäre, sich in diese Bekanntschaft mischen kann." (*Briefe* II, 252)

[20] Dorothea Henriette von Runckel to Johann Christoph Gottsched, September 9, 1755. The original is in the Handschriftenabteilung of the university library (Bibliotheca Albertina) in Leipzig, Nachlaß Gottsched, Ms 0342. I quote here from Heusers transcription in "Sprache," 64–6, this quotation 64–5: "Ich erfahre bey dem Vergnügen welches ich mir bey Eröfnung Dero geehrtesten Schreibens versprach, daß die Aufrichtigkeit nicht allemahl die beste Wirckung thut. Ich hofte die Versicherung zu lesen, in den zärtlichen Hertzen Ihrer und meiner Freundinn; noch eben den Platz zu besitzen, den mir diese vortrefliche Frau, an den glücklichsten Tage meines Lebens einzuräumen beliebet hatte; und gesetzt daß Sie mich nur damit geschmeichelt hätten, so wäre mir diesesmahl nichts lieber gewesen, als auf eine so erwünschte Weise hintergangen zu werden; Aber wie sehr beunruhigen mich jetzo die Wahrheiten die ich niemahls wünschte erfahren zu haben!

Ich sehe wohl, daß die Furcht vor so eine gefährliche Rivale nicht gantz ungegründet gewesen ist, welche bey der Ankunft der Gräfinn in Leipzig mein gantzes Hertze bemeisterte. Ist sie so listig gewesen, dem Apollo zu schmeicheln um seine liebste Muse zu gewinnen, und ist ihr dieser Anschlag gelungen; wie leicht wird es seyn, eine entfernte Freundinn aus dem Hertzen zu verdrängen, welches die gefährliche Gräfinn gantz allein zu besitzen wünschet. . . .

Das Vorspiel welches Dero gelehrte Freundinn der Gräfinn zu Gefallen verfertiget, ein Stück welches wie Sie sagen, Sie und ich nicht würden erbeten haben, dieses ist noch kein Beweis daß wir denjenigen Platz verlohren hätten, darauf wir mit Recht stoltz seyn können. . . . Sie Hochgeehrtester Herr, Sie mein vertrauter Rival, Sie und ich würden in unsern Verlangen bescheidener gewesen seyn und unserer zärtlichen Freundinn nichts zugemuthet haben was Derselben nur die geringste Bemühung verursachen könte. . . .

Sehn Sie nur mein hochgeehrtester Herr Profeßor, wie ich alles sorgfältig herbey suche um den schmertzlichen Gedancken zu unterdrücken, daß wir unserer Feindinn in dem uns bekannten vortrefflichen Hertzen, nachstehen müsten. Ich beschwöre Dieselben bey allem was heilig ist, den guten Vorsatz nicht zu ändern, und nächsten Winter mit Dero vortrefflichen Gemahlinn nach Dresden zu kommen."

[21] Letter to Runckel, July 28, 1756: "Wenn diese vortrefliche Fürstin nicht schon erfahren hätte, daß nicht eben alle Glückseligkeit den Fürstenstühlen vermacht ist; so würde sie aus Ihrem Briefe sehen, daß zwo Freundinnen in ihrer gegenseitigen Gesinnung alles das genießen, was oft, nur allzuoft, den Großen dieser Erde abgeht." (*Briefe* III, 33–4)

[22] Gottsched also complained bitterly to Runckel about this particular commission, which resulted in the one-act play *Der beste Fürst* (The Best Ruler, 1755) — her last play. Cf. *Briefe* II, 295.

[23] May 29, 1755: "les hommes connoissent rarement la delicatesse de l'amitié." (*Briefe* II, 289)

[24] October 4, 1755: "es wäre schlecht, wenn zwo Seelen, die sich so lieben wie wir, die Grundregeln der Freundschaft von jenem meyneidigen Geschlechte lernen sollten." (*Briefe* II, 304–5)

[25] Letter to "Herr S." (name withheld by Runckel), 1748: "Mein Freund findet vor gut, mich keine Stunde unbeschäftiget zu lassen." (*Briefe* I, 349)

[26] Cf. Bennholdt-Thomsen/Guzzoni and the interpretation by Kerth/Russell in their introduction to their translation of her comedies, xvi.

[27] Letter to Runckel, June 26, 1753: "Geben Sie acht, man wird mich einst mit der Feder in der Hand begraben, damit sie, wie Addison von den Zungen der Französinnen sagt, auch im Grabe nicht ruhe." (*Briefe* II, 118)

[28] Letter to Runckel, March 4, 1762: "Sie fragen nach der Ursache meiner Krankheit? Hier ist sie. Acht und zwanzig Jahre ununterbrochene Arbeit, Gram im Verborgenen und sechs Jahre unzählige Thränen...." (*Briefe* III, 167)

This passage is quoted in Kerth's and Russell's introduction to their translation of her comedies with an admission as to the context in which it was written (xxviii), but also paraphrased as follows: "At the end of her life, she wrote to her friend Dorothea von Runckel that she could look back on twenty-eight years of uninterrupted work" (xvi). In my view, this paraphrase implies a pride on the author's part in her life's work that is nowhere apparent in the actual letter.

[29] At the time of this writing, Runckel still lived in Görlitz, thirteen miles from Dresden, which was approximately the same distance from Leipzig. Gottsched's journey to Dresden, in other words, cut the distance between the two in half. Runckel's vicinity to the goal of their journey undoubtedly lead to Gottsched's renewed attempt to persuade her husband to permit her a visit with Runckel.

Runckel moved from Görlitz to Dresden in July 1755 (cf. *Briefe* II, 290).

[30] Letter to Runckel, August 10, 1754: "Sie laden mich so freundschaftlich ein, auf meiner Reise nach Dresden Sie in G. zu besuchen; daß ich alles emp-

finde, was die Freundschaft empfinden kann, die einen geheimen Trieb zu dem fühlet, was meine Freundin wünschet. Im Geiste habe ich schon Ihre feurigste Umarmung empfunden, in Ihrem Zimmer geschlafen, an Ihrem Tische gegessen, in hundert Unterredungen mit der güthigsten Wirthin, mich und die vorgelegten Speisen auf meinem Teller, für Vergnügen vergessen, und kurz, ich bin seit dem Empfang Ihres letzten Schreibens, schon ganz bey Ihnen gewesen. Bey diesen metaphysischen Genusse wird es aber auch diesmal wohl bleiben, zur Strafe, weil mein Freund Professor der Metaphysick ist. Er ist aber auch Professor der Logick, und hier sind die Gründe die er meinen Bitten entgegen setzt:
1) Sechs und zwanzig Meilen sind gerade noch einmal so weit als dreizehn.
2) Meine Geschäffte erlauben mir nicht länger als acht Tage von Leipzig abwesend seyn, da nothwendig vierzehn Tage zu einer Reise nach G. erfordert werden. ergo — — —
Alles dieses ist wahr, liebste Freundin, und ich muß Ihnen noch einen Hauptsatz anführen, der alle meine Einwendungen vereitelt: *Dein Wille soll deinen* — — —"
(*Briefe* II, 230–1; the emphasis and ellipsis are original.)

[31] Letter to Runckel, October 4, 1755: "Ich sage es noch einmal, unser Asmodi ist ein böser Bube. Kehren Sie sich an nichts, was er sagt; er hat den alten Groll von der überlegenen Freundschaft des Frauenzimmers noch auf dem Herzen . . . . Sein Versprechen mich noch dies Jahr nach Dresden zu führen, hat er schon unter vielerley Vorwand aufgehoben. Geben Sie nur acht, ob die Asmodis Wort halten." (*Briefe* II, 303)

[32] Asmodi (Hebrew for Aschmodai) is an evil demon in the Old Testament (cf. Kording's commentary 348). Gottsched possibly also alludes here to Alain René Le Sage's novel *Le Diable Boiteux* (1707), an adaptation of Luis Velez de Guevara's *El Diablo cojuelo* (1641), in which the devil Asmodeo promises the scholar Don Cleofas to show him humanity in all its variety, which results in a satirical exhibit of every human vice. The novel's popularity and Luise Gottsched's extensive knowledge of contemporary French literature make it likely that she knew of the novel.

[33] March 9, 1754: "Die Wunderkraft der Freundschaft kann also elende Ueberbleibsel in Reliquien verwandeln." (*Briefe* II, 177)

[34] The tragedy and all other ancillary texts that Runckel included in her edition of Gottsched's letters (among them *Der beste Fürst* and Gottsched's translations of Horace's odes) were not reprinted in Kording's edition of the letters.

[35] Cf. Heuser, "Das beständige Angedencken," 161–2. Runckel's writing likewise focused on the development of women's epistolary style and paradigmatic editions of letters; cf. her *Sammlung* and *Moral*, which contains a chapter on friendship.

[36] Cf. Becker-Cantarino, "Bildung," "Luise Adelgunde Victorie Gottsched," and "Outsiders"; Bohm; Brüggemann, ed., *Gottscheds Lebens- und Kunstreform*; Critchfield; Crüger; Danzel; Dawson; Johann Christoph Gottsched, "Leben" and "Nachricht"; Groß I, 28–43; Heckmann; Heitner; Kord, *Ein Blick* 44–8, 94–6, 276–83 and 372–4; Petig; Ploetz; Richel; Robinson 115–34; Sanders, "Ein kleiner Umweg" and *The Virtuous Woman* 9–15 and 51–94; S. E. Schreiber 41–88; and Schlenther.

8: The Politics of Mourning: Epilogue

IMMEDIATELY AFTER LUISE GOTTSCHED'S DEATH on June 26, 1762, her husband began the task of marketing her life. The first install-ment of her biography, "Nachricht, von dem Leben, Tode und Be-gräbnisse der hochedelgebohrnen nunmehr sel. Frau, Louise Adelgunde Victoria Gottschedinn, geb. Kulmus, aus Danzig" (Report on the Life, Death and Burial of the most nobly born and now departed Frau Louise Adelgunde Victoria Gottsched, née Kulmus, from Danzig) ap-peared in August 1762, barely four weeks after her death, in his journal *Das Neueste aus der anmuthigen Gelehrsamkeit* (The Latest from the Amiable Realm of Learning); the series continued until December of that year. In 1763, he republished an expanded version of his "Report" as the introductory biography of his wife in his edition of her poetry ("Leben"). In addition, Johann Christoph Gottsched marketed his bi-ography in France[1] and wrote a number of highly publicized rhymed eulogies about her. While it was within the bounds of propriety and tradition for widowed scholars and literati to publish rhymed eulogies about their wives — previous to Johann Christoph Gottsched, both Triller and Klopstock had celebrated their deceased wives in a very similar fashion (Hanstein I, 309) — Johann Christoph's behavior was highly unusual in several respects. For one thing, the woman thus honored was not only, as had been the case with Triller and Klopstock, his muse, but an author in her own right. The fact alone that he could reasonably hope to find readers for a biography of his wife in both Germany and France attests to her fame as a literary figure. Another unusual factor in Johann Christoph's posthumous celebration of his wife is the fact that, within the bounds of tradition, he not only produced a number of rhymed eulogies about her, he also commissioned them from others. That he must have extended such requests to many members of his and her cir-cle of literary acquaintances occasionally becomes apparent in the in-troductory excuses of answer letters containing commissioned eulogies: "Forgive me, dearest friend, for being unable to deliver something better."[2] A long list of the authors who wrote rhymed eulogies on Gottsched's passing is published in his biography ("Nachricht," De-cember 1762, 939), and in his edition of her *Sämmtliche Kleinere Ge-dichte* (Complete Smaller Poems, 1763), he published not only poetry authored by her, but also poetry written in her honor, both during her lifetime (195–365)[3] and after her death. These eulogies number literally in the hundreds and comprise well over one hundred pages of the edition (366–484), and the editor hastens to assure readers that even this impressive collection is far from complete. The difference between Johann Christoph Gottsched's manner of proceeding and that of famous precursors like Triller or Klopstock is simply that whereas they sought to establish the personal merits of the deceased, Johann Christoph Gottsched did everything he could to increase Luise Gottsched's literary fame — by publicizing Luise Gottsched's life as broadly as possible and by establishing her, even by employing the questionable method of commissioning poetry of mourning for her from others, as a widely mourned literary figure. The final aspect of his behavior that has struck previous scholars as highly unusual is that unlike Triller and Klopstock, whose eulogies confined themselves to a celebration of the virtues of the deceased, Johann Christoph Gottsched placed a very clear emphasis on his own feelings. Apparently oblivious of his own poor taste, he relegated Leipzig with tales of his insomnia and how much weight he had lost due to his deep distress over her death (Schlenther 21). Equally infamous is what is now his best known eulogy about Luise Gottsched:

> You have possessed my heart entire,
> In future, none shall own it more!
> . . .
> You still reside within my heart,
> You are and will remain my joy,
> I cannot and will not forget you.
> You have possessed my heart entire,
> In future, none shall own it more.[4]

Goethe's remark on the near-universal contempt to which Johann Christoph Gottsched was exposed toward the end of his life[5] could be read as a general expression of Johann Christoph Gottsched's waning public status as an intellectual and literary presence or, more specifically, as evidence that his somewhat sanctimonious self-representation as the mourning widower was not received entirely uncritically. Interestingly enough, it was precisely this tradition of rhymed, published eulogies on deceased wives which had also drawn severe criticism from both Luise Gottsched and, decades later, Dorothea Henriette von Runckel. Luise Gottsched, in a letter written in 1734, indirectly accused a distraught lover who had voiced his grief in a rhymed obituary of his love of embellishing his feelings for poetic purposes. In her sarcastic suspicion that said lover might sing as tenderly for his "second and third bride as he mournfully cooed and moaned on this occasion,"[6] she made it clear that the hypocrisy involved was not lost on her. The same issue is taken up in Dorothea Henriette von Runckel's epistolary exchange with Johann Christoph Gottsched. In this remarkable correspondence, Runckel and Johann Christoph Gottsched seem to have engaged in a scholarly dispute in the tradition of the erudite *quérelles*, as the belligerent tone of her letters to him (up to about 1755) attests. One of the points of dispute was apparently the fidelity of famous men towards their wives, certainly a sensitive subject of discussion in view of Johann Christoph Gottsched's infamous escapades. Runckel tackles the problem head on, and with a great amount of irony and spirit:

> Most Nobly Born Sir,
> Highly Esteemed Herr Professor,
> Have you determined to squabble with me incessantly, or do you perhaps believe that the language of my sex is never richer than when it is used to contradict and that all eloquence leaves us when we do not find cause for quarrel?
> ... Concerning the second point about which Your Grace thinks that I have insulted your entire sex, I have to admit that I am very stubborn in my opinion and that you will never move me to an admission that I am not right in this. The only aspect in which I was wrong was that I was speaking of the entirety of masculine persons, whereas I should have spoken of men alone. The first truly deserve an apology from me, for they are the ones who revere everything about us except our flaws: but as soon as they look at us with men's eyes, they hardly find the good qualities, which at times we actually possess, worthy of their approval. Your Grace has called my judgment entirely flawed and wishes to prove this to me through the evidence of von Beßer, von Canitz, Richey, von Haller, Werlhoff and Triller.[7] You will permit that I view all of these great poets as indifferent husbands and the most tender widowers.
> Was it not the death and loss of their wives that inspired their pens with the most excellent poems? Were they ever moved in this manner by their worth until their loss seemed irrevocable? Triller alone found his Henriette worthy while she was alive to be the subject of his muse; all the others prove to you the truth of my assertions. A widower's tender remembrances of the past and a tender lover's pleasant hopes for the future both have the same effect, for both show you the beloved at her highest perfection. I will here include for you the public testimony of a widower, which will prove my point, cast in stone, that he did not appreciate his wife until after her death, and until then not at all in the manner which she deserved ....[8]

Runckel's modus operandi mirrors Luise Gottsched's in that she manages to dismantle a contemporary discourse, the rhymed eulogies of famous men, couched in the terms of another, that of the scholarly *quérelles*. Her *quérelle* with Johann Christoph Gottsched manages to expose a popular literary tradition as self-serving and hypocritical. Her good-humored men-bashing is in the best tradition of the heated debate on gender roles in the moral weeklies. Nonetheless, her employment of public discourse carries a personal message; underlying her scholarly dispute with the professor of logic is a succinct message to her best friend's husband, at that point still nine years away from becoming a widower himself: "I have told you that Your Grace has the most perfect wife. Is it possible that you can, even for a moment, pretend that you are not entirely convinced of this?"[9] Johann Christoph Gottsched's manner of proceeding after his wife's death can be read as the precise opposite of the modus operandi that both Runckel and Luise Gottsched had adopted. Whereas in the women's writing, public discourse and developments are explored for their personal significance and potential or used in negotiations of personal relationships, Johann Christoph Gottsched turned his wife's personal life, illness and death into public discourse.

He did this most effectively in his biography, begun immediately after her death, and significant beyond anything else that would ever be written about her. It was this document that established the dominant discourse on Luise Gottsched and furnished future readers with a series of significant anecdotes that substituted in subsequent life stories of Luise Gottsched for empirical knowledge as well as interpretive acumen. The central aspect of his biography is his historicization of his wife's authorship, and it is this assessment that stands in strange contrast to his obvious attempts to publicize her *as* an author through publication of his own biography and authored and commissioned poems of mourning. From childhood on, Luise Gottsched appears in his biography as a kind of wunderkind who learned English effortlessly, "as if in game,"[10] who "played around" on a lute despite the fact that it barely had any strings left,[11] and whose industry and mental agility was marvelled at wherever she appeared.[12] Her utter lack of formal instruction, counterbalanced only by her "natural affinity"[13] for music and languages, becomes a recurring theme in her biography. The fact that Johann Christoph Gottsched takes such care to emphasize that she learned all languages "without having enjoyed further instruction by a language teacher" and "more from speaking and practice than from rules"[14] indicates that it was a central concern of his text to establish

Luise Gottsched as talented, but simultaneously unspoiled by "masculine" erudition:

> Her disposition was simple, or more accurately, modest . . . . She never boasted of her erudition, especially not in the presence of women; in order to never disgust them . . . . Certainly, she never burdened anyone with her knowledge.[15]

His own courtship and marriage are described using fairy tale vocabulary ("and on the fourteenth of May, they happily arrived in Leipzig"[16]), a description that establishes firmly the context in which Luise Gottsched has nearly exclusively been read by future scholars: that of Luise Gottsched as Johann Christoph's pupil and "helpmate." His mentorship role began early in their engagement, during which he furnished her with appropriate reading material ("Nachricht," *Das Neueste* [August 1762]: 469–70) and continued into their marriage, at the outset of which she learned Latin at his behest. Lest this clear breach of feminine propriety come as a shock to his readers, Johann Christoph hastened to assure his readership that Luise Gottsched's knowledge of the language merely enabled her to "understand an easy author" and to "lend a helping hand to her husband with the German edition of Bayle's dictionary."[17] While she attempted, in her "leisure hours," to "transcend somewhat the common accomplishment of women" in music,[18] she wrote and published several "little works"[19] on commission by her husband. Throughout the biography, Luise Gottsched's life's work is historicized as incidental (produced during her "leisure hours" or "to while away the time," "Leben"), unimportant ("little works") and secondary: she did not write for calling, money or fame, but to render "her husband most important services."[20] It was he who made the intellectual decisions governing her authorship, indeed, her entire intellectual life. It is for that reason that Johann Christoph Gottsched consistently emphasizes his wife's "industry" and "natural affinity" for languages or music, rather than her genius, learning, or intellectual acumen. All of her accomplishments appear in the diminutive and as outer-directed (compare his anecdote about the genesis of *Die Pietisterey* in "Leben," in which he describes her decision to translate Bougeant's play as inspired by her own childhood experiences). While the author of this first biography of Luise Gottsched almost entirely ignores her dramatic work, he places great emphasis on her occasional poetry (in itself considered an inferior genre), works she had written on a dare, and menial labor in her husband's service, such as her triple proofreading of their joint translation of Bayle's dictionary.[21] Occasional poetry is the single genre in which he regarded her as "unsurpassed"; ironically, Johann Christoph goes on to epitomize Luise Gottsched's extraordinary talent in this despised genre by pointing to her rhymed eulogies — precisely the tradition of which Luise Gottsched herself had been so contemptuous.[22]

It is probably not an exaggeration to suspect that the primary concern of Johann Christoph Gottsched's biography of Luise Gottsched was less the augmentation of her literary fame than that of his own. His strong emphasis on his own role in her life, the minute detail with which he describes his mentorship of her, and the near-total disregard he showed for all aspects of her life that were independent of his influence establish his text almost as much as an autobiography as a biography of his wife. That this biography became not only the first, but clearly the most influential document about Luise Gottsched's life to future scholars can be documented by several instances of both omission and commission in this text that reappear, unchanged over the centuries, in nearly every future rewrite of Luise Gottsched's life. The most obvious explanation for the complete omission of Dorothea Henriette von Runckel from Luise Gottsched's life in *all* scholarship until Magdalene Heuser's articles on the subject is the simple fact that Johann Christoph Gottsched never mentions her in his biography[23] — in all likelihood, because Runckel was a part of Gottsched's life that was independent from his influence and therefore immaterial to the story as he told it. In this story, he established himself as a solicitous husband on the personal level and the great author, the intellectual leadership behind their remarkable partnership, on the public level. His personal concerns are evidenced by the embarrassingly minute manner in which he describes every moment and aspect of Gottsched's two-year-long final disease and death (during which the reader is even informed at what point she stopped menstruating), the defensiveness with which he attributes her loss of love for him to the war and her "sickly physical disposition" ("kränkliche Leibesbeschaffenheit," "Leben"), and his elaborate description of his own mourning after her death (in his own words, Johann Christoph Gottsched mourned so pointedly and publicly "that it was visible to the whole town"[24]). His public self-representation as the intellectual leadership of their collaboration is clearly reflected in the manner in which he discredits his wife's authorship as occasional, incidental, unoriginal, and largely commissioned by himself — a trend that continued in subsequent scholarship on both authors. This first interpretation of Luise Gottsched's authorship is embedded in the mentorship relationship, for which Johann Christoph Gottsched cites an early poem written by his wife in a personal letter to him as proof that this view was shared by the deceased:

> My Gottsched, you alone
> And that you loved me shall be my laurel crown.
> The fact that you have taught, that you've instructed me
> Shall be my song of praise writ for posterity.
> Whoe'er has such a master won't die in obscurity:
> Although the pupil be unworthy of eternity.
> Thus, I live through you: how could I live to more acclaim?
> Through your esteem, I will gain praise, honor, even fame.[25]

The eradication of all possible consideration of Luise Gottsched as an author "worthy of eternity" is of course central to future interpretations of her work, and it is important to note that this interpretation of her authorship is carefully formulated as originating with Luise Gottsched herself. Johann Christoph Gottsched, in his biography of his wife, splendidly succeeded in establishing a tradition. This tradition has, until very recently, read expressions of "feminine" modesty as biographical fact, read severely edited and literalized correspondence as trustworthy biographical material, and read her entire published work as "little works" — little detours, distractions from her more central life's work as her husband's housewife and industrious helpmate. Initially with prompting from Johann Christoph Gottsched, this interpretation of Luise Gottsched as a secondary, derivative author was reiterated in numerous eulogies about her, most notably that composed by the brothers Walz in the year of her death:

> The pen sinks low, the lay of our laments
> displaced by our sighs. But hark! what gives
> Sweet consolation to our hearts? Providence
> Hath so ordained: her husband lives![26]

Her husband lived until 1766 and remarried shortly after her death.

Notes

[1] Cf. Heckmann. Following some difficulty in finding a publisher, the biography finally appeared in a very limited edition under the title *Le Triomphe de la Philosophie par Feue Madame Gottsched, Traduit de L'Allemand par Madame C. S. Heck nee Pairiere. Avec L'Eloge de l'auteur par Monsieur Formey.* (Paris 1767). Although the publication date reads 1767, the work must have appeared before Johann Christoph Gottsched's death in December 1766.

The only library known to own this work is the Bayrische Staatsbibliothek in Munich (Heckmann 339).

[2] Letter from Frau Kessel to Johann Christoph Gottsched, written in Breslau in the summer of 1762 and quoted in Hanstein I, 310. The letter contains a rhymed eulogy about Luise Gottsched and, revealingly, acknowledges receipt of a brief biography of Luise Gottsched as well as several sample eulogies sent by Johann Christoph Gottsched — both of which strongly suggest that Frau Kessel did not know Luise Gottsched personally and knew very little of her. It is therefore highly unlikely that she would have produced her eulogy without direct prompting from the widower.

[3] Some others were collected in Baensch's and Buchwald's 1908 collection.

[4] "Du hast mein ganzes Herz besessen,
Hinfort besitzt es keine mehr!

. . .

Du lebest noch in meiner Brust;
Du bist und bleibest meine Lust,
Ich kann und will dich nicht vergessen;
Du hast mein ganzes Herz besessen,
Hinfort besitzt es keine mehr." (Quoted in Hanstein I, 310)

[5] Goethe visited Johann Christoph Gottsched in Leipzig in 1766 and supposedly noted in his journal: "All of Leipzig despises him." The incident is related in Schlenther 21. It is unclear from the text or attribution whether Goethe's verdict is a direct quotation or Schlenther's paraphrase.

[6] *Briefe* I, 134; cf. discussion in chapter 3.

[7] Johannes von Besser, Friedrich Rudolf von Canitz, Michael Richey, Albrecht von Haller, Paul Gottlieb Werlhof, and Daniel Wilhelm Triller all wrote poetic eulogies about their wives; cf. Heuser, "Sprache" 81–2, notes 25–30.

[8] Letter from Dorothea Henriette von Runckel to Johann Christoph Gottsched, January 31, 1753, transcribed in Heuser, "Sprache" 54–8, this excerpt 54–5:
"HochEdelgebohrner Herr
Hochgeehrtester Herr Professor
Haben Sie sich denn vorgesetzt beständig StreitSchriften mit mir zu wechseln, oder glauben Sie vielleicht das die Sprache meines Geschlechts niemahls reicher als im Widersprechen ist und daß uns alle Beredsamkeit verläst, so bald wir nichts zu streiten finden?
. . . Was nun den zweyten Punct betrift, dadurch Ew. HochEdelgeb. meynen daß ich Dero gantzes Geschlecht beleidiget hätte; so gestehe ich Ihnen, daß ich sehr verstockt in meiner Meynung bin und daß Sie mich nimmermehr zu einem Bekenntniß bringen werden, daß ich nicht von den RechtGläubigen wäre. Das einzige habe ich neulich versehen, daß ich nemlich die Welt der MannsPersonen genennet da ich gantz allein von Männern reden wolte. Diese ersten verdienen würcklich eine Abbitte von mir, denn sie sind diejenigen,

so alles bis auf unsere Fehler an uns verehren: so bald sie uns aber mit Män-
ner=Augen ansehen, finden sie kaum das Gute, welches wir zuweilen würcklich besitzen ihres Beyfalls werth. Ew. HochEdelgeb. nennen meinen Satz
gäntzlich falsch, und wollen mir dieses durch die Zeugniße, derer von Beßer,
von Canitz, Richey, von Haller, Werlhoff und Trillers beweisen. Sie werden
mir erlauben daß ich diese großen Dichter allerseits als gleichgültige Ehe
Männer und die zärtlichsten Wittber ansehe.

Hat nicht der Tod und Verlust ihrer Gattinnen ihnen erst die vortreflich-
sten Gedichte in die Feder geleget? Sind Sie jemahls so, von ihren Werth gerühret worden, bis ihnen der Verlust unersetzlich geschienen? Der einzige
Triller hat seine Henriette bey ihren Leben der Mühe werth geachtet eine Beschäftigung seiner Muse zu seyn; Die andern allerseits beweisen Ihnen vielmehr die Wahrheit meiner Meynung. Das zärtliche Andencken des Vergang-
enen bey einen Wittber und die angenehme Hoffnung des Zukünftigen, bey
einen zärtlichen Liebhaber, sind von einerley Würckung, denn beydes zeiget
ihnen die geliebte Person in der grösten Vollkommenheit. Ich lege Ihnen hier
das öffentliche Zeugnis eines Wittbers bey, welches zu meinem Beweis dienet,
und in Stein gegraben ist, daß er seine Frau nicht höher als nach ihren Leben
geschätzet hat, und vorhero gar nicht so wie sie es verdienet."

[9] Ibid: "Ich habe Ihnen gesagt daß Ew. HochEdelgeb. die vollkommenste
Gattin hätten. Ist es möglich daß Sie sich einen Augenblick so verstellen können, als wenn Sie nicht völlig davon überzeuget wären?"

[10] "Von ihrem noch lebenden Halbbruder . . . begriff sie nachmals, gleichsam
spielend, das Englische . . . ." Johann Christoph Gottsched, "Nachricht," *Das
Neueste* (August 1762): 466.

[11] "Sie stahl sich oft weg, um auf einer Bodenkammer, auf der alten Laute ihres Vaters, so wenig Seyten sie auch noch hatte, zu klimpern." "Nachricht,"
Das Neueste (August 1762): 467.

[12] "Hier zeigte sie nicht nur allen Kindern ihres Geschlechtes, sondern auch
allen Knaben der Johannisschule, ein besonderes Beyspiel des Fleißes und der
Hurtigkeit ihres Geistes. Dieses währte etliche Jahre hindurch, zu großer
Verwunderung der Gemeine . . . ." "Nachricht," in *Das Neueste* (August
1762): 466.

[13] "Gleichwohl ersetzte ihr Naturell alles übrige . . . ." "Nachricht," *Das
Neueste* (August 1762): 467.

[14] "Dieses setzte sie nun, in der so schweren Rechtschreibung dieser Sprache
[French, S. K.], so fest, daß sie nachmals, ohne einen fernern Unterricht eines
Sprachmeisters genossen zu haben, auch in langen Briefen sehr schwerlich ei-
nen Fehler darinn begehen konnte: ob sie gleich dieselbe mehr aus dem Re-
den und der Uebung, als nach Regeln gelernet hatte." "Nachricht," in *Das
Neueste* (August 1762): 468.

[15] "Ihre Gemüthsart war von blöder, oder besser zu sagen, von bescheidner Art. . . . Mit ihrer Gelehrsamkeit pralte sie auch niemals; zumal in Gegenwart des Frauenzimmers; um demselben niemals zum Ekel zu werden. . . . . . . ist sie gewiß mit ihrer Kenntniß . . . niemanden beschwerlich gefallen." ("Leben," unpaginated)

[16] "und den 14 May kamen sie . . . glücklich in Leipzig an." "Nachricht," in *Das Neueste* (August 1762): 470. Throughout both this document and the expanded version ("Leben"), Johann Christoph Gottsched refers to himself in the third person.

[17] "Seine geschickte Art . . . brachten sie in kurzem so weit, daß sie bald einen leichten Schriftsteller verstehen [konnte] . . . Diese Kenntniß gab ihr hernach keine geringe Hülfe, als sie bey der deutschen Ausgabe des baylischen Wörterbuchs ihrem Gatten hülfliche Hand leistete . . . ." "Nachricht," in *Das Neueste* (September 1762): 552–3.

[18] "Da die Wohlselige noch immer die Musik zur Abwechselung ihrer Nebenstunden zu brauchen pflegte: so bemühte sie sich auch darinnen die gemeine Bahn des Frauenzimmers in etwas zu überschreiten." "Nachricht," in *Das Neueste* (September 1762): 558.

[19] Johann Christoph Gottsched consistently refers to her works as "Werkchen," cf., for example, "Nachricht," in *Das Neueste* (August 1762): 471; (October 1762): 636 and 637.

[20] "Nach diesem allen wird man sich nicht wundern, daß die Wohlselige auch ihrem Gatten, bey der Ausgabe des verdeutschten baylischen Wörterbuches, die wichtigsten Dienste leisten konnte." "Nachricht," *Das Neueste* (October 1762): 637–8.

[21] "Nachricht," *Das Neueste* (October 1762): 631; 633; 638.

[22] "On the early death of a friend, the late Frau Professor Richter, née Börner, she wrote a very moving eulogy: a genre of poem in which very few German poets have proven proficient, and in which none has ever surpassed her." ("Nachricht," in *Das Neueste* [October 1762]: 631–2: "Auf einer erblaßten Freundinn, der sel. Fr. Prof. Richterinn, einer geb. Börnerinn, frühen Tod, verfertigte sie eine sehr bewegliche Elegie: eine Art von Gedichten, darinn sich sehr wenige deutsche Dichter stark gewiesen, und noch keiner sie übertroffen hat.")

[23] Runckel's name does not appear in "Nachricht"; in the expanded version, "Leben," Runckel is mentioned only once — not as a personal friend of Luise Gottsched's, but as the translator of the second volume of Beaumelle's *History of Madame de Maintenon*, of which Luise Gottsched translated the first volume (unpag.).

[24] "So daß es der ganzen Stadt sichtbar gewesen." ("Leben," unpaginated)

[25] "Mein Gottsched, Du allein

Und daß Du mich geliebt, das soll mein Lorbeer seyn.
Daß Du mich hast gelehrt, daß Du mich unterwiesen,
Das wird der Nachwelt noch, durch manches Blatt gepriesen.
Wer solche Meister hat, da stirbt der Schüler nicht:
Wenn ihm gleich das Verdienst zur Ewigkeit gebricht.
So leb ich denn durch Dich: wie könnt ich schöner leben?
Dein Ansehn wird mir schon, Lob, Ruhm und Ehre geben."
(Quoted in "Leben," no pagination)

[26] "Die Feder sinkt, die lauten Seufzer stöhren
    Den Klageton. Doch was erhebt
    Schnell unser Herz? O sanfter Trost! wir hören
    Der Vorsicht Ruf: Ihr Gatte lebt!"

(From a eulogy by Johann Theophilus Walz and Heinrich Carl Gottlieb
Walz, quoted in *Sämmtliche Kleinere Gedichte* 484.)

9: Conclusion

THE MULTIPLE IMAGES OF LUISE GOTTSCHED as the "first" female playwright in Germany, as "prototype" Enlightenment woman author, as erudite phenomenon, and as housewife extraordinaire all originated in a tradition that began shortly after her death. Central to my discussion of her is the idea that her "self-image" as an author, as perhaps created and certainly refined by Dorothea Henriette von Runckel, is diametrically opposed to the image that has come down to us through the scholarly tradition, and that both images are careful constructions which were initiated by the two people closest to her: her "self-image" by Dorothea Henriette von Runckel, whose edition of her letters is problematic because it purposely shaped this image, and the other image — no less problematic, but much more popular with subsequent scholars — by the author's husband, Johann Christoph Gottsched. On the one hand appears the woman philosopher whose primary literary accomplishments are embodied in her epistolary writing and in her single tragedy; on the other, a derivative author of "little works" such as occasional poems, an indefatigable cataloguer and proofreader, a "helpmate" to her husband who spent her entire life subordinating her scholarly and literary existence to his. One side of the equation shows us the author as a potential influence on the writings of other women, the other ultimately ends in a reading of the author as an important, if incompetent, precursor of "great" male writers like Lessing, Schiller and Goethe. It is obvious which of these interpretations emerges as the now-dominant one, and it is my hope that it has become equally obvious, in the course of my discussion of her works, how many aspects of her multi-faceted work and personality had to be suppressed or ignored to arrive at this interpretation. My interest, my tactic and ultimately my objective throughout this project have been to put the context of women's literature and culture back into the discussion of Luise Gottsched's life and work. As the eternal sameness of interpretations over the course of the past 238 years demonstrates, Luise Gottsched, paradigmatic or not, "first" or not, is clearly not an author who can be productively read the way she has been read so far, that is, exclusively in the context of the Enlightenment and her husband's literary activity and standing. Her work and life are equally embedded in several other contexts which have remained, to this day, scandalously underresearched: women's literature in general, women's dramatic and epistolary writing in particular, the socio-historical contexts governing women's writing and publishing (among them the widespread use of anonymity and pseudonymity among women authors), and the female Cult of Friendship, as it manifested itself throughout both the eighteenth and the nineteenth centuries in countless personal and literary histories.

Interpretations of Gottsched's life and literature that do consider these essential contextual issues would necessarily come to different conclusions from those arrived at by traditional Enlightenment scholars so far. It is only these contexts that enable us to see Luise Gottsched as a complex and independent dramatic and epistolary author, despite her lifelong literary servitude to her husband. Read in the new context, her letters, however compromised, provide not so much the biographical information for which they have traditionally been mined, but more importantly evidence of her passionate friendship with Runckel — a relationship that remains, certainly in Germany, the best-documented same-sex attachment among women of either the eighteenth or the nineteenth centuries. Only this context of the female Cult of Friendship, a scholarly context that as yet barely exists, enables us to read Gottsched's letters, as well as her relationship with Runckel, as early expressions of a newly emerging literary culture.

A reading of Gottsched's dramatic work can be revitalized substantially by both an emancipation from the context in which it is usually considered, that of Enlightenment dramaturgy and of her husband's direct influence as dramatic theorist and commissioner of these texts, and an inclusion of the context of women's dramatic activity throughout the century. Both Gottsched's comedies and her tragedy, as I hope to have shown, deviate significantly from her husband's poetological doctrine. Her comedies, while following some of Johann Christoph Gottsched's rules for the genre and employing many aspects of contemporary stock comedy, are nonetheless highly unusual for her time in that they privilege their own narrative structure over generic demands. In their elimination of marriage as the Happy Ending of comedy, they refuse to make the inevitable appear plausible and simultaneously implicitly pose the crucial question of what, if not marriage, could constitute a Happy Ending for women. Thematically, they are surprisingly modern in that they not only demonstrate, as many other contemporary plays do, the utter powerlessness of women, but also in that the recurring portrayal of feminine hypochondria can be read as an illustration of women's complicity and participation in the processes that keep them dependent.

Gottsched's single tragedy *Panthea* is no less deviant from her husband's poetology in its refusal to portray morally mixed characters and its absolute abandonment of the concept of poetic justice, on which tragedy traditionally rests. The commendable suicide and senseless murder of the virtuous hero(in)es and the inexplicable escape of the villain portrayed in the tragedy amount to a purposeful denial of the benevolent dramatic world order, an order that is ultimately supplanted by a theology of love in which the victims of the old world order reign supreme. The denial of viewer edification and the withholding of any discernible "moral" make *Panthea* less a tragedy than an aesthetic commentary on Tragedy, one that raises important questions about the universal applicability of the worldview presented in the genre.

A comparison of Gottsched's themes, structures and narrative techniques with women's subsequent dramatic writing in both genres establishes Gottsched as an important pioneer in both areas. While no such connection can be drawn to men's drama of the age, the elimination of marriage as the Happy Ending of comedy, the denial of poetic justice, the destruction of the benevolent world order in tragedy, and the privileging of narrative over generic concerns all reappear in women's plays in the second half of the eighteenth century.[1] Reading Luise Gottsched as she has been read, as a precursor to male "greats" like Lessing, Schiller and Goethe, seems inadequate in this context: neither her themes nor her narrative techniques are taken up by any of these authors, and none of them ever acknowledged her as an influence. (Lessing's vituperative assessment of her dramatic writing makes the opposite more probable.) Such an interpretation would have to be rooted in the context of her husband's attempts at creating a National Theater (an effort which was indeed still central to the dramatic writing and poetologies of Lessing, Schiller and Goethe, among many others). It would thus not only ignore the context of women's writing of the age, but also — and this is where I take issue with most scholars who have written on Luise Gottsched thus far — subsume her literary activity under her husband's, a move that would necessarily blind the reader to every autonomous aspect of her literary work.

Perhaps most unusual for an author of her age is Luise Gottsched's conceptualization, in both non-dramatic and dramatic texts, of women's authorship as a concept. Her portrayal of women's authorship as harnessed and guided by male editors and mentors, even as a form of directed writing (*Das Testament*), as *inescapably* subject to masculine sanction and legitimation (*Pietisterey; Das Testament*) is far from merely autobiographical: it can instead be read as an analysis of women's authorship per se. The self-abnegation, the revocation of authorship in the pretense of "innocent" translatorship or simply the now-infamous "Discourse of Modesty" (*Bescheidenheitstopos*) which asserts that the work was written for the personal edification of its author, that it was not intended for publication, that someone else wrote it, that it wrote itself, and that (regardless of the genesis of this particular work) its author is much more skilled with the needle than with the pen — all of these reappear, in near-identical phraseology, in the forewords of hundreds of women authors after Luise Gottsched.[2] While her portrayal of women's authorship is undoubtedly also "autobiographical" in the sense that Luise Gottsched's own authorship was tightly harnessed to her husband's projects, the inclusion of women's literary history would enable us to read her discussion of authorship not only as an autobiographical issue, but as a historical phenomenon.

It makes sense, then, to rediscover Luise Gottsched not as the incompetent precursor to male giants of subsequent ages, but as the beginning of a tradition of women's epistolary writing on the one hand — a tradition that features names like Bettina von Arnim, Karoline von Günderrode, Rahel Varnhagen von Ense, Karoline Pichler, Therese Huber and many others — and of women's drama on the other. Making this connection is vital not only for a fair reassessment of Luise Gottsched's life and work in particular, but for the continued discovery, analysis and assessment of the rich and varied tradition of women's writing in general. In my view, the two central prerequisites to making this connection are conscientious *archival* research and its precursor, a consistent, all-encompassing and critical awareness of how women's lives and works have been (mis)represented in scholarship. Previous scholarship, and this is perhaps the most daunting aspect of researching women's lives and literature, cannot simply serve as a source of information, biographical, interpretive or otherwise, but must be read with a high degree of skepticism, continuously examined for errors, prejudices, assumptions, omissions and commissions both intentional and subconscious. While the argument could be made that this naturally applies to scholarship on male authors as well, I would maintain — and I hope to have demonstrated paradigmatically in my analysis of Luise Gottsched's distorted and prejudicial reception — that scholarship on women's writing, particularly older and non-feminist scholarship, is compromised in this manner to an incomparably greater degree.[3] Until there is a reliable body of scholarship on Luise Gottsched or any other woman writer before the twentieth century, researching early women's writings will be a very different affair from researching famous male writers. By "reliable" I mean: inclusive of and centered on women's literary history, based on archival source materials, and critically aware of the distortion of men's literary history when that of women has been ignored, as well as of the distortion of women's literary history in the few cases where it has been discussed. Like its object of inquiry, the findings of such scholarship are likely to be tentative rather than authoritative; like women's writings, the emphasis, for a time at least, is more likely to be on discovery, presentation, and initial interpretation and analysis rather than on the authoritative and sweeping establishment of encompassing "traditions"; like women's literature, its scholarly investigation is likely to be hampered in ways that men's is not — by "little detours" through the archives necessary to obtain even the most basic biographical data, by an unreliable and prejudiced handling of the material on the part of previous scholars, and by the continued marginalization of women's literature and culture in the academic enterprise. Ultimately, any attempt to examine women's literature fairly and in adequate contexts will depend on our ability to develop alternative traditions and reading behaviors. One step in that direction would be the relativization of traditional literary history through the study not only of its content, but also of its philosophical and ideological basis and its genesis. Literary values and criteria that have always appeared universal to us (literary "quality," "talent," "masterworks," "genius") thus become quantifiable and subject to scholarly investigation themselves. Our ability to re-evaluate women's writing and the concomitant revision of the literary canon will depend on our capacity to emancipate ourselves from clichés of universality and on our capacity to assume not the mediocrity of women's literature but the mediocrity of our own literary training and knowledge. We will need to learn to read women's literature outside of contexts that presuppose its inferiority, in new contexts, with new eyes and with a new sense of aesthetic appreciation.

Notes

[1] Cf. Kord, *Ein Blick* 52–56 and 93–109 as well as "All's Well that Ends Well?"

[2] For an analysis of this phenomenon in women's forewords to their novels, cf. Heuser, "Poetologische Reflexionen."

[3] The point is made more empirically in my broad analysis of the reception of women's eighteenth- and nineteenth-century literature, for which I examined 87 literary histories published between 1836 and 1983. Cf. *Namen* 135–73.

Works Consulted

[Aichinger, K. F.] *Bemühung der Obern Pfalz den Zorn des Herrn Prof. Gottscheds zu besänfftigen.* N. p. 1750.

Anonymous. "Der Fr. Luise Adelgunde Victoria Gottschedinn, geb. Kulmus, sämmtl. kleinere Gedichte, nebst dem von vielen vornehmen Standespersonen, Gönnern und Freunden, beyderley Geschlechtes, Ihr gestifteten Ehrenmaale, und ihrem Leben, herausgegeben, von ihrem hinterbliebenen Ehegatten. Leipzig bey Bernh. Christ. Breitkopf und Sohne. 1763" [Announcement]. *Das Neueste aus der anmuthigen Gelehrsamkeit.* Ed. Johann Christoph Gottsched. Leipzig: Bernhard Christoph Breitkopf, 1762. Christmond [December] 937–9.

Aufklärung: Erläuterungen zur deutschen Literatur. Ed. Kollektiv für Literaturgeschichte. 7th ed. Berlin: Volk und Wissen, 1983.

Baensch, W. and Reinhard Buchwald, ed. *Huldigungen für Frau Gottsched in Wort und Bild aus Handschriften und Drucken.* Leipzig: n. p., 1908.

Bausinger, Hermann. "Märchenglück." *Zeitschrift für Literaturwissenschaft und Linguistik* 50 (1983): 17–27.

Becker-Cantarino, Barbara. "Bildung, Schreiben und Selbständigkeit: Christiana Mariana von Ziegler, die Gottschedin, Sidonie Hedwig Zäunemann, die Karschin." *Der lange Weg zur Mündigkeit: Frau und Literatur (1500–1800).* Munich: dtv, 1989. 259–78.

——. "Leben als Text — Briefe als Ausdrucks- und Verständigungsmittel in der Briefkultur und Literatur des 18. Jahrhunderts." *Frauen Literatur Geschichte: Schreibende Frauen vom Mittelalter bis zur Gegenwart.* Ed. Hiltrud Gnüg and Renate Möhrmann. Stuttgart/Weimar: Metzler, 1999. 129–46.

——. "Luise Adelgunde Victorie Gottsched." *Women Writers of Germany, Austria, and Switzerland: An Annotated Bio-Bibliographical Guide.* Ed. Elke Frederiksen. New York: Greenwood, 1989. 86.

——. "'Outsiders': Women in German Literary Culture of Absolutism." *Jahrbuch für internationale Germanistik* 16.2 (1984): 147–57.

Bennholdt-Thomsen, Anke and Alfredo Guzzoni. "Gelehrte Arbeit von Frauen: Möglichkeiten und Grenzen im Deutschland des 18. Jahrhunderts." *Quérelles: Jahrbuch für Frauenforschung* 1 (1996): 48–76.

Bode, Wilhelm. *Charlotte von Stein.* Berlin: Mittler, 1920.

Bodmer, Johann Jakob. *Beurtheilung der Panthea eines sogenannten Trauerspiels der Frau L. A. V. G. Nebst einem Vorberichte für die Nachkommen und einer Ode auf den Namen Gottsched.* Cologne: n. p., 1746.

Bohm, Arnd. "Authority and Authorship in Luise Adelgunde Gottsched's *Das Testament.*" *The Lessing Yearbook* 18 (1986): 129–40.

Bougeant, Guillaume Hyacinthe. *La femme docteur, ou, La théologie tombée en quenouille.* Liège: Chez la vieve Procureur, n. d.

Bovenschen, Silvia. *Die imaginierte Weiblichkeit: Exemplarische Untersuchungen zu kulturgeschichtlichen und literarischen Präsentationsformen des Weiblichen.* Frankfurt/M.: Suhrkamp, 1979.

Boy-Ed, Ida. *Das Martyrium der Charlotte von Stein: Versuch ihrer Rechtfertigung.* Stuttgart, Berlin: Cotta, 1920.

Brüggemann, Fritz. "Einführung." *Die bürgerliche Gemeinschaftskultur der vierziger Jahre. Zweiter Teil: Drama.* Ed. Fritz Brüggemann. Leipzig: Reclam, 1933. 5–32.

——. "Einführung." *Gottscheds Lebens- und Kunstreform in den zwanziger und dreißiger Jahren: Gottsched, Breitinger, die Gottschedin, die Neuberin.* Ed. Fritz Brüggemann. Leipzig: Reclam, 1935. 5–16.

——. "Einführung." *Das Weltbild der deutschen Aufklärung: Philosophische Grundlagen und literarische Auswirkung.* Ed. Fritz Brüggemann. Leipzig: Reclam, 1930. 5–24.

——, ed. *Die bürgerliche Gemeinschaftskultur der vierziger Jahre.* 2 vols. (vol. I in collaboration with Helmut Paustian). Leipzig: Reclam, 1933.

——, ed. *Gottscheds Lebens- und Kunstreform in den zwanziger und dreißiger Jahren: Gottsched, Breitinger, die Gottschedin, die Neuberin.* Leipzig: Reclam, 1935.

——, ed. *Das Weltbild der deutschen Aufklärung: Philosophische Grundlagen und literarische Auswirkung.* Leipzig: Reclam, 1930.

——, and Helmut Paustian. "Einführung." *Die bürgerliche Gemeinschaftskultur der vierziger Jahre. Erster Teil: Lyrik und Roman.* Ed. Fritz Brüggemann in collaboration with Helmut Paustian. Leipzig: Reclam, 1933. 5–28.

Bryan, George B., and Veronica C. Richel. "The Plays of Luise Gottsched: A Footnote to German Dramatic History." *Neuphilologische Mitteilungen* 78 (1977): 193–201.

Buchwald, Reinhard. "Frau Gottsched." *Deutsche Rundschau* 148 (1911): 434–40.

——, and Albert Köster. "Schlußbericht." *Luise Adelgunde Gottsched, Die Lustspiele der Gottschedin.* 2 vols. Ed. Reinhard Buchwald and Albert Köster. Leipzig: Leipziger Bibliophilen-Abend, 1908–9. Vol. II (1909), 533–43.

Bürger, Christa. *Leben Schreiben: Die Klassik, die Romantik und der Ort der Frauen.* Stuttgart: Metzler, 1990.

Campe, Joachim Heinrich. *Väterlicher Rat für meine Tochter. Ein Gegenstück zum Theophron. Der erwachseneren weiblichen Jugend gewidmet.* Vienna: J. T. von Trattnern, 1790.

Cocalis, Susan. "Der Vormund will Vormund sein: Zur Problematik der weiblichen Unmündigkeit im 18. Jahrhundert." *Gestaltet und Gestaltend. Frauen in der deutschen Literatur.* Ed. Marianne Burkhard. Amsterdam: Rodopi, 1980. 33–55.

Consentius, Ernst. "Frau Gottsched und die preußische Gesetzgebung." *Preußische Jahrbücher* 112 (1903): 288–307.

Critchfield, Richard. "Beyond Luise Gottsched's 'Die Pietisterey im Fischbein-Rocke oder die Doctormäßige Frau'." *Jahrbuch für Internationale Germanistik* 17.2 (1985): 112–20.

Crompton, Louis. "The Myth of Lesbian Impunity: Capital Laws from 1270 to 1791." *Journal of Homosexuality* 6 No. 1/2 (Fall/Winter 1980/81): 11–25.

Crüger, Johannes. "Einleitung." *Joh. Christoph Gottsched und die Schweizer Joh. J. Bodmer und Joh. J. Breitinger.* Ed. Johannes Crüger. Darmstadt: Wissenschaftliche Buchgesellschaft, 1965 [Rprt. of the edition Berlin & Stuttgart 1884]. i-ci.

——, ed. *Joh. Christoph Gottsched und die Schweizer Joh. J. Bodmer und Joh. J. Breitinger.* Darmstadt: Wissenschaftliche Buchgesellschaft, 1965 [Rprt. of the edition Berlin & Stuttgart 1884].

Danzel, Th[eodor] W[ilhelm]. *Gottsched und seine Zeit: Auszüge aus seinem Briefwechsel.* Hildesheim & New York: Georg Olms, 1970.

Dawson, Ruth P. "Frauen und Theater: Vom Stegreifspiel zum bürgerlichen Rührstück." *Deutsche Literatur von Frauen.* 2 vols. Ed. Gisela Brinker-Gabler. Munich: Beck, 1988. I, 421–34.

Devrient, Hans. *Johann Friedrich Schönemann und seine Schauspielergesellschaft. Ein Beitrag zur Theatergeschichte des 18. Jahrhunderts.* Hamburg & Leipzig: Leopold Voß, 1895.

——. *Die Schönemannsche Truppe in Berlin, Breslau, Danzig und Königsberg 1742–1744.* Diss. (University of Jena). Hamburg: L. Voß, 1895.

Dotzler, Bernhard J. "'Seht doch wie ihr vor Eifer schäumet...' Zum männlichen Diskurs über Weiblichkeit um 1800." *Jahrbuch der deutschen Schillergesellschaft* 30 (1986): 339–82.

Duden, Barbara. "Das schöne Eigentum: Zur Herausbildung des bürgerlichen Frauenbildes an der Wende vom 18. zum 19. Jahrhundert." *Kursbuch* 47 (1977): 125–40.

Düntzer, Heinrich. *Charlotte von Stein: Goethes Freundin.* 2 vols. Stuttgart: Cotta, 1874.

Duncan, Bruce. "Luise Adelgunde Gottsched (1713–52 [sic])." *Bitter Healing: German Women Writers 1700–1830. An Anthology.* Ed. Jeannine Blackwell and Susanne Zantop. Lincoln & London: University of Nebraska Press, 1990. 79–84.

Eberti, Johann Caspar. *Eröffnetes Cabinet Deß Gelehrten Frauen-Zimmers. Darinnen Die Berühmtesten dieses Geschlechtes umbständlich vorgestellet werden Durch Johann Caspar Eberti.* Frankfurt/Leipzig 1706. Rprt. ed. Elisabeth Gössmann. Munich: iudicium, 1986.

Ebrecht, Angelika, Regina Nörtemann, Herta Schwarz, et. al., eds. *Brieftheorie des 18. Jahrhunderts: Texte, Kommentare, Essays.* Stuttgart: Metzler, 1990.

Edwards, John. *Abradatas and Panthea. A Tragedy in Five Acts from the Cyropaedia of Xenophon.* London: Ridgway, 1803.

Ellinger, G. "Der Einfluss des Tartuffe auf die Pietisterey der Frau Gottsched und deren Vorbild." *Archiv für Literaturgeschichte* 13 (1885): 444–7.

Eriksson, Brigitte, trans. "A Lesbian Execution in Germany, 1721: The Trial Records." *Historical Perspectives on Homosexuality.* Ed. Salvatore J. Licata and Robert P. Petersen. New York: Haworth, 1981. 27–40.

Feyl, Renate. *Idylle mit Professor.* Cologne: Kiepenheuer & Witsch, 1989.

Fichte, Johann Gottlieb. "Erster Anhang des Naturrechts: Grundriß des Familienrechts." *Johann Gottlieb Fichtes sämmtliche Werke.* Berlin: Veit & Comp, 1845. III, 304–68.

French, Lorely. *German Women as Letter Writers: 1750–1850.* Madison & London: Associated University Presses, 1996.

Frevert, Ute. "Bürgerliche Meisterdenker und das Geschlechterverhältnis: Konzepte, Erfahrungen, Visionen an der Wende vom 18. zum 19. Jahrhundert." *Bürgerinnen und Bürger: Geschlechterverhältnisse im 19. Jahrhundert.* Ed. Ute Frevert. Göttingen: Vandenhoeck & Ruprecht, 1988. 17–48.

Friederici, Hans. *Das deutsche bürgerliche Lustspiel der Frühaufklärung (1736–1750) unter besonderer Berücksichtigung seiner Anschauungen von der Gesellschaft.* Halle: Max Niemeyer, 1957.

Friedli, Lynne. "'Passing women' — A study of gender boundaries in the eighteenth century." *Sexual Underworlds of the Enlightenment.* Ed. G. S. Rousseau and Roy Porter. Chapel Hill: University of North Carolina Press, 1988. 234–60.

Gardner, Helen. "Happy Endings: Literature, Misery, and Joy." *Encounter* 57:2 (1981): 39–51.

Gellert, Christian Fürchtegott. "Gedanken von einem guten deutschen Briefe, an den Herrn F. H. v. W." *Gesammelte Schriften: Kritische, kommentierte Ausgabe*. Vol. IV. Ed. Bernd Witte. Berlin, New York: Walter de Gruyter, 1989. 97–104.

——. "Praktische Abhandlung von dem guten Geschmacke in Briefen." *Gesammelte Schriften: Kritische, kommentierte Ausgabe*. Vol. IV. Ed. Bernd Witte. Berlin, New York: Walter de Gruyter, 1989. 111–52.

Gössmann, Elisabeth. *Eva — Gottes Meisterwerk*. Munich: iudicium, 1985.

——, ed. *Das wohlgelahrte Frauenzimmer*. Munich: iudicium, 1984.

Goodman, Katherine R. *Dis/Closures. Women's Autobiography in Germany Between 1790 and 1914*. New York, Berne, Frankfurt/M.: Peter Lang, 1986.

——. "Klein Paris and Women's Writing: Luise Gottsched's Unknown Complaints." *Daphnis: Zeitschrift für Mittlere Deutsche Literatur* 25/4 (1996): 695–711.

——, and Edith Waldstein, eds. *In the Shadow of Olympus: German Women Writers Around 1800*. Albany: State University of New York Press, 1992.

Gottsched, Johann Christoph. "Ausgewählte Stücke aus den ersten Gründen der gesamten Weltweisheit." *Das Weltbild der deutschen Aufklärung: Philosophische Grundlagen und literarische Auswirkung*. Ed. Fritz Brüggemann. Leipzig: Reclam, 1930. 196–219.

——. "Leben." Luise Adelgunde Gottsched, *Der Frau Luise Adelgunde Victoria Gottschedinn, geb. Kulmus, sämmtliche Kleinere Gedichte, nebst dem, von vielen vornehmen Standespersonen, Gönnern und Freunden beyderley Geschlechtes, Ihr gestifteten Ehrenmale, und Ihrem Leben, herausgegeben von Ihrem hinterbliebenen Ehegatten*. Ed. Johann Christoph Gottsched. Leipzig: B. C. Breitkopf & Sohn, 1763.

——. "Nachricht, von dem Leben, Tode und Begräbnisse der hochedelgebohrnen nunmehr sel. Frau, Louise Adelgunde Victoria Gottschedinn, geb. Kulmus, aus Danzig." *Das Neueste aus der anmuthigen Gelehrsamkeit*. Ed. Johann Christoph Gottsched. Leipzig: Bernhard Christoph Breitkopf, 1762. Brachmond [August] 465–80; Heumond [September] 552–60; Aerntemond [October] 631–8; Windmond [November] 878–80; Christmond [December] 937–9.

——. "Von Comödien oder Lustspielen." *Versuch einer Critischen Dichtkunst. Ausgewählte Werke VI*, 2. Ed. Joachim and Brigitte Birke. Berlin, New York: Walter de Gruyter, 1973. 337–60.

——. "Von Tragödien oder Trauerspielen." *Versuch einer Critischen Dichtkunst. Ausgewählte Werke VI*, 2. Ed. Joachim and Brigitte Birke. Berlin, New York: Walter de Gruyter, 1973. 309–35.

——, ed. *Die Vernünftigen Tadlerinnen 1725–1726.* 2 vols. Vol. 1: Halle (Magdeburg): Johann Adam Spörl, 1725; Vol. 2: Leipzig: Johann Friedrich Brauns Erben, 1726. (Rprt. ed. Helga Brandes. Hildesheim, Zurich, New York: Georg Olms, 1993.)

Gottsched, Luise Adelgunde. *Briefe der Frau Louise Adelgunde Victorie Gottsched gebohrne Kulmus.* 3 vols. Ed. Dorothea Henriette von Runckel. Dresden: Harpeter, 1771–2.

——. *Herr Witzling. Deutsche Dichterinen und Schriftstellerinen in Wort und Bild.* Ed. Heinrich Groß. 3 vols. Berlin: Fr. Thiel, 1885. I, 29–43.

——. "Lob der Arbeit." *Die vernünftigen Tadlerinnen. Der erste Theil.* Ed. Johann Christoph Gottsched. Leipzig & Hamburg: Conrad König, 1738 (second edition of the edition of 1725). Rprt. ed. Helga Brandes. 2 vols. Hildesheim, Zurich, New York: Georg Olms, 1993. Vol. II. 8. Stück, 60–9.

——. *Louise Gottsched — mit der Feder in der Hand. Briefe aus den Jahren 1730 bis 1762.* Ed. Inka Kording. Darmstadt: Wissenschaftliche Buchgesellschaft, 1999.

——. "Luise Gottsched an Dorothee Henriette von Runckel." *Briefe berühmter Frauen. Von Lieselotte von der Pfalz bis Rosa Luxemburg.* Ed. Claudia Schmölders. Frankfurt/M.: Insel, 1993. 181–2.

——. "Luise Gottsched an das Fräulein Thomasius." *Briefe berühmter Frauen. Von Lieselotte von der Pfalz bis Rosa Luxemburg.* Ed. Claudia Schmölders. Frankfurt/M.: Insel, 1993. 269–73.

——. "Luise Kulmus an Johann Christoph Gottsched." *Briefe berühmter Frauen. Von Lieselotte von der Pfalz bis Rosa Luxemburg.* Ed. Claudia Schmölders. Frankfurt/M.: Insel, 1993. 111–2.

——. *Die Lustspiele der Gottschedin.* 2 vols. Ed. Reinhard Buchwald and Albert Köster. Leipzig: Leipziger Bibliophilen-Abend, 1908–9.

——. *Pietism in Petticoats and Other Comedies.* Trans. and with an introduction by Thomas Kerth and John R. Russell. Columbia, S. C.: Camden House, 1994.

——. *Die Pietisterei im Fischbein-Rocke oder Die doktormäßige Frau. Ein Lustspiel aus dem Jahre 1737. Gottscheds Lebens- und Kunstreform in den zwanziger und dreißiger Jahren: Gottsched, Breitinger, die Gottschedin, die Neuberin.* Ed. Fritz Brüggemann. Leipzig: Reclam, 1935. 137–215.

——. *Die Pietisterey im Fischbein-Rocke. Komödie.* Ed. Wolfgang Martens. Stuttgart: Reclam, 1968.

——. "Die Rolle der Frau als Gattin, Mutter, Hausfrau." *Die vernünftigen Tadlerinnen. Der erste Theil.* Ed. Johann Christoph Gottsched. Leipzig & Hamburg: Conrad König, 1738 (second edition of the edition of 1725). Rprt. ed. Helga Brandes. 2 vols. Hildesheim, Zurich, New York: Georg Olms, 1993. Vol. II. 29. Stück, 248–59.

——. *Der Frau Luise Adelgunde Victoria Gottschedinn, geb. Kulmus, sämmtliche Kleinere Gedichte, nebst dem, von vielen vornehmen Standespersonen, Gönnern und Freunden beyderley Geschlechtes, Ihr gestifteten Ehrenmale, und Ihrem Leben, herausgegeben von Ihrem hinterbliebenen Ehegatten.* Ed. Johann Christoph Gottsched. Leipzig: B. C. Breitkopf & Sohn, 1763.

——. "Selected Letters." Trans. Bruce Duncan. *Bitter Healing: German Women Writers 1700–1830. An Anthology.* Ed. Jeannine Blackwell and Susanne Zantop. Lincoln & London: University of Nebraska Press, 1990. 118–23.

——. *Das Testament, ein deutsches Lustspiel in fünf Aufzügen. Die bürgerliche Gemeinschaftskultur der vierziger Jahre. Zweiter Teil: Drama.* Ed. Fritz Brüggemann. Leipzig: Reclam, 1933. 83–164.

——. *Das Testament, ein deutsches Lustspiel in fünf Aufzügen von Luise Adelgunde Victorine Gottsched. Joh. Christoph Gottsched und die Schweizer Joh. J. Bodmer und Joh. J. Breitinger.* Ed. Johannes Crüger. Darmstadt: Wissenschaftliche Buchgesellschaft, 1965 [Rprt. of the edition Berlin & Stuttgart 1884]. 255–337.

——. "Wahre Tugend ist frei von Ehrsucht." *Die vernünftigen Tadlerinnen. Der erste Theil.* Ed. Johann Christoph Gottsched. Leipzig & Hamburg: Conrad König, 1748 (third edition of the edition of 1725). Rprt. ed. Helga Brandes. 2 vols. Hildesheim, Zurich, New York: Georg Olms, 1993. Vol. II. 34. Stück, 295–305.

——. "Wechselrede zwischen Damon und Urania." *Deutsche Dichterinen und Schriftstellerinen in Wort und Bild.* Ed. Heinrich Groß. 3 vols. Berlin: Fr. Thiel, 1885. I, 28.

——. *The Witling.* Trans. Bruce Duncan. *Bitter Healing: German Women Writers 1700–1830. An Anthology.* Ed. Jeannine Blackwell and Susanne Zantop. Lincoln & London: University of Nebraska Press, 1990. 85–117.

Groß, Heinrich, ed. *Deutsche Dichterinen und Schriftstellerinen in Wort und Bild.* 3 vols. Berlin: F. Thiel, 1885.

Haberland, Helga, and Wolfgang Pehnt, eds. "Frau Gottsched." *Die Frauen der Goethezeit in Briefen, Dokumenten und Bildern. Eine Anthologie.* Ed. Helga Haberland and Wolfgang Pehnt. Stuttgart: Reclam, 1960. 35–61.

Hacker, Hanna. *Frauen und Freundinnen: Studien zur 'weiblichen Homosexualität' am Beispiel Österreich 1870–1938.* Weinheim, Basel: Beltz, 1987.

Hahn, Barbara. *Unter falschem Namen. Von der schwierigen Autorschaft der Frauen.* Frankfurt/M.: Suhrkamp, 1991.

Hanstein, Adalbert von. *Die Frauen in der Geschichte des Deutschen Geisteslebens des 18. und 19. Jahrhunderts.* 2 vols. Leipzig: Freund & Wittiz, [1900?].

Hart, Gail. "A Family Without Women: The Triumph of the Sentimental Father in Lessing's Sara Sampson and Klinger's Sturm und Drang." *The Lessing Yearbook* 22 (1990): 113–32.

Hausen, Karin. "Die Polarisierung der 'Geschlechtscharaktere' — Eine Spiegelung der Dissoziation von Erwerbs- und Familienleben." *Sozialgeschichte der Familie in der Neuzeit Europas.* Ed. Werner Conze. Stuttgart: Ernst Klett, 1976. 363–93.

Heckmann, Hannelore. "Auf der Suche nach einem Verleger: Aus Gottscheds Briefwechsel." *Daphnis: Zeitschrift für Mittlere Deutsche Literatur* 17.2 (1988): 327–45.

Hegel, Georg Friedrich Wilhelm. *Grundlinien der Philosophie des Rechts. Sämtliche Werke: Jubiläumsausgabe in 20 Bänden.* Vol. 7. Stuttgart: F. Frommanns, 1952.

——. *Vorlesungen über die Ästhetik.* 3 vols. Sämtliche Werke: Jubiläumsausgabe in 20 Bänden. Vols. 12–14. Stuttgart: F. Frommanns, 1953.

Heitner, Robert H. *German Tragedy in the Age of Enlightenment: A Study in the Development of Original Tragedies, 1724–1768.* Berkeley & Los Angeles: University of California Press, 1963.

Heuser, Magdalene. "'Das beständige Angedencken vertritt die Stelle der Gegenwart.' Frauen und Freundschaften in Briefen der Frühaufklärung und Empfindsamkeit." *Frauenfreundschaft — Männerfreundschaft: Literarische Diskurse im 18. Jahrhundert.* Ed. Wolfram Mauser and Barbara Becker-Cantarino. Tübingen: Max Niemeyer, 1991. 141–65.

——. "Das Musenchor mit neuer Ehre zieren: Schriftstellerinnen zur Zeit der Frühaufklärung." *Deutsche Literatur von Frauen.* 2 vols. Ed. Gisela Brinker-Gabler. Munich: Beck, 1988. I, 293–313.

——. "'Das die Sprache meines Geschlechts niemahls reicher als im Widersprechen ist': Dorothea Henriette von Runckels Briefe an Johann Christoph Gottsched 1753–1756." *Lichtenberg-Jahrbuch* (1996): 51–89.

——. "'Ich wollte dieß und das von meinem Buche sagen, und gerieth in ein Vernünfteln': Poetologische Reflexionen in den Romanvorreden." *Untersuchungen zum Roman von Frauen um 1800.* Ed. Helga Gallas and Magdalene Heuser. Tübingen: Niemeyer, 1990. 52–65.

——. "Neuedition der Briefe von Louise Adelgunde Victorie Gottsched." *Chloe: Beiheft zum Daphnis. Editionsdesiderate zur Frühen Neuzeit*. Ed. Hans-Gert Roloff, in collaboration with Renate Meincke. Amsterdam: Rodopi, 1998. 319–39.

Hinck, Walter. "Vom Ausgang der Komödie: Exemplarische Lustspielschlüsse in der europäischen Literatur." *Zwischen Satire und Utopie: Zur Komiktheorie und zur Geschichte der europäischen Komödie*. Ed. Reinhold Grimm and Walter Hinck. Frankfurt/M.: Suhrkamp, 1982. 126–36.

Höfer, Edmund. *Goethe und Charlotte von Stein*. 9th ed. Berlin, Leipzig: B. Behr, 1923.

Hof, Walter. *Goethe und Charlotte von Stein*. Frankfurt/M.: Insel, 1979.

Hollmer, Heide. *Anmut und Nutzen: Die Originaltrauerspiele in Gottscheds 'Deutscher Schaubühne'*. Tübingen: Max Niemeyer, 1994.

Humboldt, Wilhelm von. "Plan einer vergleichenden Anthropologie." *Werke*. Stuttgart: J. G. Cotta, 1960. I, 337–75.

——. "Über den Geschlechtsunterschied und dessen Einfluß auf die organische Natur." *Werke*. Stuttgart: J. G. Cotta, 1960. I, 268–95.

——. "Über männliche und weibliche Form." *Werke*. Stuttgart: J. G. Cotta, 1960. I, 296–336.

Jameson, Anna, ed. and trans. *Social Life in Germany, Illustrated in the Acted Dramas of Her Royal Highness the Princess Amelia [sic] of Saxony*. 2 vols. London: Saunders & Otley, 1840.

Joeres, Ruth-Ellen B. "'We are adjacent to human society': German Women Writers, the Homosocial Experience, and a Challenge to the Public/Domestic Dichotomy." *Women in German Yearbook* 10 (1995): 39–57.

Kahn-Wallerstein, Carmen. "Charlotte von Stein und Christiane von Goethe." *Goethe-Kalender* (1932): 108–37.

Kaiser, Nancy. "In Our Own Words: Dramatizing History in L. A. V. Gottsched's Pietisterey im Fischbein-Rocke." *Thalia's Daughters: German Women Dramatists from the Eighteenth Century to the Present*. Ed. Susan Cocalis and Ferrel Rose in collaboration with Karin Obermeier. Tübingen & Basel: Francke, 1996. 5–15.

Kallin, Britta. "Amalie von Sachsen. Darstellung der Frauencharaktere in ausgewählten Lustspielen." M. A. Thesis, University of Cincinnati. Cincinnati, OH: 1994.

Kant, Immanuel. "Anthropologie in pragmatischer Hinsicht." *Kants Werke*. Berlin: Walter de Gruyter & Co., 1968. VII, 117–334.

——. "Die Metaphysik der Sitten." *Kants Werke*. Berlin: Walter de Gruyter & Co., 1968. VI, 203–494.

Kerth, Thomas, and John R. Russell. "Introduction." Luise Adelgunde Gottsched, *Pietism in Petticoats and Other Comedies.* Trans. and with an introduction by Thomas Kerth and John R. Russell. Columbia, S. C.: Camden
House, 1994. xi-xxxi.

Kittler, Friedrich A. *Aufschreibesysteme. 1800/1900.* Munich: Fink, 1985.

*Klag-Lied des Herrn Professor Gottscheds über das rauhe Pfälzer-Land in einer
Abschieds-Ode.* N. p., 1750.

Knigge, Adolph Freiherr von. *Über den Umgang mit Menschen.* Nen-
deln/Liechtenstein: KTO Press, 1978 (Rprt. of the 5th edition, Hanover:
Christian Ritscher, 1796). Vol. 2.

Köster, Albert. *Die deutsche Literatur der Aufklärungszeit.* Heidelberg: Carl
Winter, 1925.

Kord, Susanne. "All's Well That Ends Well? Marriage, Madness and Other
Happy Endings in Eighteenth-Century Women's Comedies." *The Lessing
Yearbook* 28 (1996): 181–97.

——. *Ein Blick hinter die Kulissen: Deutschsprachige Dramatikerinnen im 18.
und 19. Jahrhundert.* Stuttgart: Metzler, 1992.

——. "Eternal Love or Sentimental Discourse? Gender Dissonance and
Women's Passionate 'Friendships'." *Outing Goethe and His Age.* Ed. Alice
Kuzniar. Stanford: Stanford UP, 1996. 228–49.

——. "Frühe dramatische Entwürfe: Drei Dramatikerinnen im 18. Jahrhundert." *Frauen Literatur Geschichte.* Ed. Hiltrud Gnüg and Renate Möhrmann. Stuttgart: Metzler, 1998. 231–46; 694–7.

——. "Die Gelehrte als Zwitterwesen in Schriften von Autorinnen des 18.
und 19. Jahrhunderts." *Quérelles: Jahrbuch für Frauenforschung* I (1996):
158–89.

——. "The Innocent Translator: Translation as Pseudonymous Behavior in
Eighteenth-Century German Women's Writing." *The Jerome Quarterly*
9/4 (August/Sept. 1994): 11–3.

——. "Luise Gottsched." *Women Writers in German Speaking Countries.* Ed.
Elke Frederiksen. Westport, CT: The Greenwood Press, 1997. 160–70.

——. "Not in Goethe's Image: The Playwright Charlotte von Stein." *Thalia's
Daughters: German Women Dramatists From the Eighteenth Century to the
Present.* Ed. Susan Cocalis and Ferrel Rose. Tübingen: Francke/Narr,
1996. 53–75.

——. *Sich einen Namen machen: Anonymität und weibliche Autorschaft 1700–
1900.* Stuttgart: Metzler, 1996.

——. "Tugend im Rampenlicht: Friederike Sophie Hensel als Schauspielerin
und Dramatikerin." *The German Quarterly* 66/1 (1993): 1–19.

Kording, Inka. "Kommentar." *Louise Gottsched — mit der Feder in der Hand. Briefe aus den Jahren 1730 bis 1762*. Ed. Inka Kording. Darmstadt: Wissenschaftliche Buchgesellschaft, 1999. 315–75.

——. "Zu dieser Ausgabe." *Louise Gottsched – mit der Feder in der Hand. Briefe aus den Jahren 1730 bis 1762*. Ed. Inka Kording. Darmstadt: Wissenschaftliche Buchgesellschaft, 1999. 376–9.

Kraft, Helga. "Emilia und ihre Schwestern: Das seltsame Verschwinden der Mutter und die geopferte Tochter." *Mütter — Töchter — Frauen: Weiblichkeitsbilder in der Literatur*. Ed. Helga Kraft and Elke Liebs. Stuttgart/Weimar: Metzler, 1993. 53–70.

Kuzniar, Alice. *Delayed Endings: Nonclosure in Novalis and Hölderlin*. Athens & London: University of Georgia Press, 1987.

Lange, Adolf. *Über die Sprache der Gottschedin in ihren Briefen*. 2 vols. Upsala: Almquist & Wiksells, 1896–1901.

Le Sage, Alain René. *Le Diable Boiteux or the Devil upon Two Sticks*. Translated from the Last Edition at Paris, with several Additions. London: Printed for Jacob Tonson, within Grays-Inn Gate next Grays-Inn Lane, 1708. (Rprt. with a new introduction by Josephine Grieder. London/New York: Garland Publishing, 1972.)

Lehms, Georg Christian. *Teutschlands Galante Poetinnen. Mit ihren sinnreichen und netten Proben; Nebst einem Anhang Ausländischer Dames, So sich gleichfalls durch Schöne Poesien Bey der curieusen Welt bekannt gemacht, und einer Vorrede. Daß das Weibliche Geschlecht so geschickt zum Studieren/als das Männliche, ausgefertiget Von Georg Christian Lehms*. 2 vols. Frankfurt/M.: Samuel Tobias Hocker, 1715.

Lessing, Gotthold Ephraim. *Hamburgische Dramaturgie*. In: *Lessings Werke*. Ed. Kurt Wölfel. 3 vols. Frankfurt/M.: Insel, 1967. II, 121–533.

Linke, Evelyn. "Emanzipation der Protagonistinnen in den Lustspielen der Gottschedin." M. A. Thesis, University of Waterloo. Waterloo, Ontario: 1985.

Loster-Schneider, Gudrun. "Louise Adelgunde Gottscheds 'Testament'. Ein 'parodistisches' Vermächtnis zur Gottschedschen Komödienpoetik." *Formzitate, Gattungsparodien, ironische Formverwendung: Gattungsformen jenseits von Gattungsgrenzen*. Ed. Andreas Böhn. St. Ingbert: Röhrig Universitätsverlag, 1999. 59–83.

Martens, Wolfgang. *Die Botschaft der Tugend: Die Aufklärung im Spiegel der deutschen Moralischen Wochenschriften*. Stuttgart: Metzler, 1971.

——. "Nachwort." *L. A. V. Gottsched, Die Pietisterey im Fischbein-Rocke. Komödie*. Ed. Wolfgang Martens. Stuttgart: Reclam, 1968. 151–67.

Martin, Bernhard. *Goethe und Charlotte von Stein: Gnade und Tragik in ihrer Freundschaft*. Kassel, Basel: Bärenreiter, 1949.

Maurer, Doris. *Charlotte von Stein. Ein Frauenleben der Goethezeit.* Bonn: Keil, 1985.

Mauser, Wolfram, and Barbara Becker-Cantarino, eds. *Frauenfreundschaft — Männerfreundschaft. Literarische Diskurse im 18. Jahrhundert.* Tübingen: Niemeyer, 1991.

Mitchell, P[hillip] M[arshall]. *Johann Christoph Gottsched (1700–1766): Harbinger of German Classicism.* Columbia, S. C.: Camden House, 1995.

Möhrmann, Renate, ed. *Verklärt, verkitscht, vergessen: Die Mutter als ästhetische Figur.* Stuttgart/Weimar: Metzler, 1996.

Montrose, Louis A. "Professing the Renaissance: The Poetics and Politics of Culture." *The New Historicism.* Ed. H. Aram Veeser. New York, London: Routledge, 1989. 15–36.

Nenon, Monika. *Autorschaft und Frauenbildung: Das Beispiel Sophie von La Roche.* Würzburg: Königshausen & Neumann, 1988.

Nickisch, Reinhard M. G. "Briefkultur: Entwicklung und sozialgeschichtliche Bedeutung des Frauenbriefs im 18. Jahrhundert." *Deutsche Literatur von Frauen.* 2 vols. Ed. Gisela Brinker-Gabler. Munich: Beck, 1988. I, 389–409.

Nörtemann, Regina. "Brieftheoretische Konzepte im 18. Jahrhundert und ihre Genese." *Brieftheorie des 18. Jahrhunderts: Texte, Kommentare, Essays.* Ed. Angelika Ebrecht, Regina Nörtemann, Herta Schwarz, et. al. Stuttgart: Metzler, 1990. 211–24.

O'Connor, Pat. *Friendships Between Women: A Critical Review.* New York/London: The Guilford Press, 1992.

Pailer, Gaby. "Luise Adelgunde Victoria Gottsched in der biographischen Konstruktion." *Studia Germanica Gedansensia: 1000 Jahre Danzig in der deutschen Literatur.* Ed. Marek Jaroszewski. Gdansk: Instytut Filologii Germanskiej Universytetu Gdanskiego, 1998. 45–60.

Pataky, Sophie, ed. *Lexikon deutscher Frauen der Feder: Eine Zusammenstellung der seit dem Jahre 1840 erschienenen Werke weiblicher Autoren, nebst Biographien der lebenden und einem Verzeichnis der Pseudonyme.* 2 vols. Berlin: C. Pataky, 1898. Rprt. Berne: Herbert Lang, 1971.

Paullini, Christian Franz. *Das Hoch- und Wohlgelahrte Teutsche Frauen-Zimmer. Nochmahls mit mercklichem Zusatz vorgestellet.* Frankfurt & Leipzig: J. C. Stösseln, 1705.

Pehnt, Wolfgang. "Einleitung." *Die Frauen der Goethezeit in Briefen, Dokumenten und Bildern. Eine Anthologie.* Ed. Helga Haberland and Wolfgang Pehnt. Stuttgart: Reclam, 1960. 5–33.

Petersen, Julius. "Goethe und Charlotte v. Stein." *Aus der Goethezeit: Gesammelte Aufsätze zur Literatur des klassischen Zeitalters.* Leipzig: Quelle & Meyer, 1932. 19–48.

Petig, William E. "Forms of Satire in Antipietistic Dramas." *Colloquia Germanica: Internationale Zeitschrift für Germanische Sprach- und Literaturwissenschaft* 18.3 (1985): 257–63.

Pfeiffer, Peter C. "Geschichte, Leidenspathos, feminine Subjektivität: Marie von Ebner-Eschenbachs Autobiographie Meine Kinderjahre." *Monatshefte* 87.1 (1995): 68–81.

Ploetz, H. "Ein Lebensbild: Adelgunde Gottsched, geb. Culmus (1713–1762)." *Geistige Arbeit: Zeitung aus der wissenschaftlichen Welt* 2.15 (1935): 12.

Pockels, Carl Friedrich. *Versuch einer Charakteristik des weiblichen Geschlechts. Ein Sittengemählde des Menschen, des Zeitalters und des geselligen Lebens.* 5 vols. Hanover: Christian Ritscher, 1797–1802.

Rasch, Wolfdietrich. *Freundschaftskult und Freundschaftsdichtung im deutschen Schrifttum des 18. Jahrhunderts: Vom Ausgang des Barock bis zu Klopstock.* Halle/Saale: Max Niemeyer, 1936.

Reichel, Eugen. *Gottsched.* 2 vols. Berlin: Gottsched-Verlag, 1908–12.

——, ed. *Kleine Gottsched-Halle. Jahrbuch der Gottsched-Gesellschaft.* Vol. 7. Berlin: Gottsched-Verlag, 1910.

Richel, Veronica C. *Luise Gottsched: A Reconsideration.* Berne & Frankfurt: Peter Lang, 1973.

——. "Luise Gottsched's Der Lockenraub and Alexander Pope's The Rape of the Lock: A Comparative Analysis." *Neuphilologische Mitteilungen* 76 (1975): 473–87.

Rieck, Werner, Paul Günter Krohn, Hans-Heinrich Reuter and Regine Otto. *Geschichte der deutschen Literatur vom Ausgang des 17. Jahrhunderts bis 1789.* Berlin: Volk und Wissen, 1979.

[Robinson, Therese]. "Deutschlands Scnriftstellerinnen bis vor hundert Jahren. Von Talvj [pseud.]." *Historisches Tagebuch* 32 (Leipzig, 1861): 1–141.

Runckel, Dorothea Henriette von. *Moral für Frauenzimmer nach Anleitung der moralischen Vorlesungen.* Dresden: Runckel, 1774.

——. *Sammlung freundschaftlicher Originalbriefe.* Dresden: Harpetersche Schriften, 1777/1779.

——. "Vorbericht" to her *Sammlung freundschaftlicher Originalbriefe zur Bildung des Geschmacks für Frauenzimmer.* In *Brieftheorie des 18. Jahrhunderts: Texte, Kommentare, Essays.* Ed. Angelika Ebrecht, Regina Nörtemann, Herta Schwarz, et. al. Stuttgart: Metzler, 1990. 137–8.

Russ, Joanna. *How to Suppress Women's Writing.* Austin: University of Texas Press, 1983.

——. "She Wasn't, She Isn't, She Didn't, She Doesn't, and Why Do You Keep On Bringing It Up?" *What Are We Fighting For? Sex, Race, Class, and the Future of Feminism*. New York: St. Martin's Press, 1998. 104–25.

Sanders, Ruth H. "'Ein kleiner Umweg:' Das literarische Schaffen der Luise Gottsched." *Die Frau von der Reformation zur Romantik: Die Situation der Frau vor dem Hintergrund der Literatur- und Sozialgeschichte*. Ed. Barbara Becker-Cantarino. Bonn: Bouvier, 1980. 170–94.

——. "The Virtuous Woman In the Comedies of the Early Enlightenment." Dissertation. Stony Brook: State University of New York, 1975.

Schenck, Ernst von, ed. *Briefe der Freunde: Das Zeitalter Goethes im Spiegel der Freundschaft*. Berlin: Verlag die Runde, 1937.

Schlenther, Paul. *Frau Gottsched und die bürgerliche Komödie: Ein Kulturbild aus der Zopfzeit*. Berlin: Wilhelm Hertz, 1886.

Schlueter, June. *Dramatic Closure: Reading the End*. London: Associated University Presses, 1995.

Schmidt, Henry J. *How Dramas End: Essays on the German Sturm und Drang, Büchner, Hauptmann, and Fleisser*. Ann Arbor: University of Michigan Press, 1992.

Schmölders, Claudia, ed. *Briefe berühmter Frauen. Von Lieselotte von der Pfalz bis Rosa Luxemburg*. Frankfurt/M.: Insel, 1993.

Schreiber, Sara Etta. *The German Woman in the Age of Enlightenment: A Study in the Drama from Gottsched to Lessing*. New York: Kings Crown Press, 1948.

Seillière, Ernest. *Charlotte von Stein und ihr antiromantischer Einfluß auf Goethe*. Trans. Lydia Jacobs. Berlin: Hermann Barsdorf, 1914.

Spender, Dale. *The Writing or the Sex? Why You Don't Have to Read Women's Writing to Know It's No Good*. New York: Pergamon Press, 1989.

Steinhausen, Georg. *Geschichte des deutschen Briefes: Zur Kulturgeschichte des deutschen Volkes*. 2 vols. in 1. Dublin & Zurich: Weidmann, 1968 [Rprt. of the edition 1889–1891].

Steinmetz, Horst. *Das deutsche Drama von Gottsched bis Lessing: Ein historischer Überblick*. Stuttgart: Metzler, 1987.

——. *Die Komödie der Aufklärung*. 3rd ed. Stuttgart: Metzler, 1978.

Stone, Lawrence. *The Family, Sex and Marriage in England 1500–1800*. New York: Harper & Row, 1977.

Suchier, Wolfram. *Gottscheds Korrespondenten: Alphabetisches Absenderregister zur Gottschedschen Briefsammlung in der Universitätsbibliothek Leipzig*. Leipzig: Zentralantiquariat der DDR, 1971.

Susmann, Margarethe. *Deutung einer großen Liebe: Goethe und Charlotte von Stein.* Zurich: Artemis, 1957.

Tubach, Sally Patterson. "Female Homoeroticism in German Literature and Culture." Dissertation. University of California, Berkeley, 1980.

Voß, Lena. *Goethes unsterbliche Freundin (Charlotte von Stein): Eine psychologische Studie an der Hand der Quellen.* Leipzig: Klinkhardt & Biermann, 1922.

Vulliod, A[médée]. *Guillaume Hyacinthe Bougeant, La Femme Docteur. Mme. Gottsched et son modèle français Bougeant: ou, Jansénisme et piétisme.* Lyon: A. Rey, 1912.

Walter, Eva. *Schrieb oft, von Mägde Arbeit müde: Lebenszusammenhänge deutscher Schriftstellerinnen um 1800 — Schritte zur bürgerlichen Weiblichkeit. Mit einer Bibliographie zur Sozialgeschichte von Frauen 1800–1914 von Ute Daniel.* Ed. Annette Kuhn. Düsseldorf: Schwann, 1985.

Waniek, Gustav. *Gottsched und die deutsche Litteratur seiner Zeit.* Leipzig: Breitkopf & Härtel, 1897 [Rprt. Leipzig: Zentralantiquariat der DDR, 1972].

Waters, Michael. "Frau Gottsched's 'Die Pietisterey im Fischbein-Rocke': Original, Adaptation or Translation?" *Forum for Modern Language Studies* 11 (1975): 252–67.

Wicke, Günter. *Die Struktur des deutschen Lustspiels der Aufklärung: Versuch einer Typologie.* Bonn: Bouvier, 1965.

Wiegler, Paul. "Vorwort zur neuen Auflage." *Briefe deutscher Frauen. Neu bearbeitet und herausgegeben von Paul Wiegler.* Berlin: Ullstein, 1936. 5–6.

Wieland, Christoph Martin. *Araspes und Panthea. Eine moralische Geschichte in einer Reyhe von Unterredungen.* Zurich: Ovell, 1760.

——. *Cyrus, Araspes und Panthea.* Karlsruhe: Christian Gottlieb Schneider, 1804.

Wolff, Christian. "Rede von der Sittenlehre der Sineser." *Das Weltbild der deutschen Aufklärung: Philosophische Grundlagen und literarische Auswirkung.* Ed. Fritz Brüggemann. Leipzig: Reclam, 1930. 174–95.

——. *Vernünfftige Gedancken von Gott, der Welt und der Seele des Menschen, auch allen Dingen überhaupt.* 2 vols. Ed. Charles A. Gorr. *Gesammelte Werke* I/2 and I/3. Hildesheim, Zurich, New York: Georg Olms, 1983.

——. *Vernünfftige Gedancken von der Menschen Thun und Lassen, zu Beförderung ihrer Glückseeligkeit.* Ed. Hans Werner Arndt. *Gesammelte Werke* I/4. Hildesheim, Zurich, New York: Georg Olms, 1976.

——. "Von einer allgemeinen Regel der menschlichen Handlungen und der Gesetze der Natur." *Das Weltbild der deutschen Aufklärung: Philosophische Grundlagen und literarische Auswirkung.* Ed. Fritz Brüggemann. Leipzig: Reclam, 1930. 140–61.

——. "Von Gott." *Das Weltbild der deutschen Aufklärung: Philosophische Grundlagen und literarische Auswirkung.* Ed. Fritz Brüggemann. Leipzig: Reclam, 1930. 99–139.

——. "Von dem Vertrauen auf Gott." *Das Weltbild der deutschen Aufklärung: Philosophische Grundlagen und literarische Auswirkung.* Ed. Fritz Brüggemann. Leipzig: Reclam, 1930. 162–73.

Zelle, Carsten. "Zur 'Quérelle du théâtre' in der Frühaufklärung: Eine englisch-französisch-deutsche Literaturbeziehung." *Arcadia: Zeitschrift für vergleichende Literaturwissenschaft* 19.2 (1984): 165–9.

Zobeltitz, Fedor von, ed. *Briefe deutscher Frauen. Neu bearbeitet und herausgegeben von Paul Wiegler.* Berlin: Ullstein, 1936.

Der Zorn des Herrn Professor Gottscheds über das rauhe Pfälzer-Land. N. p., 1750.

Index